Susan Richmond is Associate Professor of Art History at Georgia State University.

‘In this monograph, Richmond has successfully reinstated the work of Lynda Benglis, providing a broader reading […] that is both rigorous in its examination and considered in its interpretation […]. This book is a welcome and enlightened addition to the literature.’

Mo white, ***Cassone***

‘*Beyond Process* celebrates a life in arts that has been full of beautifully twisted and messy moments.’

BOMB Magazine

‘Scholarly […] thorough […] a good introduction.’

Victoria Thorson, ***Woman’s Art Journal***

Lynda Benglis

Beyond Process

Susan Richmond

BLOOMSBURY VISUAL ARTS
LONDON • NEW YORK • OXFORD • NEW DELHI • SYDNEY

BLOOMSBURY VISUAL ARTS
Bloomsbury Publishing Plc
50 Bedford Square, London, WC1B 3DP, UK
1385 Broadway, New York, NY 10018, USA
29 Earlsfort Terrace, Dublin 2, Ireland

First published in Great Britain 2013 by I.B.Tauris & Co Ltd
Reprinted by Bloomsbury Visual Arts 2021, 2023

Cover image: Lynda Benglis, Omnicron, 1974, mylar sparkles and sculp-metal on plaster, cotton bunting and aluminium screen, 68 × 36 × 16 in (172.7 × 91.4 × 40.6 cm). Private Collection, Courtesy Locks Gallery, Philadelphia. © Lynda Benglis/Licensed by VAGA, New York, NY.

A catalogue record for this book is available from the British Library.

A catalog record for this book is available from the Library of Congress.

ISBN: PB: 978-1-3502-9006-8
ePDF: 978-0-8577-2853-1
eBook: 978-0-8577-2854-8

Contents

Illustrations

Figures

Plates

14. Lynda Benglis, *Omega*, 1973, acrylic, glitter, and gesso on plaster, cotton bunting and aluminum screen, 33 x 17 ½ x 11 ¼ in. (83. 8 x 44.5 x 28.6 cm). Collection of the Portland Museum of Art, Oregon; purchased with Robert Hale Ellis Jr. Fund for the Blanche Eloise Day Ellis and Robert Hale Ellis Memorial Collection. © Lynda Benglis/Licensed by VAGA, New York, NY.
15. Lynda Benglis, *Omnicron*, 1974, mylar sparkles and sculp-metal on plaster, cotton bunting and aluminum screen, 68 x 36 x 16 in. (172.7 x 91.4 x 40.6 cm). Private Collection, Courtesy Locks Gallery, Philadelphia. © Lynda Benglis/ Licensed by VAGA, New York, NY.
16. Lynda Benglis, *Peter*, 1974, spray paint on aluminum foil and screen, 60 x 17 x 11 in. (152.4 x 43.2 x 27.9 cm). Greenville County Museum, Greenville, SC; museum purchase from the Arthur and Holly Magill Fund. © Lynda Benglis/ Licensed by VAGA, New York, NY.
17. Lynda Benglis, *Lagniappe: Bayou Babe*, 1977, polypropylene, acrylic, glitter, and gesso on plaster, cotton bunting, and aluminum screen, 32 x 8 x 9 in. (81.3 x 20.3 x 22.9 cm). Courtesy of Andrea Rosen Gallery, New York. © Lynda Benglis/Licensed by VAGA, New York, NY.
18. Cover, *Feather Flowers and Arrangements* (Temple City, CA: Craft Course Publishers, 1967; 1964). Printed permission by Tiffany Windsor, www.Cool2Craft.com.
19. Lynda Benglis, *Untitled C*, 1993, glazed ceramic, 12 ½ x 8 ½ x 7 in. (31.8 x 21.6 x 17.8 cm). Courtesy of the artist and Cheim & Read Gallery, New York. © Lynda Benglis/Licensed by VAGA, New York, NY.
20. Lynda Benglis, *Blansko*, 1996, hand blown glass, 5 x 34 x 5 in. (12.7 x 86.4 x 12.7 cm) Courtesy of the artist and Cheim & Read Gallery, New York. © Lynda Benglis/Licensed by VAGA, New York, NY.
21. Benglis, *Eclat*, 1990, aluminum on stainless steel mesh, 65 x 105 x 31 in. (165.1 x 266.7 x 78.7 cm). Courtesy of the artist and Cheim & Read Gallery, New York. © Lynda Benglis/Licensed by VAGA, New York, NY.
22. Benglis, *Swinburne Egg I*, 2009, tinted polyurethane, 41 x 28 x 15 in. (104.1 x 71.1 x 38.1 cm). Courtesy of the artist and Cheim & Read Gallery, New York. © Lynda Benglis/Licensed by VAGA, New York, NY.
23. Lynda Benglis, *Figure 4*, 2009, bronze, black patina, 98 ½ x 66 ½ x 25 in. (250.2 x 168.9 x 63.5 cm). Courtesy of the artist and Cheim & Read Gallery, New York. © Lynda Benglis/Licensed by VAGA, New York, NY.
24. Lynda Benglis, *Come*, 1969/74, bronze, 13 x 49 x 30 in. (33 x 124.4 x 76.2 cm). Courtesy of the artist and Cheim & Read Gallery, New York. © Lynda Benglis/Licensed by VAGA, New York, NY.
25. Lynda Benglis, *Wave of the World*, 1983–4, bronze, 108 x 108 x 204 in. (274.3 x 274.3 x 518.2 cm). Louisiana World Exposition, New Orleans, Louisiana. © Lynda Benglis/Licensed by VAGA, New York, NY.

Acknowledgments

I am grateful to a number of people for their support during the completion of this book. Since it began as a dissertation at the University of Texas at Austin, my project could not have happened without the advice and encouragement of Ann Reynolds, to whom I am deeply appreciative. I would also like to thank the other members of my dissertation committee for their input at an early stage: Ann Cvetkovich, Linda Henderson, John Clarke, and Richard Shiff. I likewise extend my gratitude to Lynda Benglis, for giving generously of her time and for welcoming me into her studio on several occasions.

Over the years I have been fortunate to have several individuals read and comment on portions of my manuscript, including Roberta Weston, Erina Duganne, Margo Hobbs Thompson, Kimberly Cleveland, and Matthew Roudane. I am also grateful to Sonia Fulop for her help with copy-editing, and to Dermot Smyth for sharing his passion and insights about Lynda Benglis's work with me. I look forward to seeing his film project on the artist come to fruition.

A summer fellowship at the Georgia O'Keeffe Museum and Research Center in Santa Fe gave me an extended period of time to think and write without distractions. I especially thank Barbara Buhler Lynes and Eumie Imm-Stroukoff for their assistance during my residency at the Center. At Georgia State University I have been fortunate enough to work with a wonderful group of colleagues and students; I thank them for their support over the years. Not least, both the Ernest G. Welch School of Art & Design and the College of Arts & Sciences at GSU provided funding for research and writing; the School of Art & Design likewise granted a publication subvention for the inclusion of colour plates.

Portions of the introduction and chapter 3 have previously appeared in *n.paradoxa* and *Camera Obscura*. I extend my thanks to these journals for the initial opportunity to publish on Benglis's work. I am likewise grateful to Liza Thompson at I.B.Tauris for her interest in and encouragement of this project, and for seeing it through to completion as a book.

My family has been a constant source of support for me, for which I will always remain grateful. Over the years, many dear friends have also provided welcome relief from the solitary work of scholarship. I feel very lucky in that regard. Most of all, I thank Josef Cillo for his love, patience, and humour – and not least, his expert assistance with several of the images reproduced here. Joe's unwavering belief in me has been invaluable and profound. I dedicate this book to him and to the memory of Idgie, whose steadfast companionship over the years was also a true gift.

Introduction

An early assessment by the art historian and critic Robert Pincus-Witten sums up a popular and often-voiced sentiment regarding Lynda Benglis's career: the artist, he wrote in 1974, 'contributes to new options in American art – my reluctance to admit this is tied to her extravagance. Few talents today are so alert to the weights and balances of the actual moment and no artist seems more capricious, more casual'.[1]

As an early proponent and frequent reviewer of Benglis's art, Pincus-Witten believed it to be timely and relevant to contemporary artistic practices, yet he also found himself somewhat discomfited by its wilful divergences and by the artist's seeming refusal to stay the course. Subsequent writers have echoed this ambivalence, citing Benglis's penchant for visceral forms and her apparent indifference to perceived artistic standards as reasons for both delight and consternation. Though critics have been responsive to her procedural innovations, the perceived discontinuities in the artist's career have likewise challenged those seeking a unifying theme or perspective. As curator Susan Krane consequently observed on the occasion of a 1991 retrospective exhibition of Benglis's work at the High Museum of Art in Atlanta, the artist embodies a spirit of independence and provocation that 'refuses easy historical typecasting'.[2]

The present book heeds Krane's assessment: rather than attempt to square the artist's career with prevailing art-historical paradigms of postwar art in the United States, I approach Benglis's art on its own terms in the hopes that in so doing, I convey something of its individual vitality and specificity without eliding its potent contradictions. That ambivalence characterises much of Benglis's critical reception over the decades is argument for rather than against looking closely at the salient features of the artist's career; for identifying how, more specifically, Benglis generates such contradictions; and, ultimately, for considering her significance in positing new or overlooked interpretative narratives of contemporary US art. Through close formal and contextual consideration of works that have been paid scant attention outside exhibition catalogues, I thus broaden an understanding of Benglis's eclectic career and demonstrate how it serves as a striking but not singular example of the complex interrelationship between an individual artistic practice and the contemporary cultural and artistic structures within and through which it becomes meaningful.

the *Artforum* controversy

Any art-historical attempt to assess Benglis's career must necessarily contend with the artist's most notorious and oft-mentioned project: the November 1974 *Artforum* dildo advertisement. At no time was the ambivalence over Benglis's work (and person) more palpable than in the aftermath of the publication of this two-page ad. Appearing in the same issue of *Artforum* as Robert Pincus-Witten's aforementioned assessment, it infamously included a glossy colour photograph of the artist posing naked save for a pair of sunglasses and a large double-headed dildo thrusting outward from her tanned and oiled body (fig. 1). Set against an expansive black background,

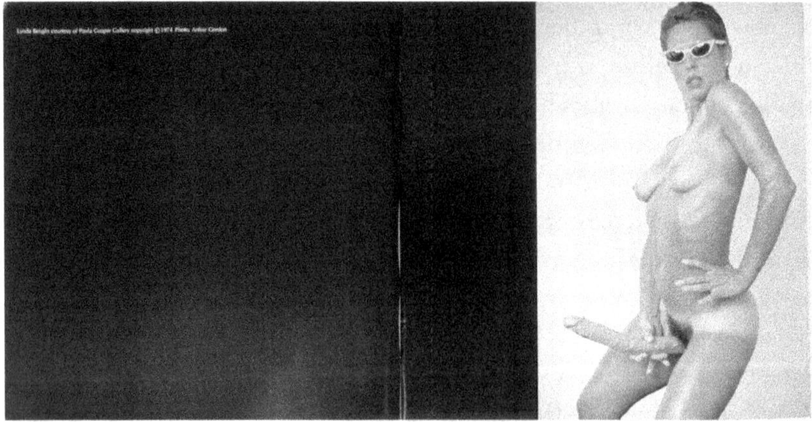

1. Lynda Benglis, advertisement in *Artforum*, November 1974. Photograph by Arthur Gordon. © Lynda Benglis/Licensed by VAGA, New York, NY.

the image was accompanied by only a small line of copy reading: 'Lynda Benglis courtesy of Paula Cooper Gallery copyright © 1974 Photo: Arthur Gordon'.

The photograph of the naked, phallus-wielding artist was the last and most provocative in a series of promotional projects conceived by Benglis in 1974. The first was produced as a gallery ad in conjunction with a 1974 solo exhibition at Paula Cooper Gallery in New York. Published in *Artforum* in April 1974, it consisted of a snapshot of the artist striking what she calls her 'macharina' (in a pun on the word 'macho') pose: leaning against her Porsche with one arm akimbo, the other stretched along the top of the car, an androgynous-looking Benglis appears casual and confident in aviator glasses, a button-down shirt, a neatly tailored jacket, and slicked-back hair (fig. 2).[3] For her second promotional image, which was reproduced as a postcard for the same show at Paula Cooper Gallery, Benglis hired photographer Annie Leibovitz to capture her irreverently mooning the camera in an updated version of Betty Grable's famous cheesecake pinup from the 1940s, the artist's bare posterior, shortly cropped and dyed hair, and pencilled-in eyebrows substituting a subcultural glam rock style for Grable's friendly all-American beauty (fig. 3).[4] Six months later, Benglis's dildo self-portrait debuted in the opening pages of the November 1974 issue of *Artforum*.

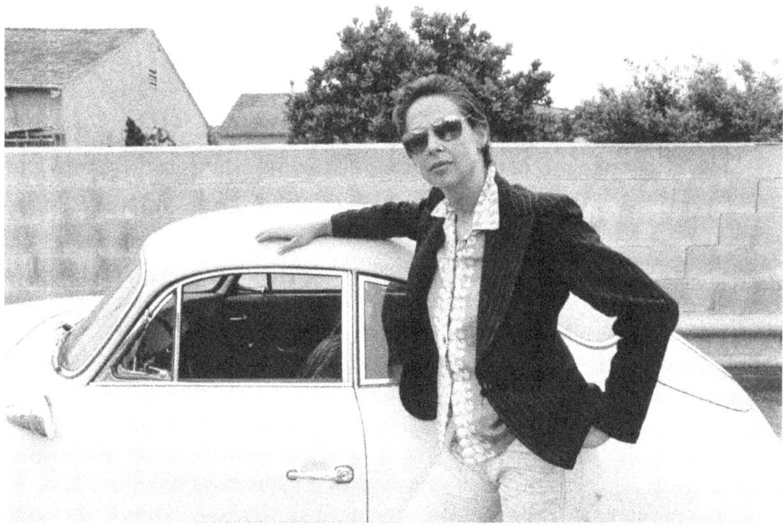

2. Lynda Benglis, advertisement in *Artforum*, May 1974. © Lynda Benglis/ Licensed by VAGA, New York, NY.

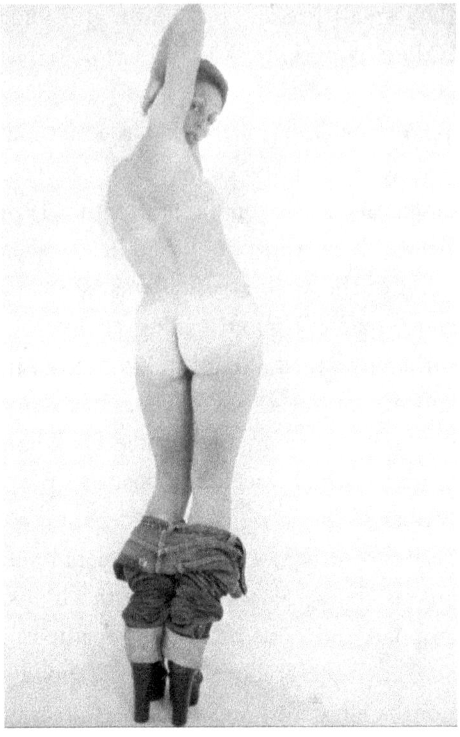

3. Lynda Benglis, invitation for *Lynda Benglis Presents Metallized Knots*, Paula Cooper Gallery, New York, May 1974. Photograph by Annie Leibovitz. © Lynda Benglis/Licensed by VAGA, New York, NY.

These 'sexual mockeries', as Benglis has dubbed them, reflected a growing trend among contemporary artists of promoting their work through provocative publicity imagery, with notable examples by Edward Ruscha, Judy Chicago, and Hannah Wilke, to name but a few published in the 1960s and 1970s. In blatantly coupling art and commerce, such images marketed the artists' edgy personae as much as, if not more so than, their artwork. For women artists, however, the fashioning of a public artistic identity had its paradoxes, given both the masculine gendering of the modern American artist and the objectification of the female body in popular culture and high art alike. Mindful of these issues, Benglis originally intended for her third sexual mockery, her nude portrait with the dildo, to appear in *Artforum* as an artistic project, specifically in the form of a centrefold pinup accompanying Robert Pincus-Witten's feature article. However, because the magazine's chief editor, John Coplans, was unwilling to give editorial space over to an individual artist, he and Benglis reached a compromise: for double the typical cost to advertise in *Artforum*, she was allowed to publish her image in the magazine's commercial space. With the approval of her dealer, Paula Cooper, Benglis proceeded with the advertisement. In making no mention of a specific show or opening, however, the resulting ad gave *Artforum* readers the impression that it was the artist, not her work, for sale.

The fallout from Benglis's gesture was immediate: *Artforum* received dozens of letters both penned in support of and expressing outrage over the artist's project, and a number of commentaries and essays quickly followed in other publications.[5] Consequently, the ad has become Benglis's best-known artistic statement; it is discussed in numerous contexts, from historical surveys of contemporary art to critical histories of the female pinup.[6] With only a few exceptions, however, most historical accounts suffer from a narrow focus and broad-stroke characterisations. In particular, the majority of the retellings of the image's production and the ensuing controversy focus on the vitriolic response Benglis received from the editorial staff at *Artforum*. In a rare moment of solidarity, five of the magazine's associate editors wrote a letter of protest outlining a number of concerns, foremost of which was their collective consternation over the 'extreme vulgarity' of Benglis's project and the perceived complicity of their magazine in its publication.[7] By couching their approbation in such terms, the editors fashioned themselves – and the magazine's readership – as unwitting victims of Benglis's tasteless publicity statement.[8] More specifically, their letter deemed the artist's ad a brutal insult to women, and thus to the magazine's commitment to feminist issues. In concluding that it made 'a shabby mockery' of the women's movement, the editors effectively cast Benglis's project as politically retrograde.

Though the editors were not alone in their condemnation of Benglis's ad, few of the other published responses or subsequent references to the image matched their tone of moral outrage. In revisiting their response to Benglis, the art historian Amelia Jones has convincingly argued that the editors' collective indignation proved symptomatic of other unacknowledged anxieties, specifically over the artist's aggressive and unapologetic flaunting of female sexuality. As Jones writes, 'Displaying the sexual excess of the threateningly active female subject in wild abandon, [Benglis] becomes that which *should not be seen*: woman as desirable body, woman with penis, woman with phallus, woman as self-producer, woman in control of the critical gaze'.[9] As a perceived threat to the editors' authority, Benglis's naked female body elicited fears that had to be 'rechanneled into critical opprobrium by those (male and female) invested in the masculine, heterosexual, modernist paradigm'.[10]

To make her point about Benglis's transgression and the disproportionate anxieties it incited from the *Artforum* staff, Jones compared its reception to the critical silence that greeted the appearance of an equally provocative publicity image by the artist Robert Morris in the spring of 1974, a few months prior to the publication of Benglis's dildo ad. Produced in conjunction with a solo exhibition at Castelli-Sonnabend Gallery in New York, Morris's self-image pictures the artist from the waist up, bare chested and wearing a German military helmet, aviator glasses, and wrist cuffs shackled to a length of chain draped around his neck (fig. 4). The photograph, taken by *Artforum* associate editor Rosalind Krauss, not only construed the artist as a sadomasochist but also transformed his upper body into a large phallus. Yet the virtual silence around its public appearance, Jones contends, offered proximate proof that the art world employed, and continues to employ, a different set of criteria for judging male and female artists. As she concludes,

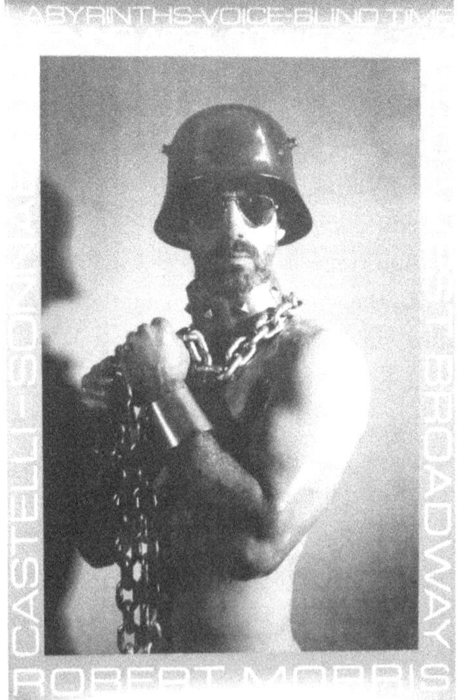

4. Robert Morris, poster for *Robert Morris: Labyrinths–Voice–Blind Time*, Castelli-Sonnabend Gallery, New York, April 1974, offset poster printed in two colours, 36 x 24 in. Photograph by Rosalind Krauss. Published by Castelli-Sonnabend, New York. Courtesy of Susan Inglett Gallery, NY. © 2011 Robert Morris/Licensed by Artists Rights Society (ARS), New York, NY.

'While Morris safely – if certainly ironically – reconstructs the male artist as penis ... the scandal Benglis's advertisement provoked at the time provides further proof of the threatening nature of her appropriation of power'.[11] As such, the responses to the two artists' projects effectively exposed the lack of gender neutrality in the production and reception of contemporary art.

Though not the first to recuperate Benglis's ad as a powerful feminist statement, Jones's assessment has done much to secure it as a popular progenitor of more contemporary feminist and queer body art, with Cindy Sherman and Mike Kelley, among others, citing its direct influence.[12] Indeed, the artist's phallus-wielding self-image has acquired an iconic status, its defiant 'fuck you' gesture – to borrow the words of feminist artist and scholar Joanna Frueh – overwhelmingly lauded as a visually powerful assertion of female sexual agency.[13] This recuperation, however, is not without problems, not least of which are the ways in which it tacitly disempowers the artist.

In the early 1990s, for example, Benglis's *Artforum* project was cast as a prescient forerunner to the postfeminist 'bad girls' phenomenon sweeping the contemporary art world. A much-debated term, 'bad girl' proved to be a short-lived but popular epithet for a new generation of in-your-face women artists, many of whom produced explicit body-oriented imagery and performances.[14] For proponents, the strength of 'bad girl' art lay in its subversive use of bawdy humour, wilful cultural appropriations, and unconventional expression of female sexuality. And as the curator Marcia Tanner avows, Benglis's ad deserved a heartfelt 'Thanks, Mom' for helping to inspire insouciant badness in a younger generation of women.[15]

While it is inevitable that pithy labels are useful for initial attempts to identify and historicise contemporary artistic practices, a number of feminist writers have been quick – rightfully so, I believe – to challenge the 'bad girl' label for its negative cultural connotations. Though appreciative of its sexy and recuperative edge, the US artist Barbara Pollack astutely asked in an article of 1991 if calling a woman 'bad' was truly empowering, or whether it remained shorthand for accusing her of possessing a 'bad reputation': as she concedes, it is 'a fine line to read that one is "bad" in her art but not "bad" in her life'.[16] Pollack's observation has relevance not only for the historicisation of Benglis's *Artforum* image but also for Benglis's subsequent reputation as a 'bad girl'. In particular it sheds light on the persistent impression that the artist's project stemmed directly from her personal entanglement with Robert Morris. For instance, Amelia Jones alludes to a romantic liaison between the two artists, as does the feminist artist and writer Mira Schor.[17]

Likewise, and according to several of the accounts included in Amy Newman's *Challenging Art: Artforum, 1962–1974*, a compilation of interviews about the magazine's first decade of operation, Benglis not only created her dildo ad in response to Morris's sadomasochistic poster but, in so doing, made an unseemly and unreciprocated (read: 'bad girl') bid for his attention. The critic Barbara Rose, for instance, contends that Benglis was 'trying to one up [Morris] all the time and probably also to torture him, and this ended with her taking out that ad'.[18] In contrast to such accounts, Benglis's own assertion to Newman that she 'was *not* doing it' in response to Morris, or in an attempt to garner his attention, rings hollow.[19] Despite her objections, Benglis comes across as (yet another) female artist whose significance is measured in terms of her relation to a high-profile man. The literature on Morris's career, conversely, never makes mention of Benglis as a potential collaborator or interlocutor in any capacity.

As an oral history of *Arforum*'s first decade of publication, Newman's *Challenging Art* clearly indulges in uncensored opinion and innuendo. In offering us a glimpse into the magazine's daily operations, it demonstrates how memory as a form of gossip is, as the cultural theorist Irit Rogoff claims, an exchange not of facts but of points of view. Gossip, continues Rogoff, traditionally deals with intimate relational knowledge of sexual identities and relationships; it is knowledge that is accompanied by 'certain qualifying frames' that act to disrupt master narratives.[20] Though gossip often serves as a policing agent, it also potentially compels our psychic fantasies for 'transgression and unruly excess'.[21] As an unruly and excessive sexual image, Benglis's ad fosters fantasies that necessarily exceed the artist and the specifics of her project; this is not in question. Yet rooted as they are in gossipy points of view, such fantasies also have concrete implications for an artist's critical reception, for the trajectory of her career, and for her subsequent historical assessment. In this instance, the fantasies repeatedly return to Benglis's personal 'badness' in a way that conflates her private and professional lives.

For example, while none of the first-person accounts in Newman's book openly describe a romantic entanglement between Benglis and Morris, a number of subsequent assessments, including those by Jones and Schor, have pointedly raised the issue, not as speculation, but as fact, and again despite the artist's claim to the contrary.[22] To be certain, I am not especially concerned to determine the 'truth' behind Benglis – Morris relationship, if only because memories are notoriously unreliable and personal histories are often rewritten with good intentions. However, I believe that repeated references to Morris's role as a sexual or artistic partner actually diminish the power and significance of Benglis's ad, specifically by foreclosing further consideration of other relationships, subjects, and experiences that have informed its production. While these may not inspire the same level of gossip and intrigue as the possible connection to Morris, they do help to flesh out the larger artistic and cultural contexts in which the artist created her project. In moving beyond Morris, and beyond the vicious editorial response, the present book thus considers how the dildo ad may be understood to dramatise issues and concerns central to Benglis's broader practice and milieu. It is, in the end, the artist's rich and diverse object production that forms the focus of the book.

the frozen gesture

When Benglis arrived in New York in 1964, a young painter from Louisiana with a BFA in hand from the H. Sophie Newcomb Memorial College for Women at Tulane University in New Orleans, she encountered a diverse range of artists and artistic practices. Though retrospectively distinguished under such labels as neo-dada, pop, minimalism, colour-field painting, and conceptualism, these practices shared a number of artistic and intellectual concerns, their distinctions proving less significant than their crosscurrents. For example, many of the artists now associated with these movements openly eschewed the conceit of painterly self-expression associated with postwar abstract expressionism. This is important to note with respect to Benglis, for though she gravitated towards gestural painting early on, the artist responded equally to the lexicon of new forms and materials to which these other practices were giving rise in New York in the mid-to-late 1960s.

Once in New York, Benglis befriended a group of artists that included Gordon Hart (to whom she was briefly married), Ron Gorchov, Marilyn Lenkowsky, Jennifer Bartlett, Stanton Kaye, Michael Goldberg, and Carl Andre. Through Hart, she soon met Annalee and Barnett Newman and socialised with the couple until the latter's death in 1970. Both Newman's friendship and his art made a lasting impression on the young artist. After a brief stint at the Brooklyn Museum School of Art (1964–5), Benglis abandoned her formal artistic education in favour of teaching at the secondary school level but soon left that career as well when opportunities came up in the professional art world. From 1966 to 1968, she worked as an assistant at the newly opened Bykert Gallery, owned by Klaus Kertess and Jeffrey Byers. It was a fortuitous affiliation, as she began to participate in shows at Bykert in 1968, exhibiting first a series of encaustic paintings and eventually her floor-bound latex pours. By 1969, Benglis was also exhibiting regularly at Paula Cooper Gallery, one of the first galleries to open in the Soho neighbourhood. The next few years brought a flurry of opportunities in New York, and in other US cities and abroad in Germany, and Benglis's work was exhibited alongside that of Eva Hesse, Robert Morris, Richard Van Buren, Alan Shields, Jennifer Bartlett, Judy Chicago, and Brice Marden, among others. By the time Robert Pincus-Witten offered his equivocal appraisal of her work in 1974, Benglis had shifted rapidly from one material to another, and from one body of work to another. Though these shifts seemed to yield different and seemingly 'capricious' results, to recall Pincus-Witten's term, each similarly stemmed from the artist's interest in using fluid and malleable materials to realise what she has called the 'frozen gesture'.

Over the years, the term 'frozen gesture' has persisted as a characterisation of Benglis's work. It forms the subtitle of Pincus-Witten's 1974 *Artforum* feature article and is given brief but helpful consideration by him in this context. The critic rightly observes that the term not only speaks to Benglis's interest in utilising fluid materials and gestural actions but also accounts for the cultural connotations embedded in her work; it acknowledges how gesture functions as a social mannerism – a 'beau geste', as Pincus-Witten writes. Not only are Benglis's frozen gestures, then, simply records of material processes but just as importantly, they are visual statements rich with cultural signification. A 'beau geste', according to *The Oxford English Dictionary*, entails 'a display of magnanimity', a definition that usefully captures the emotional tenor of Benglis's frozen gestures. This second connotation of the frozen gesture likewise conveys something of the artist's risk-taking approach, her intrepid aplomb, and her openness to new influences. While this amenability has generated an eclectic body of work, it has also allowed Benglis to go where less confident artists might fear to tread: towards the decorative, the theatrical, and the vulgar, for instance. With a healthy dose of humour and respect, the artist has tackled cherished artistic values and hierarchies.

the feminist problematic

In exploring the multiple implications of Benglis's 'frozen gestures', this book offers no overarching theoretical framework. Instead, I have allowed each body of work under discussion to dictate the direction of my analysis. However, an important topic that weaves through each chapter concerns the artist's gendered identity and its significance for both her artistic production and her critical reception. That the early years of Benglis's career coincided with the burgeoning US women's movement suggests one reason for this emphasis, as does her subsequent positioning as a 'bad mother' to younger generations of women and queer artists.

To be certain, however, my interest in parsing the feminist politics of Benglis's career rubs up against the artist's open eschewal of a feminist identity. A comment she made in a 1979 interview sums up her position in this regard: 'I don't wish to separate myself from [feminism], I don't wish necessarily to be a part of it, but I am a part of it whether I want it or not'.[23] Here the artist admits to some reluctance even as she recognises the inevitability of being caught up in circumstances larger than she. Given her sexual mockeries project, this stated position might seem disingenuous, or at the very least, it downplays those instances in which Benglis has seemed anything but reluctant to enter the fray of sexual politics. Nonetheless, I take seriously the artist's desire to problematise a straightforward classification of either her artwork or her artistic identity, while simultaneously admitting to my own investment in writing as a feminist art historian.

In a 1981 essay entitled 'Reviewing Modernist Criticism', the US artist Mary Kelly employed the term 'feminist problematic' in order to ask how and where to locate the feminist character of an artwork. In wanting to identify the ways in which the social, the material, and the sexual are embodied in a visual form, Kelly usefully moved away from the issue of intentionality and from the idea of a work of art as a discrete and autonomous entity to allow for a broader consideration of the ideologies that structure social practices and systems of representation.[24] Expanding on Kelly's initial distinction, the British art historian Griselda Pollock has proffered that a feminist perspective (or problematic) is determined not by the gender or political identity of the artist but rather by the 'effect' of the work: 'the way the work acts upon, makes demands of, and produces positions for its viewers. It is feminist because of the way it works as a text within a specific social space in relation to dominant codes and conventions of art and to dominant ideologies of femininity'.[25] Here Pollock considers how the viewing positions solicited by a work enable or, conversely, undermine certain institutional frameworks and discourses around femininity. As I argue throughout this book, there are important moments when Benglis's practice, whether intentionally or not, may be understood to challenge viewers' perceptions of existing aesthetic values and hierarchies in which the feminine is inextricably caught up, and in ways significant for writing feminist histories of contemporary art.

The emergence of feminist art history and criticism in the 1970s brought with it a healthy scepticism of the value of the artistic monograph. Scholars including Griselda Pollock have argued convincingly for rejecting a monographic approach because it perpetuates biased notions of individual genius and success and imposes a coherent and unified narrative on an artist's oeuvre.[26] In heeding these concerns, I have nonetheless chosen to focus this book around an individual career. In so doing, I concur with art historian Amy Schlegel's reassessment of the value of the monograph. In particular, she notes that when it abandons a strictly biographical structure in favour of a thematic focus, the single-artist study performs important feminist work: it redresses the dearth of scholarly material that still plagues the work of contemporary women artists while simultaneously expanding the methodological scope of feminist art-historical scholarship.[27] Building on this cogent argument, I would add that because in-depth analyses of specific practices presume that the artist under consideration is both representative and exceptional – the paradox that ultimately underlies the monograph, Schlegel notes – it necessitates new ways of looking at a given context and thus potentially chips away at period generalisations and master art-historical narratives.[28]

* * *

The five chapters of this book are roughly chronological in their examination of key bodies of art in Benglis's oeuvre. In penning the first, book-length art-historical examination of her practice, I have not attempted an exhaustive treatment of the artist's output over the past forty years. Instead I have chosen first to return to previously neglected aspects of her early career before then positing some readings of more current projects. While each chapter focuses on an issue or set of issues in relation to specific artworks, my interpretations often implicitly extend to other moments across the artist's career. For instance, my consideration in chapter 2 of the corporeal character of Benglis's encaustic lozenge paintings of the early 1970s suggests only one way in which the artist's work as a whole models the sensate body and embodied modes of subjectivity. Likewise, in chapter 4, I use a series of knotted relief sculptures from the mid-1970s to elaborate on Benglis's engagement with perceptions of taste and decorative aesthetic values, though arguably these issues are relevant to the majority of her output.

Accordingly, in chapter 1, I examine the role of process in Benglis's latex and polyurethane pours of the late 1960s and early 1970s. The pours marked the artist's professional entry into the New York art world, where she was quickly classified as a process artist working in the legacy of Jackson Pollock's famous drip technique. The circulation of two early sets of images documenting Benglis at work on her pours helped to secure this narrative of process and inheritance. However, as I argue here, this account comes at the expense of more careful consideration of the resulting artwork. Beginning with an analysis of the latex pieces and continuing with the polyurethane installations that followed, I indicate how the works produce broader artistic and contextual associations than the emphasis on artistic process and inheritance reveals. At the chapter's end, I examine Benglis's response to the 1971 publication in *Art News* of Linda Nochlin's feminist essay 'Why Have There Been No Great Women Artists?' in order to address the artist's growing awareness of the sexual politics of her critical reception, notably as it was repeatedly configured through the connection to Pollock.

Concurrent to the poured latex and polyurethane projects, Benglis produced a series of small encaustic relief paintings, the intimate and tactile character of which have inspired claims for the gendered nature of the artist's practice, and for identifying the bodily allusions in her work as specifically female. Chapter 2 examines the contexts in which the gendered readings of the wax paintings first emerged in the early 1970s before then proposing that these works posit a more fluid conception of corporeal identifications and subjective encounters. Drawing on interviews Benglis gave in the early 1970s, and developing a close formal reading of the encaustic paintings, I argue that their corporeal effects necessarily exceed the body of the artist, presenting instead an androgynous eroticism that shifts depending on the viewer's embodied relation to the art.

I devote chapter 3 to an analysis of Benglis's video production. Like many of her peers, Benglis turned to video in the 1970s as a seemingly natural extension of her sculptural practice, producing over a dozen works between

1972 and 1977. As critics and writers attempted to grapple with the theoretical implications of early video technology, the artist's output was a significant reference point. For women practitioners, video represented an arena of artistic production not yet territorialised by male artists, however it was a medium that also enabled them to engage with existing cultural and artistic conventions concerning female identity, the body, and self-representation. In looking at the unique possibilities video afforded Benglis, this chapter assesses her efforts against the backdrop of contemporary debates about technologically mediated experiences, as well as feminist conversations about women's autobiographical narrations of self. Specifically, I demonstrate how Benglis employed different formal and conceptual techniques to call into question the documentary realism enabled by the video medium.

Several related series of knotted relief sculptures from the 1970s form the main subject of chapter 4. Evidencing Benglis's expanded material repertoire, these works pleasurably challenge established perceptions of taste and artistic value. In pinpointing the sources of their transgressions, I argue that the sculptures demonstrate Benglis's recourse to cultural and artistic practices persistently coded as feminine and middle class in the post-war era. As such, the artist productively reworked this feminine 'middle' in a manner that I identify as campy. Though largely associated with gay subcultural practices, by the 1960s, camp represented a sophisticated mode of cultural politics that appealed to a range of practitioners. Its indulgence in feminine decoration, artifice, and theatricality rendered camp especially appealing to women artists interested in reworking denigrated modes of visual production.

Chapter 5 analyses several bodies of work that Benglis has produced since the late 1970s. In assessing three decades' worth of material, this chapter is necessarily broader in scope than the previous ones. It outlines a number of new directions while also demonstrating the continuation of certain formal and conceptual concerns in the artist's mature work. The introduction of new materials and techniques is significant here, as is the artist's attention to sensual surface embellishments and decorative effects. I conclude the chapter with an examination of Benglis's use of metal casting, notably in a series of public fountain projects undertaken since the mid-1980s. The fountains illuminate the artist's desire to produce work that is more expressly interactive: to that end, I consider how the element of process becomes a factor of the viewer's perceptual experience.

Overall, this book makes a case for looking anew at Lynda Benglis's career and, by implication, for assessing its place in histories of contemporary art. To state it slightly differently: I choose to take Pincus-Witten's aforementioned assessment – that the artist is 'capricious' and 'casual' in her approach – as indication not of carelessness or arbitrariness on the artist's part (as his words connote) but of a need to challenge the evaluative frameworks that appear to buckle and fold so easily under pressure from an individual artistic practice.

1 Boundless Forms and Continuous Imagery

'Some artists use a brush. Miss Benglis uses a pour'.[1] With this simple distinction, the author of the 1971 article 'Latex: One Artist's Raw Material' captured one of the most compelling aspects of Benglis's use of liquid latex, namely, her technique of pouring the medium from cans directly onto the floor to create large and boldly coloured spills (fig. 5). Each pour was the product of a complex choreography, necessitating a balance of spontaneity and precision, not to mention physical endurance, as the artist frequently wielded five-gallon cans of the pigmented medium. Benglis had opportunities to produce some of her pours *in situ*, such that the condition of the gallery floor and the parameters of the architectural space became important variables in the artistic process. Indicative of the expanded definitions of materials and techniques that typified US art of the late 1960s, her latex pieces were immediately aligned with a sensibility variously identified at the time as post-minimal, anti-formal, and process art.[2]

Benglis did not, however, consider process to be the central conceit of the pours. Rather, she envisioned her gestural technique as a means simply to free the work from a fixed armature and, in some cases, to integrate it into a specific architectural environment. In a statement for the 1969 exhibition *Art in Process IV* at Finch College Museum of Art in New York, Benglis voiced a position that she would repeat over the years: 'The image varies with the materials used. ... I am not involved with just process. I am involved in all the associations with material'.[3] Significantly, the privileging of process has tended to occlude considerations of the work itself, and of the viewer's experience of it. Indeed, the issue

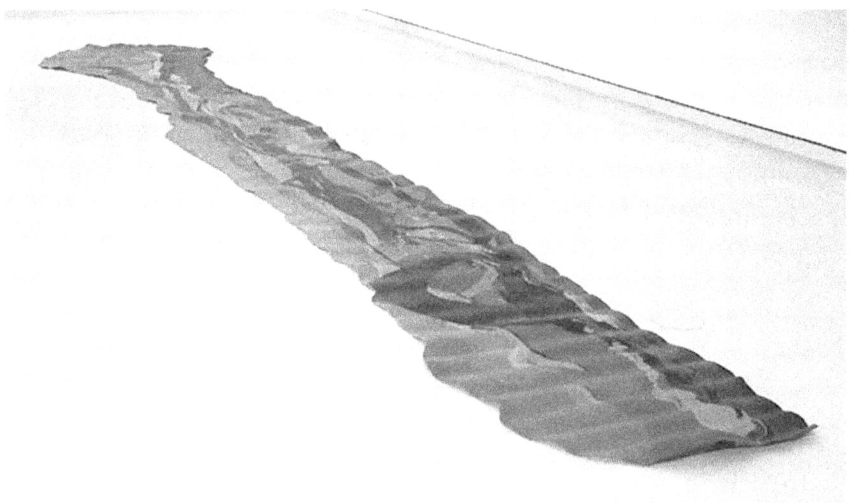

5. Lynda Benglis, *Fallen Painting*, 1968, poured pigmented latex, 355 x 69 ¼ in. (901.7 x 175.9 cm). Albright-Knox Art Gallery, Buffalo, NY; gift of Michael Goldberg, Lynda Benglis, and Paula Cooper, 1992. © Lynda Benglis/Licensed by VAGA, New York, NY.

of spectatorship has largely fallen away as art-historical accounts instead stress what is now largely described as the 'performative' nature of Benglis's pouring process. In this context, the performative encompasses the original concept of process as a physical interaction with artistic mediums while also accounting for issues of artistic identity, as enacted through the material process.

I believe that this privileging of process and, in turn, of the performative dimension of Benglis's technique is largely due to the publication and subsequent circulation of two sets of photographs documenting the artist at work: the first was taken in the context of a 1969 exhibition at the Whitney Museum of American Art, the second to accompany an article published in *Life* in 1970. These photographs, and notably the second set, are frequently reproduced in art-historical studies, where they serve not only to emphasise the act of making over the finished work but also, significantly, to reveal the similarities of Benglis's procedure to Jackson Pollock's famous dripping technique.[4] Consequently, a convincing narrative of process and inheritance has developed, one dramatised by the younger artist's status as a woman reworking the masculinist legacy of gestural abstract expressionism. The 1974 publication of Benglis's infamous *Artforum* dildo advertisement, which I discuss in the introduction, further codified this art-historical narrative by placing the artist's mobile and performative body at the centre of her practice.

In acknowledging that the performative (and the performance of gender) remains a compelling lens through which to consider Benglis's pours, however, this chapter shifts focus to reconsider the actual works of art, their formal innovations, and the viewer's experience of them. Beginning with the latex pieces and continuing with an analysis of the polyurethane installations that immediately followed, I examine the significance of Benglis's dramatic staging in her work of a series of interrelated formal and conceptual tensions. These tensions, I argue, inscribe the viewer into different viewing modalities and give rise to broader artistic and contextual associations than the emphasis on artistic process, performativity, and inheritance suggests.[5]

fallen paintings

Benglis discovered the formal possibilities of liquid latex during a visit in 1967 to Sol LeWitt's New York studio, where she saw a small work that Eva Hesse had executed in preparation for her larger sculpture *Schema* (1967). The study, comprising nine moulded hemispheres arranged in a grid on a square latex mat, impressed Benglis with its glossy suppleness and highly textured, skin-like surface, the latter an effect Hesse emphasised by painting additional coats of latex over the moulded spherical forms (fig. 6).[6] The work also evidenced a fundamental tension between its geometric ordering and its labile materiality. Benglis had been exploring a similar juxtaposition in a series of encaustic relief paintings she initiated around 1966. This work, coupled with the introduction to Hesse's latex study, contributed to her eventual dissatisfaction with the constraints of a painting armature. As Benglis recounts in her statement for *Art in Process IV*, 'With the firing of the wax paintings, I realized that the idea of directing matter logically was absurd. Matter could and would take, finally, its own form. This is the reason I felt it necessary to make in pigmented latex several large paintings that were boundless in form and continuous in imagery'.[7] The method of pouring latex directly onto the floor was, for Benglis, a pragmatic solution to what she considered to be an illogical attachment to a rectilinear ground. The constrictions of the conventional painting format prohibited the kinds of compositions she sought to achieve with her material processes; by attending to the interactions of colour on colour, rather than colour on canvas, she effectively dissolved the two-dimensional surface and its assertion as a physical ground. The resulting latex pieces, which the artist dubbed 'fallen paintings', evidenced the integration of material, process, colour, and image she had been unable to

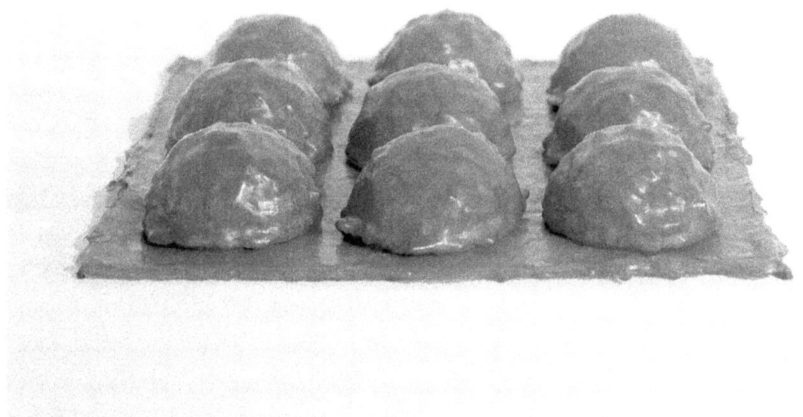

6. Eva Hesse, *No title*, 1967, latex, 9 ½ x 9 ½ in. (24 x 24 cm); nine hemispheres, each diameter 2 ½ in. (6.4 cm). The LeWitt Collection, Chester, CT. © The Estate of Eva Hesse. Courtesy Galerie Hauser & Wirth, Zurich. Photo: Abby Robinson, New York.

achieve with paint or wax. Thus, while Hesse continued to use latex to mould forms and paint surfaces, Benglis took advantage of its viscosity at the moment of the pouring to generate amorphous and seemingly boundless spills.

The shift to latex also involved one of scale for Benglis. Though she continued to produce smaller encaustic works in her studio (see chapter 2), the artist directed much of her artistic energy during this period to producing latex pours in large interior spaces. A single work entitled *Fallen Painting* (1968) demonstrates the boundless configurations to which the artist aspired with her new material (fig. 5). With a length of approximately thirty feet, the pour pools noticeably at either end in a manner that suggests extended pauses in Benglis's movements. Like all the extant latex pieces, over the years *Fallen Painting* has succumbed to age and storage constraints. While it would have originally hugged the floor, with passing time the once-glossy latex has rippled and no longer lies flush. Under gallery lighting, its wavy surface and softly turned edges cast shadows and create literal depth, while an accretion of dirt and other detritus draws unintended attention to a now matte and pocked surface.

In contrast to these signs of aging, the fluorescent pigments Benglis used in *Fallen Painting* – a marbleised blend of bright green, dark blue, tangerine orange, canary yellow, and cherry red – have retained much of their initial saturation and offer some sense of the work's original chromatic effect. Benglis recognised early on that her bold Day-Glo palette not only illuminated the variables of the pouring process but also defied a clear reading of spatial relations. As she once noted, her pieces may have been 'down on the floor, but the color was up'.[8] On another occasion she described the effect of the colouration in terms of 'bouncing', even titling a latex pour with this description in mind (plate 1).[9] As it was originally installed in a corner of Bykert Gallery in New York, the vibrant Day-Glo hues in *Bounce* (1969) no doubt seemed to ricochet off the adjoining walls like a rubber bouncy ball. Or, as critic Peter Schjeldahl observed in writing about the Bykert show, Benglis's colourful choices deny 'the eye a precise reading of the work's shape and consistency and thus heighten the confusion of painting, sculpture, and "other" to an exquisite pitch'. What most struck the critic about *Bounce*, however, was Benglis's 'nearly exact repetition' of Pollock's painting technique.[10] Schjeldahl was not alone in this assessment: overwhelmingly, curators and critics found that the younger artist's pours singularised gestural process in a manner highly reminiscent of the abstract expressionist's style.

This attention to process earned Benglis an invitation to participate in *Anti-Illusion: Procedures/Materials*, the 1969 landmark exhibition organised by Marcia Tucker and James Monte for the Whitney Museum of American Art. The exhibition was the first in a major US museum to showcase process-oriented practices, and it helped to establish the definitive set of criteria for such work. For Monte, writing in the *Anti-Illusion* catalogue, the selected artists epitomised an important shift away from modernist formal aesthetics. Their commitment to investigating material procedures, proposed the curator, opened up a series of radical questions about 'how art should be seen, what should be done with it and finally, what is an art experience'.[11]

Robert Morris's artwork and writings constituted an acknowledged springboard for the *Anti-Illusion* exhibition. In particular, his 1968 essay 'Anti Form', published in *Artforum*, proffered a description of process-oriented art to which the Whitney curators were clearly indebted. Here Morris first observed that a number of his peers were abandoning predetermined idealised forms in favour of work arrived at through unpredictable, non-hierarchical and seemingly random configurations. Utilising unconventional materials and elemental physical procedures, they allowed such variables as gravity and chance to inflect the working process, the end results of which no longer conformed to clear-cut categories of painting and sculpture. According to Morris, an important genesis for these tendencies could be found in the work of Jackson Pollock and, to a somewhat lesser degree, Morris Louis. Each painter's technique, he argued, retained the artistic process as 'part of the end form' of the artwork. Their practices demonstrated to a subsequent generation of artists that a 'disengagement with preconceived enduring forms and order for things is a positive assertion'.[12] Within the paradigm of process and anti-formal art, the object status of the works proved less significant than the highly experimental and experiential dimensions of their production.

Monte and Tucker subsequently echoed Morris's critical emphasis on the phenomenological and situational contexts of 'anti-formal' artistic procedures. In planning for the exhibition, the curators invited several artists to create their work on site, and though Benglis was not one of them, she poured *Contraband* (1969) in her studio with the Whitney space in mind (plate 2). Tucker and Monte also commissioned the photographer Robert Fiore, a participant in the show, to document all the artists at work in their studios. Published in the accompanying exhibition catalogue, these images detail individual working methods but rarely afford clear views of the finished artwork. Fiore's photographs of Benglis at work in her Baxter Street studio capture the artist's balletic movements and the fluid streaming of the latex, the two actions neatly and inevitably aligned (fig. 7). However, while Fiore's photographs of Benglis underscore how well the artist's material process aligned with Tucker and Monte's curatorial vision, the resulting artwork proved more difficult to accommodate in the exhibition. Just prior to the opening of *Anti-Illusion*, Benglis withdrew *Contraband*.

There appears to be no consensus on the circumstances leading up to the removal of *Contraband* from the Whitney exhibition. Benglis recalls that the curators were unhappy with her strident colour choices, and in particular her inclusion of bubble-gum pink, and they expressed concern that the latex pour would deflect attention away from other works in the exhibition, none of which contained a comparable degree of colouration.[13] Marcia Tucker, in turn, recollects that the initial decision to invite Benglis was based on a much smaller work that the curators had seen in the artist's studio, and that *Contraband* – its length approximately thirty-four feet – simply exceeded the space originally allocated to it.[14] As a compromise, during the final installation of the show, the curators decided to move Benglis's work out of the main gallery and into the atrium. In its new location, however, the pour had to be partially elevated on a ramp so as not to impede the flow of traffic in a crowded area of the museum.[15] This last-minute alteration to its installation directly refuted Tucker's catalogue description of Benglis's pours as floor-bound projects that

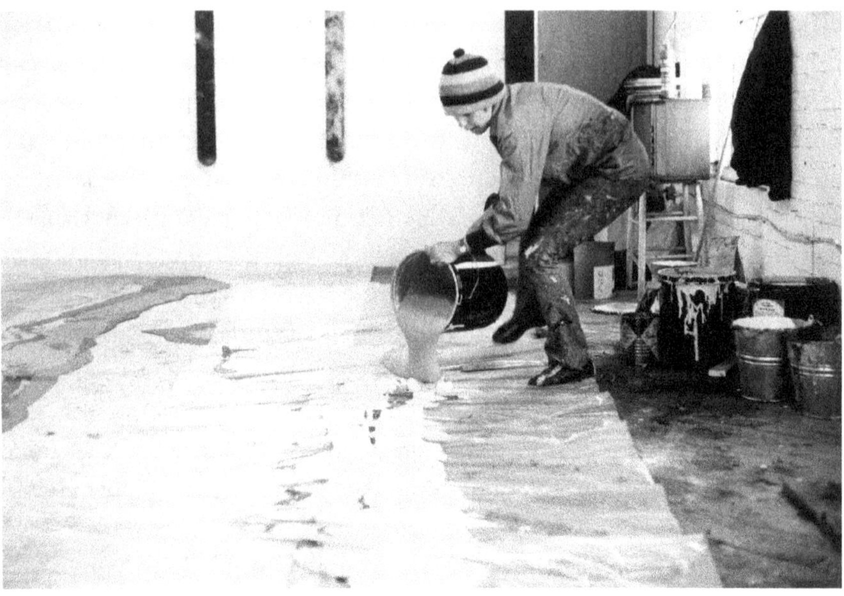

7. Lynda Benglis creating the art work *Contraband*, 1969. Photograph by Bob Fiore. Courtesy Whitney Museum of American Art Archives, New York. © Lynda Benglis/Licensed by VAGA, New York, NY.

were 'neither stretched nor hung' nor presumably placed on a support of any kind.[16] Changing the horizontal orientation of the latex likewise undermined Tucker and Monte's mutual assertion that site-specificity was essential to the conception and display of 'anti-illusion' works.

In the end, however, the choice to alter *Contraband*'s installation revealed a fundamental difference in how Benglis and the curators perceived the work. Presumably, for Monte and Tucker, the frozen swirls of coloured latex effectively conveyed 'process' whether the work was placed on the floor or positioned on a ramp. For Benglis, conversely, the elevation destroyed the work's visual illusion, its 'image' of a colourful and somewhat toxic-looking spill on the museum's black-tiled floor.[17] Illusion *and* allusion were, in fact, germane to Benglis's conceptualisation of her practice, and as I discuss in the following pages, her exploration of new processes and materials served that end.

Benglis later deemed the Whitney curators' decision to elevate her latex pour 'totally dishonest'. In retrospect, the artist conceded that she did not handle the situation very well: 'I'd had no previous showing experience and I was just ... this mad girl'.[18] This decision to withdraw from the museum exhibition, however, had no perceivable negative impact on the artist's early career opportunities and critical reputation: later that same season, Benglis poured *Bounce* for a group show at Bykert Gallery, and in September of 1969, she exhibited *Contraband* in another group exhibition at the newly opened Paula Cooper Gallery, marking the beginning of a long professional and personal relationship between Cooper and Benglis. And though her work was absent from the Whitney galleries in the spring of 1969, the museum's annual painting exhibition in December included *Bullitt*, one of the artist's new polyurethane foam pours (fig. 9). The next few years, in fact, brought Benglis a significant number of invitations for national and international exhibitions and commissions, as well as a flurry of reviews and interviews in both art publications and the popular press. A subtext of many of these opportunities, the connections to Pollock, were rarely overlooked. The comparison undeniably worked in Benglis's favour, providing a critical frame of reference for the artist's bold reinterpretation of a painterly idiom.

fling, dribble, and dip

Indicative of her growing reputation, in February 1970 Benglis was featured along with Eva Hesse, Richard Serra, and Richard Van Buren in a photo-essay in *Life* entitled 'Fling, Dribble and Dip', the premise of which was the ongoing vitality of Pollock's legacy for contemporary art.[19] Gracing the article's opening layout were six large colour photographs depicting Benglis executing a latex piece at the University of Rhode Island in Kingston (plate 3). From the initial pour of red along one gallery wall to the final moment when Benglis stood back, one arm akimbo, to appraise the results, the *Life* reader could watch the piece unfurl from the corner of the gallery in a succession of colourful rivulets and puddles against a dull grey floor. Forty gallons of rubber in all went into the pour, the artist's palette consisting mainly of fluorescent red and yellow, with lesser areas of green, blue, pink, and orange.

To underscore the connection to Pollock, the *Life* essay also included one of Hans Namuth's well-known photographs from 1950 of the painter at work in his East Hampton studio. Captured from above, Pollock leans in to distribute paint onto his floor-bound canvas. *Life* photographer Henry Groskinsky also shot Benglis from an elevated position, and in one photo in particular, in which she is seen stepping carefully into her work to pour a bucket of yellow latex, the artist's pose uncannily echoes the scene captured by Namuth's camera. Based on this visual comparison alone, a reader could easily extrapolate the commonalities between the two artists: both utilised a fluid medium, both exploited gravity, and both literally entered their large-scale artworks in a manner that brought artist and material together in a common physical space.

More so than any of the other artists documented in 'Fling, Dribble and Dip', the images of Benglis at work prioritised what Richard Serra would elsewhere ascribe to advertising photography more generally, namely, 'high image content ... [and] easy Gestalt reading'.[20] Conversely, while Serra's method of splashing molten lead afforded an equally compelling variation on Pollock's flinging of paint, neither the documentation of the respirator-clad artist nor the resulting work – jagged strips of monochromatic lead – made for as spectacular a visual juxtaposition as the images of Benglis at work on her pour (plate 4). In fact, for some *Life* readers, it may have proven difficult to determine the exact character of Serra's pieces, their rough-hewn forms seeming to blend in with the scuffed floors, metal plates, and surrounding studio detritus. Simply put, Benglis's graceful execution and colourful results offered a more 'camera-friendly' reiteration of Pollock's drip technique than did Serra's splashed lead castings, Van Buren's fibreglass sculptures, or Hesse's latex-coated rope sculpture. Likewise, her bold colour combinations – with hues reflecting the cultural tastes of the time – evidenced another kind of fashionability, one associated with consumerism and popular commodities rather than avant-garde experimentation. If the decorative overtures of Benglis's latex pours worried the colour-cautious *Anti-Illusion* curators, as the artist has claimed, such associations fit comfortably into a contemporary magazine such as *Life*.

In three early and significant contexts – the *Anti-Illusion* catalogue, Schjeldahl's review of the Bykert Gallery exhibition, and the *Life* feature essay – the connection between Pollock and Benglis emphasised the centrality of process to both artists' work. Each likewise positioned the abstract expressionist as the ultimate source of the younger artist's poured process, thereby establishing a procedural debt that, while propitious, would prove difficult to shed. Though Benglis did not reject the connection, on the occasions when she spoke of it, she gave it a slightly different inflection. Pollock, she told a reporter in 1971, 'pioneered the movement of dealing with materials used by the artist as the prime manifestation of imagery. ... He drew with paint by dipping into cans of liquid colour and making an image on canvas placed on the floor, which was subsequently framed and hung. This was a new way of thinking'.[21] Pollock's process, in other words, remained tied to the production of an image, a claim Benglis advanced about her own working method in her 1969 statement for *Art in Process IV* and again in 1983, her assertion even more emphatic with the passage of time: 'I was not interested in isolating each pour in the installation pieces – I was interested in the final image.... Artists such as myself were exploring new materials in art in order to make different kinds of images'.[22] Such images, her words tacitly suggest, were to be found not through the photographic documentation of her working process but in a more direct engagement with the work itself.

Benglis voiced a not-uncommon concern at the time about the limitations of photography in capturing the experience of the artwork. Serra's reference to the 'easy Gestalt reading' of advertising imagery made a similar point about the contrivances of the photographic document. By bracketing the artwork into an easily consumable picture, the camera's elevated eye could not adequately convey the actual encounter between the artist and his or her materials, or between the spectator and the resulting artwork.[23] Robert Morris also elaborated on the problem of photographic documentation and the production of images in his 1969 article 'Notes on Sculpture, Part IV: Beyond Objects'. The substitution of a photograph of the artwork for the actual experience of it, he averred, confuses the 'record with the thing' and relegates the art to a static and essentially 'dead' form. Contending that the reliance on photography revealed a 'conservative' preoccupation with closed systems of analysis, Morris distinguished it from the 'image' afforded by the actual artwork. While the tendency for process artists to employ 'stuff, substances in many states – from chunks, to particles, to slime, to whatever' – largely undermines the pictorial character of the work, Morris conceded that the resulting art 'does in fact provide a general sort of image'.[24] Thus it was not 'image' per se that Morris repudiated in favour of process, but simply the one subject to the conventions of photographic imaging or gestalt principles.

For all these artists, including Benglis, photographic documents not only potentially misrepresented the artistic process but also presented a contrived view of the work, as professional photographers often relied on ladders to obtain the 'best' perspective. In the context of the gallery, Benglis's latex pours staged a more complex encounter for the mobile viewer than the elevated camera's view suggests. That the firsthand experience of the work did not simply reproduce the camera's gestalt image is clear from Peter Schjeldahl's review of *Bounce* and his description of his inability to discern the exact nature of the work – recall, for instance, his observation that the pour initially forbade 'the eye a precise reading of the work's shape and consistency'. Eventually, however, the critic was able to give structure to his experience, first by comparing Benglis's pour to a 'prodigious volcanic pool, sulphurous and beautiful', then by conceding that the materiality of the pigmented rubber, and perhaps too its loud Day-Glo colouration, rendered such 'romantic reveries difficult'.[25]

Schjeldahl's impressions of Benglis's work did not necessarily occur sequentially or cumulatively and indeed may have oscillated as he manoeuvred around the pour and the space in which it was located. His review does indicate how difficult it can be to resist analogizing an abstract work of art through previously known (or even imagined) categories of experience. Indeed, Benglis's latex pours have generated a number of associations, largely but not exclusively to natural phenomena: in addition to Schjeldahl's reference to a 'volcanic pool', critic Emily Wasserman once compared them to 'amoeba' and 'protoplasm', Klaus Kertess to an 'oil spill', and Benglis herself to both Louisiana bayous and planetary bodies.[26] The artist has noted retrospectively that the NASA space mission of the late 1960s was a significant point of reference for her, even inspiring some of the titles for her works. She explains:

> We had arrived on the moon and our photographs from that vantage point began to show our planet and the depiction of the both real and synthesized landing by video which was broadcast throughout the world showed our expansion of the world, [there] appeared to me to be a great distancing of the way we perceive matter. ... We were looking back at ourselves. My latex floor paintings called *Planet* and *Contraband* have to do with that sense of the visualization of matter, of that distancing of ourselves from the material world and they expressed a kind of phenomenological, otherworldly viewing.[27]

For Benglis, the moon landing induced a feeling of spatial dislocation and dematerialisation that she sought to express in her latex pours. In downplaying her actual handling of the latex – by relying on the bucket to distribute the material – the artist literally distanced herself from the medium, allowing it to follow its own liquid inclinations with minimal interference. Likewise, and just as the images of the earth suspended in space temporally undermined Benglis's sense of embodied viewing, and of recognisable coordinates from which to anchor herself, so too do the more successful latex pieces convey something of this sensation: the vibrant fluorescent colours temporarily disorient, while the works' indeterminate scale (as opposed to their actual size) also effects a momentary instability. Their 'scalelessness' affords the viewer no definitive sense of his or her own embodied relation to the works. The pours are by turns the variegated topography of a distant planet, the surface of a pond and the microscopic structure of an amoeba. Immense or microscopic: the difference between the two collapses. Further, and as Benglis intimates with reference to the actual and staged moon landings, a sense of what constitutes reality is momentarily thrown off kilter. In turn, the latex pours engender a tension between the natural and the contrived.

In 1966, the artist Peter Hutchinson coined the term 'abstract mannerism' to describe an emerging artistic sensibility he felt reflected an intellectualised response to the breakdown of artistic, social, scientific, and political certainties in the mid-1960s. Though written about artists more closely aligned with minimalism than Benglis, including Dan Flavin, Robert Smithson, and Charles Hinman, Hutchinson's account captures something of the formal and affective impact of the latex pours. Characterised by 'elegance, high technique, acid colour, drama, [and] use of the cliché', abstract mannerism turned to artifice and exaggeration as a means to counter certainty and reason. Stemming from a place of despair and doubt, it parodically pictured 'a world in intellectual hysteria, punctuated by frozen inactivity, a world where space-time cease to have meaning, a world of soundless gestures, where humans do not live'.[28] While Benglis's pours are neither cynical nor hysterical to the degree described by Hutchinson, their 'mannerist' qualities are self-consciously affected and as such exist in tension with the works' expressionistic and romantic overtures.

For the critic Emily Wasserman, however, the emotional overtures of Benglis's latex pours proved less significant than their formal status, and specifically their failure to convince as either a painterly image or a floor-bound object. As she writes of *Bounce*, 'It is not strong enough as that protoplasmic mat... nor does it hold its own as a kind of painting entirely freed from an auxiliary ground. ... Its irresolution suggests some of the conceptual and methodological problems which concern Miss Benglis: aiming to reconstitute one's perception of the art object, she has not yet clearly realized her own conception of exactly what it is that she is making to elicit that radical reorganization of visual, mental, or somatic responses'.[29] Whether or not we agree, Wasserman's qualification recalls Benglis's initial impetus with the latex. In wanting to breach the limitations of conventional painting, the artist necessarily moved into the literal space of sculpture. Though this move allowed her to dramatise the pictorial character of her work, as Wasserman opines, it did not necessarily entail a sufficient level of materiality to justify its presence on the floor. This is not a question of success or failure, but one of recognising the pivotal role of the latex pours in the artist's early oeuvre: in resolving one set of problems, the work opened the door to others. In many respects, Benglis's subsequent use of polyurethane foam picked up where the latex left off. The shift enabled the artist to continue to explore pictorial concerns, but with a material possessing greater physicality than latex. 'I suppose I found myself a sculptor', Benglis conceded to an interviewer in 1982 about her work in polyurethane.[30]

plastic tensions

Just as she had done with the latex, Benglis initially poured liquid polyurethane directly on the floor, where it formed low-lying, semi-flexible mounds. By adjusting her recipe as well as the timing of the actual pouring process, the artist was able to control the volume of the foaming that occurred.[31] The majority of the floor-bound polyurethane pours of 1968–9 are brightly pigmented with Day-Glo, the vivid colours functioning as both a surface condition and a structural component of the work. A comparison between an untitled work (1969) and *Bounce* demonstrates the different effects that Benglis achieved with each medium (plates 1, 5). No longer a flattened mat, the polyurethane version is a softly modulated topography of rainbow hues. Colour still generates optical 'bouncing', but now it also possesses a greater sense of physical materiality. In Benglis's untitled piece, photographed here in indirect light in the artist's Baxter Street studio, the presence of shadows confirms the work's three dimensionality, yet at the same time some of the individual fluorescent colours appear to expand and constrict of their own accord: the pour is thus both defined by and exceeds the actual space it occupies.

Even more so than the latex pours, Benglis's foam pieces traffic in formal and perceptual contradictions: the works appear soft but are rigid to the touch, look bulky but are lightweight, appear organic but are synthetic. These 'series of ironies', as Benglis calls them, are largely the result of using plastic foam.[32] As Roland Barthes famously decreed, plastic is a marvellous substance, its 'prestigious free-wheeling through Nature' giving humankind a pleasurable sense of empowerment over the material world. The prosaic character of plastic may, in the eyes of many, make it 'a disgraced material'; however, for Barthes, its protean capabilities also render it the 'the stuff of alchemy'.[33] As a highly mutable chemical substance, plastic proved appealing to artists in the US art world of the 1960s and 1970s. The material readily lent itself to a seemingly infinite number of forms and contexts: from Donald Judd's use of coloured plexiglass to Claes Oldenburg's soft vinyl sculptures and Larry Bell's cast resin forms, plastic played no stylistic favourites. For some artists, the material connoted modern industry and technological advancements, and for others, it invoked mass consumerism and cultural excess, while for yet others, it was its manifold formal qualities that proved most attractive.[34] For Benglis, it often entailed all three. Not all artists, however, approached plastic on its own terms. For the critic Robert Pincus-Witten, writing in 1970, many practitioners simply used the material in 'imitative rather than innovative modes'.[35] Benglis escaped this criticism as reviewers recognised that not only did she *not* avoid its popular and industrial associations, but she well understood how to utilise polyurethane to unique structural and formal ends.[36]

Early on, Benglis's polyurethane pours inspired passing comparisons to Oldenburg's soft vinyl sculptures, both artists seen to impart bodily qualities to inanimate plastic objects and materials (fig. 8). However, while Oldenburg's sculptures are effective in the way they appear to be *like* bodies or body parts, Benglis's works invoke bodily sensations rather than figurative or substantive allusions. It is tempting to draw analogies to bodily fluids, and Benglis on occasion made pieces that conjure such associations. Generally, however, the artist sought ways to express more abstract proprioceptive bodily sensations.[37] Such experiences, she shared with an interviewer in 1977, are 'prehistoric in a way or things that people know about when

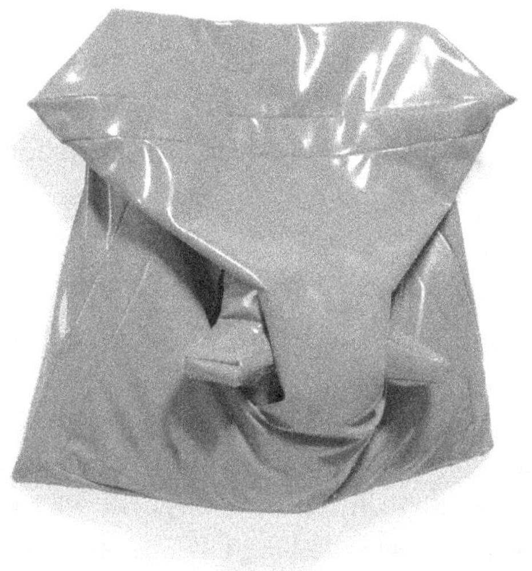

8. Claes Oldenburg, *Soft Light Switches*, 1964, vinyl filled with Dacron and canvas, 47 x 47 x 3 ⅛ in. (119.4 x 119.4 x 9.1 cm). Nelson-Atkins Museu m of Art, Kansas City; gift of Claes Oldenburg and Coosje van Bruggen. © 1964 Claes Oldenburg.

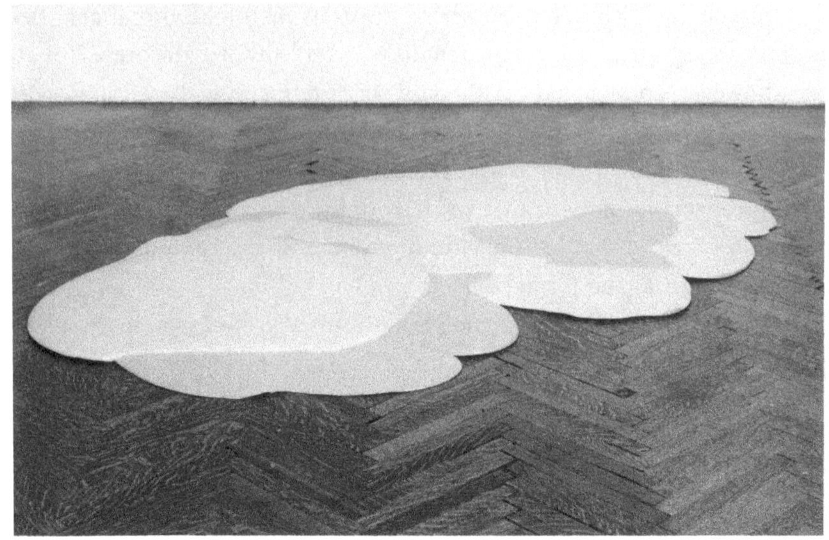

9. Lynda Benglis, *Bullitt*, 1969, pigmented polyurethane foam, 94 x 63 x 4 ½ in. (238.8 x 160 x 11.4 cm). Destroyed. © Lynda Benglis/Licensed by VAGA, New York, NY.

they look at them, although the forms are not specifically recognizable, the feelings are'.[38] On at least one occasion, Benglis compared the kinaesthetic effect of the brightly coloured pour *Bullitt* to the gut-wrenching experience of a fast-paced car ride, albeit one experienced via the 1968 Hollywood action film to which her title refers (fig. 9). Featuring Steve McQueen as a San Francisco detective, the film *Bullitt* set a new industry standard for car chase sequences by placing viewers in the middle of the action. Benglis, in turn, felt that the Day-Glo yellows and oranges in her polyurethane pour induced a comparable sensation of gravity-defying movement. In making this connection, the artist appreciated how both film and sculpture sustain an embodied encounter.

It is important to stress how Benglis coupled her interest in organic forms and natural processes with an astute understanding of popular cultural phenomena, and vice versa. At first blush, her colour choices seem timely for the period, the Day-Glo palette recalling advertisements, clothing fashions, and home décor. However, and as artificial as the psychedelic hues seem, they are not entirely without natural counterparts: not only do any number of plants, minerals, and gems possess shockingly vivid hues, but just as many also fluoresce under certain light conditions. Likewise, as contrived as a Hollywood action film sequence

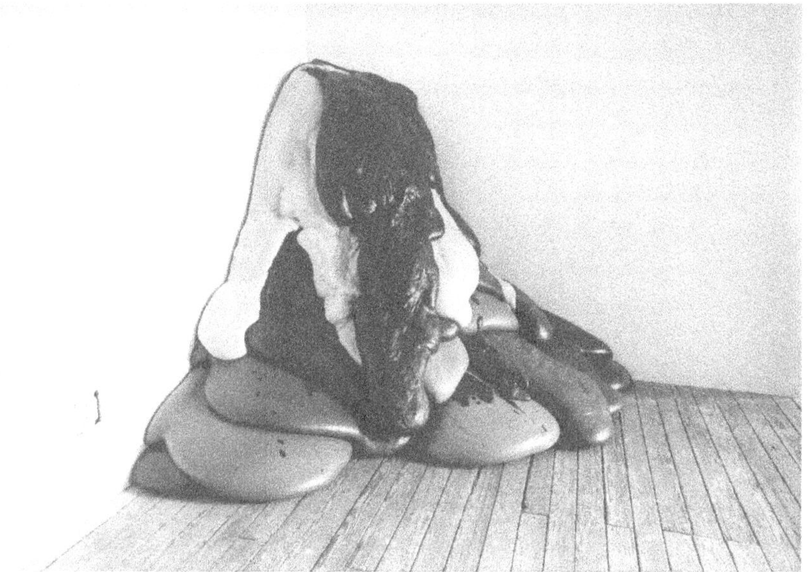

10. Lynda Benglis, *Untitled (King of Flot)*, 1969, pigmented polyurethane foam, approx 60 x 60 x 60 in. (152.4 x 152.4 x 152.4 cm). Destroyed. © Lynda Benglis/ Licensed by VAGA, New York, NY.

may actually be, the proprioceptive sensations it induces in the audience are real. For Benglis, the differences between these poles – the actual and the simulated – were not clear-cut, nor did one seem substantively superior to the other. Though her perspective foreshadows what the cultural theorist Jean Baudrillard would characterise in the early 1980s as the 'precession of simulacra' in postmodernity,[39] it differs insofar as Benglis saw a correlation between image and experience, both affording an engagement with rather than a distancing from the 'real', and each capable of generating sensory responses – a strong intake of breath, a flutter in the gut, or a tingle at the nape of the neck.

Benglis's polyurethane projects quickly grew more spatially complex and site-specific. Around 1969, the artist began to execute a number of pours in corner spaces. The corner, traditionally a neglected architectural area for sculptural production, became a favoured spot for a number of contemporary artists working in the 1960s and 1970s, and Benglis entered into a dialogue of sorts with some of the better-known precedents. For instance, one of her first corner pieces (now destroyed) was created with Robert Morris's work in mind (fig. 10).[40] Bearing the title *Untitled (King of Flot)*, in reference to the industrial 'flotsam and jetsam' he utilised in his practice, the pour may also be seen as Benglis's answer to Morris's geometric plywood

11. Robert Morris, *Untitled (Corner Piece)*, 1964, painted plywood, 78 x 108 in. (198.1 x 274.3 cm). Solomon R. Guggenheim Museum, New York; Panza Collection, 1991, 91.3791. Photograph by David Heald © The Solomon R. Guggenheim Foundation, New York. Art © 2011 Robert Morris/Licensed by Artists Rights Society (ARS), New York.

constructions, particularly *Untitled (Corner Piece)* (1964), a large triangular wedge that assertively alters the ninety-degree angles of the gallery corner, forcing attention to its literal physicality and that of the viewer in the adjacent space (fig. 11). However, because it is supported by hidden wheels and directly touches neither the walls nor the floor, Morris's piece also appears to hover rather than sit in the corner; it thus partially belies its own physical heft through an illusion of weightlessness. This subtle contradiction is echoed in Benglis's pour. Executed in a corner of Klaus Kertess's New York studio, *Untitled* (*King of Flot*) was sited directly on the floor, its pyramidal form comprising multiple layers of grey, white, and black polyurethane. Seemingly resistant to gravity, the lightweight foam appeared to flow into and out of the architectural seams behind it. Partially stemming this sense of motion, however, a final layer of glossy opaque black cascading down the front serves to anchor Benglis's piece in its place.

This impression of counter-movements also informs *For Carl Andre* (1970), a work Benglis executed at the Modern Art Museum of Forth Worth

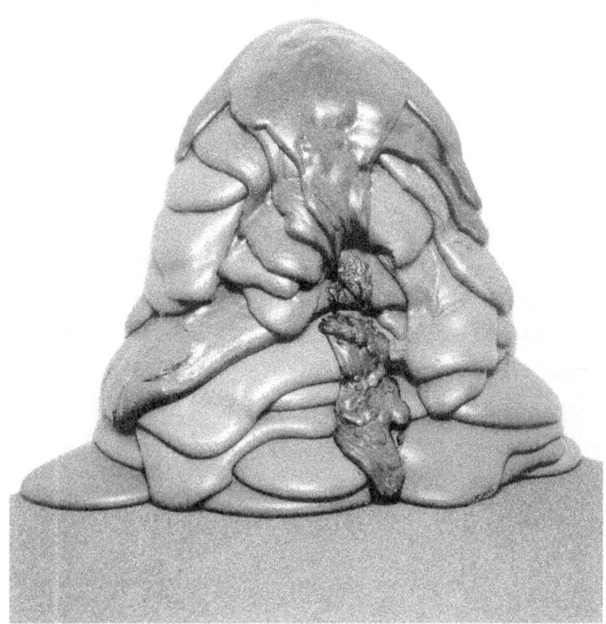

12. Lynda Benglis, *For Carl Andre*, 1970, pigmented polyurethane foam, 56 ¼ x 53 ½ x 46 ⅕ in. (142.9 x 135.9 x 117.3 cm). Modern Art Museum of Fort Worth. © Lynda Benglis/Licensed by VAGA, New York, NY.

(fig. 12). A hulking black corner piece, it was an homage of sorts to the minimalist sculptor, whose work Benglis admired. Carl Andre, she once observed, was 'one of the most pure artists because he continuously involves himself with very basic, elemental ideas that have always been about both open and closed systems'.[41] Benglis recalls how his *Lever* (1966), though not a corner piece, made a strong impression on her when she saw it at the 1966 *Primary Structures: Younger American and British Sculptors* exhibition at the Jewish Museum in New York (fig. 13).[42] Consisting of 137 identical fire-bricks arranged to form a long, low row extending along the floor of two rooms, *Lever* was installed so that viewers could experience it from two perspectives: from the side and straight on. However, the side view only allowed a partial glimpse of the work as it passed from one room to the next. *Lever* could be seen in its entirely only when one looked down its length from one end, a foreshortened perspective that destabilised the space and caused the work to appear to emerge from and disappear into the wall behind it.

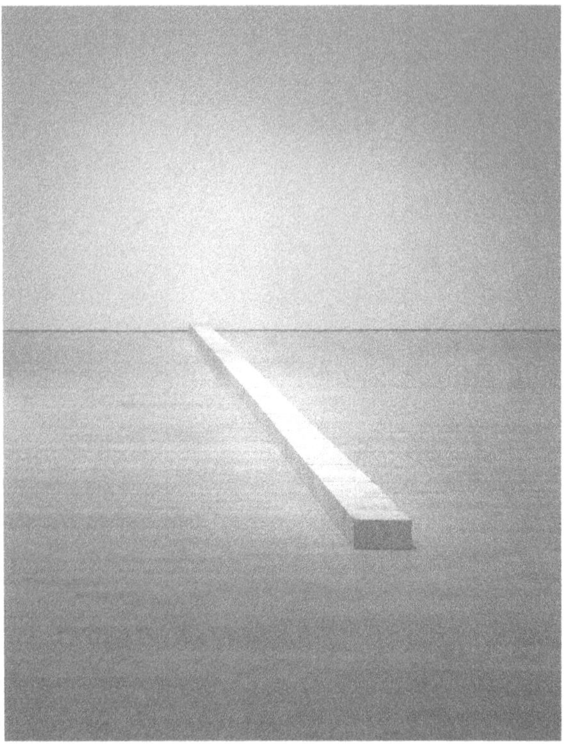

13. Carl Andre, *Lever*, 1966, 137 firebricks, 4 ½ x 8 ⅞ x 348 ½ in. (11.4 x 20.3 x 885 cm). National Gallery of Canada, Ottawa. Photo © National Gallery of Canada. © Carl Andre/Licensed by VAGA, New York, NY.

From its location in the corner of the room, Benglis's *For Carl Andre* effectively collapsed these two distinct perspectives into one. With two sides hidden by its placement against the walls, *For Carl Andre* presented only part of its form to viewers, its opaque layers of black foam held in careful tension with the illusion of rippling movement from and against the walls and floor. As in *Untitled (King of Flot)*, however, a darker top pour not only serves to anchor the Fort Worth piece into the corner but also indicates how its composition is, paradoxically, simultaneously stable and complete. Again, the connection to *Lever* is tacitly established, as Andre's work imparts a sense of 'infinite extension' even though its configuration and constituent elements were originally determined and fixed by its placement in the *Primary Structures* exhibition.[43]

The organic character of Benglis's corner pours may also be said to bring out the latent corporeal associations of *Lever*. Her work recalls Andre's proposition that his own piece be seen in relation to Constantin Brancusi's *Endless Column* (completed in 1938). If Brancusi's sculpture invokes an upright phallic form, he opined, in his own work, 'priapus is down on the floor. The engaged position is to run along the earth'.[44] Andre's erotic description, though likely related to his desire to identify his practice with artisanal labour and humble materials, finds a humorous counterpart in the excremental appearance of Benglis's oozing polyurethane pour, its frozen plastic seepage teasing out the *informe* or desublimated materiality of Andre's floor-bound sculpture.[45] In simultaneously invoking and defamiliarising distinctions between the artificial and the organic, *For Carl Andre* troubles the hierarchical structure of representation through which the corporeal is made culturally meaningful.

Around the same time that she created *For Carl Andre*, Benglis also executed an untitled polyurethane piece for the home of Vera List, a startling hot pink pour that was sited next to the toilet in the corner of the collector's white-tiled bathroom. This location, the artist later told an interviewer, reflected her interest in questioning 'the idea of vulgarity', and she chuckled at the thought of the collector's husband first encountering the work as though it were a mass of 'melted lipstick'. She continued, 'I can only assume he would have said something if he didn't like it', before adding that he was in fact very polite in subsequent meetings.[46] That List was polite about the project may have been an indication of his tacit approval of Benglis's unusual project. It may equally have been a sign that he wanted to avoid an overt discussion of the work, since melted lipstick was not its only association. Situated on the floor of the bathroom, the pour may have alluded too uncomfortably to excessive bodily secretions and processes of a decidedly female character, a connection reinforced by the pink colouration. This overt gendering of the List work is as much a product of its context as of its formal properties; I am not, in other words, making a case for the inherently feminine nature of Benglis's practice. Within the collector's personal bathroom, the artist's abstract sculpture assumes layers of meaning that might not have existed if the work were shown in a gallery. In general, however, all of the artist's corner pours impart an air of indecorum, their visceral (and proprioceptive) physicality, excessive plastic materiality, and placement along the margins of their respective architectural spaces contributing to this impression of transgression.

off the floor

Having successfully tackled the structural issues presented first by the floor and then by architectural corners, Benglis moved fairly rapidly into other areas of the gallery, specifically up the walls. While working on an installation at

Galerie Müller in Cologne in the summer of 1970, the artist devised a way to elevate one of the polyurethane pours by using an armature of chicken wire covered with plastic sheeting and stir sticks as props. The resulting wing-like form appeared to (but in actuality did not) cantilever from the wall. Importantly, it marked the beginning of a series of airborne polyurethane pours the artist executed in rapid succession over the course of the following year. With their landscape-like orientation, these eventually led Benglis to take over entire walls, and even rooms, with her polyurethane pours.

Over an eight-month period in 1971, Benglis completed six large-scale polyurethane commissions in institutions around the United States. Each installation was more complex than the last, eventually requiring a week or two to carry out and a crew to assist with the construction of the armatures and the execution of the actual pouring. As they were all conceived as temporary installations, the projects were subsequently destroyed at the end of each show; the sole exception is the first, *Phantom*, which Benglis created at Kansas State University in February.[47]

In the spring of 1971, Benglis was one of twenty-two artists invited by Martin Friedman, then director of the Walker Art Center in Minneapolis, to create a work on site for the inaugural exhibition in the museum's new building, *New Works for New Spaces*. Benglis was allocated a long wall adjacent to an installation by Dan Flavin; already in place, the latter comprised a seventy-four-foot-long corridor with a ceiling of coloured fluorescent lights. Realizing that Flavin's installation would cast a greenish glow over her work, Benglis used polyurethane pigmented with black, which she knew would generate complementary shadows in red. Entitled *Adhesive Products* after the Bronx company that supplied the material – and, more obliquely, in reference to the 'adhering' of the pours to the wall – the resulting installation included nine cantilevered forms arching diagonally out into the gallery, at least one as much as fifteen feet (plate 6). A testament to both the tensile strength of the polyurethane and Benglis's adept pouring skills, the wavelike forms were relatively thin and lightweight, though not necessarily fragile looking.

In offering no ideal vantage point from which to take it all in, *Adhesive Products* solicited and dramatised a complex viewing experience, one premised on repetition and variation, stasis and movement. As viewers traversed the long wall, the general impression of movement and flow yielded to smaller and seemingly infinite details: from plunging vectors and foreshortened forms to rounded planes, thin edges, shifting light reflections, and subtle colour modulations. In contrast to the glossy smooth top sides, the underside of each

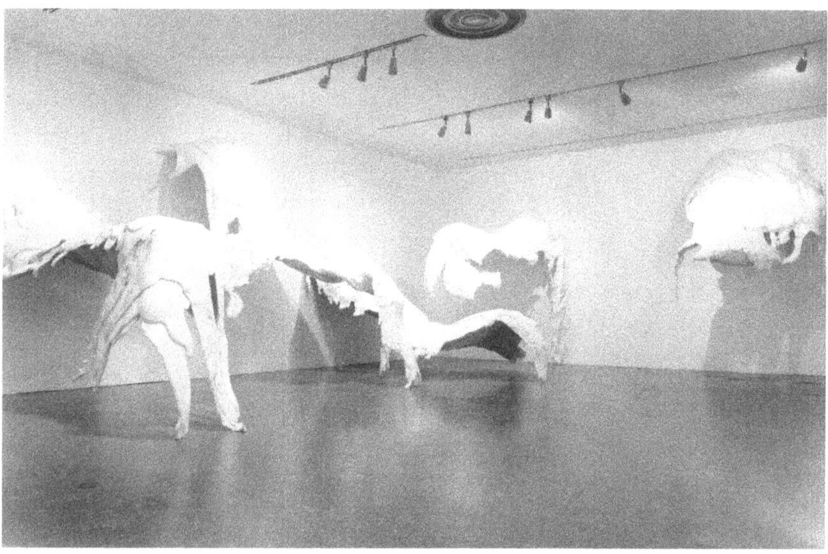

14. Installation view of *For Darkness (Situation and Circumstance)* at the Milwaukee Art Center, 1971, pigmented polyurethane foam. Destroyed. © Lynda Benglis/Licensed by VAGA, New York, NY.

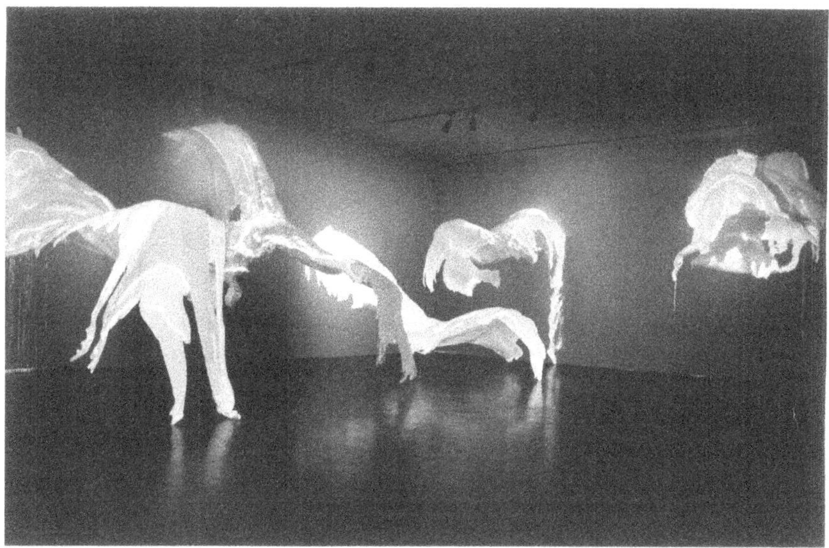

15. Installation view of *For Darkness (Situation and Circumstance)* at the Milwaukee Art Center, 1971, pigmented polyurethane foam. Destroyed. © Lynda Benglis/Licensed by VAGA, New York, NY (with lights off).

pour revealed the cross-hatched imprint of the chicken wire armature, now removed, adding yet another tactile element to the work. Just as the installation itself oscillated among the pictorial, the sculptural, and the architectural, so too did viewers experience different spatial and temporal registers, the immediate physicality of Benglis's polyurethane pieces countered by a more prolonged engagement with their formal allusions.

Highly suggestive of landscape phenomena and behemoth life forms, *Adhesive Products* inspired critics to draw both prehistoric and science-fiction analogies.[48] The aggressive tenor of the work likewise did not go unnoticed: for the critic Grace Glueck, Benglis's series of black pours evoked the foliage of a 'malevolent' swamp plant, while for Hilton Kramer the effect was 'menacing' and 'macabre'.[49] Klaus Kertess found that it expressed a 'black rage', the source of which was neither primeval nor fictional but very much of the present era: 'death and aggression on the highways, the suppression of minorities, the destruction of lives and land in Southeast Asia and all the other things the media serve with breakfast'.[50] While Kertess's politicised reading seemed tangential to the artist's stated interest in proprioception and the physical sensations of such natural occurrences as crashing waves, it nonetheless echoed Benglis's appreciation of the relation between potentially destructive natural forces and 'unnatural' contemporary social conflicts.[51] For both artist and critic, the dark and assertive character of *Adhesive Products* conveyed something of the tremendous outpouring of anger that many in the art world felt towards the Vietnam War.[52]

In June 1971, Benglis created her fourth polyurethane installation for a group show, *Directions 3: Eight Artists*, at the Milwaukee Art Center. Entitled *For Darkness* (*Situation and Circumstance*), it consisted of multiple pours that extended to three walls, thereby drawing the space in on viewers. Benglis also pigmented the material with phosphorescent salts, which were meant to be experienced under two different conditions: under normal gallery lighting and with the lights cycling completely off. In the first instance, the phosphorescent forms presented as a series of bright white waves cascading into the room and in some cases touching the floor; with the lights off, they became ghostly green entities looming from the surrounding darkness, the walls and floor all but disappearing behind them (figs. 14, 15).[53] In extending the duration of the work, the light cycle also accentuated the shifting, ephemeral nature of the phosphorescence, the latter in turn drawing out the implied movement of the individual polyurethane pours. Benglis has described the effects in terms of dynamic, opposing forces. As she explains:

> What was happening – as the piece was coming *down* in space in terms

> of visually how the foam itself would fall, the light in the phosphorus would pull up, because the light was being lit from above.... Therefore *below* the foam was not so intensely lit, and was more brightly lit from the top. So you get this pull going up, because of the light; but the piece was contradictorily, in terms of line and form, moving down. So they have an interesting, very interesting, sort of ghostly presence, as if they were constantly moving in space, both coming out at you, and away and up and down at the same time.[54]

The immersive experience of *For Darkness* (*Situation and Circumstance*) underscored the oscillation between the material and the immaterial that informs all of Benglis's polyurethane installations to one degree or another. Here the addition of the phosphorescence rendered the juxtaposition all the more theatrical, the combination of light and dark generating a vertiginous experience not unlike the sublime or, more tellingly, a 'mannerist' sublime imagined through culture: a sublime in which a feeling of awe is coupled with an appreciation for the familiarity – even the banality – of its artifice. Indeed, many reviewers, whether tacitly or not, measured their experiences of Benglis's work against a cinematic paradigm, the realms of science fiction and horror providing the corresponding images of spumid landmasses and extraterrestrial life forms used to describe *Adhesive Products* and *For Darkness*. As curator Susan Krane would later observe, these works conjoined a sense of geological time with a 'slight Hollywood twist'.[55] Benglis's works openly solicited such phantasmagorical connections even as they inspired viewers to internalise their ebb and flow through proprioception.

Benglis executed her sixth and final polyurethane installation, *Totem*, in the Hayden Gallery at the Massachusetts Institute of Technology in Boston, a fitting locale for the artist's commingling of aesthetics, chemistry, popular culture, and structural engineering. Inspired by a popular line of automotive paint recently issued by the Chrysler Corporation, she added reds and pink to a more neutral palette of black and white, with each of the six wall-mounted pours rendered in a single colour (fig. 16).[56] Tacitly recalling the artist's previous reference to the film *Bullitt*, and to Steve McQueen's famous car chase, Benglis's choices with *Totem* generated yet another 'series of ironies', this time in terms of gender, as her seemingly feminine colour palette was largely utilised in the masculine arena of American muscle cars of the era.

Because the Hayden space had a higher ceiling than previous locations, Benglis sited the pours at different heights on the walls, their irregular placement breaking with the strong horizontality of her previous installations. At the same time,

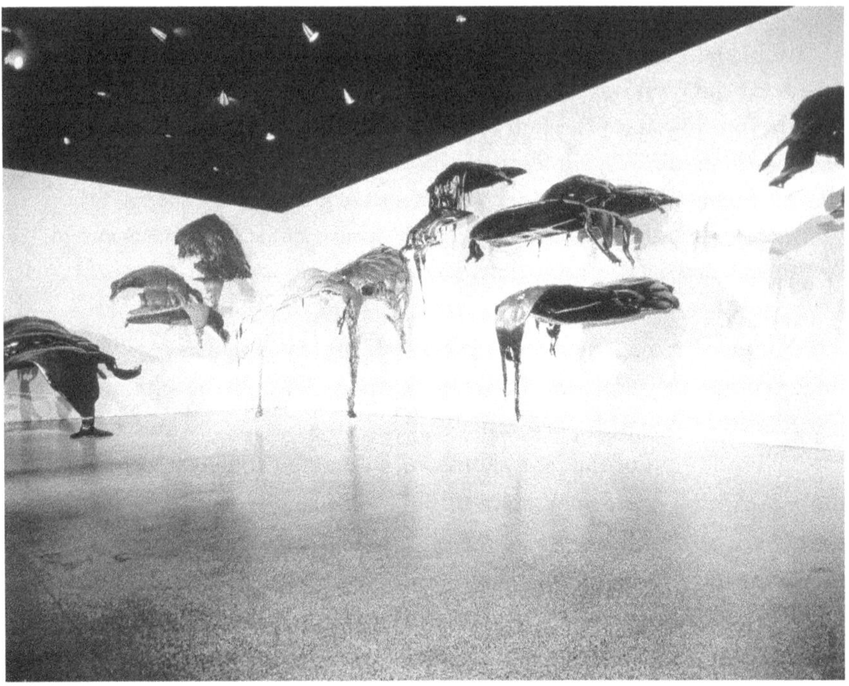

16. Installation view of *Totem* at the Hayden Gallery, Massachusetts Institute of Technology, 1971, pigmented polyurethane foam. Destroyed. © Lynda Benglis/ Licensed by VAGA, New York, NY.

rather than plunging directly down to the floor, the individual pours maintained a perpendicular alignment to the walls, with only a few delicate spindly streams of pigmented polyurethane eventually cascading down to the floor, like paint dripping off of a congealed brushstroke. As a result, the MIT installation imparted a more painterly and pictorial effect than Benglis's other projects, yet it proved no less allusive, its configurations moving viewers from the fictive to the physical, and back again. As Klaus Kertess proffered, 'I can only say that for a month there was a tropical rain forest in the middle of Cambridge that might have been a painting or maybe a sculpture'.[57] Though *Totem* was the last of Benglis's large-scale polyurethane installations, it did not mark the end of the artist's interest in utilising the wall rather than the floor. In subsequent work, she continued to exploit the tensions between painting and sculpture from this vantage point.

the (in)visible woman

Benglis received a lot of positive press coverage, both mainstream and artistic, for the polyurethane pours. Towards the end of 1971, she was one of a handful of women artists featured in a *Newsweek* article entitled 'The Invisible Woman is Visible'. Rather than artistic process or technique, the article's focus concerned the impact of the women's liberation movement on the US art world, and it lauded Benglis's career to date. In claiming that her aesthetic was not 'clearly "women's art," in any obvious sense', and was instead 'tough, sophisticated and totally at one with all "advanced" mainstream art', author Douglas Davis voiced a sentiment not dissimilar from the artist's own desire to secure her success in mainstream terms.[58] However, as much as she sought and even gained wide acclaim, Benglis remained sensitive to how her status as a woman artist figured in her professional experiences and in the reception of her work.

Benglis's perceptions of gender differences were especially acute during these early years as she witnessed the pressures exerted by the feminist movement on the institutional misogyny of the art world. Though she eschewed direct participation in feminist political organizations, she appreciated that being successful in the 'mainstream' inspired its own set of gendered paradoxes – the framing of her practice in relation to Pollock's masculinised legacy marking one such instance. On occasion she also responded by creating provocative titles for her works, which were intended to solicit specifically gendered readings. An early example is a latex pour that Benglis named *Odalisque (Hey Hey Frankenthaler)* (1969) after seeing a retrospective of Helen Frankenthaler's paintings at the Whitney Museum earlier that year (fig. 18).[59] This was not, I propose, an insignificant gesture on her part.

In many respects, Benglis's choice of title built on her general characterisation of her latex pours as 'fallen paintings'. As a literal reference to the physical orientation of her work on the floor, the phrase also alludes to the cultural trope of the fallen woman and, by turns, to women's traditional position as erotic muses to and subject matter for male creativity in modern art history. Though resolutely abstract, the sinuous lines and soft curves of Benglis's *Odalisque* invite viewers to entertain analogies not only to the exotic female subject popular in nineteenth-century academic painting but also to the female body subtending twentieth-century abstraction. As Susan Krane has observed, the allusion in the latex pour 'seems a blatant proposition of femininity and female sensuality, made within the predominantly male arena of modernism'.[60]

Benglis's interpellation, 'Hey Hey Frankenthaler', is thus a bit puzzling in this regard. On the one hand, the subtitle reads as simple homage to the older painter, as appreciation for the formal connection between her colourful diaphanous compositions and Benglis's own amorphous latex pour (fig. 17).

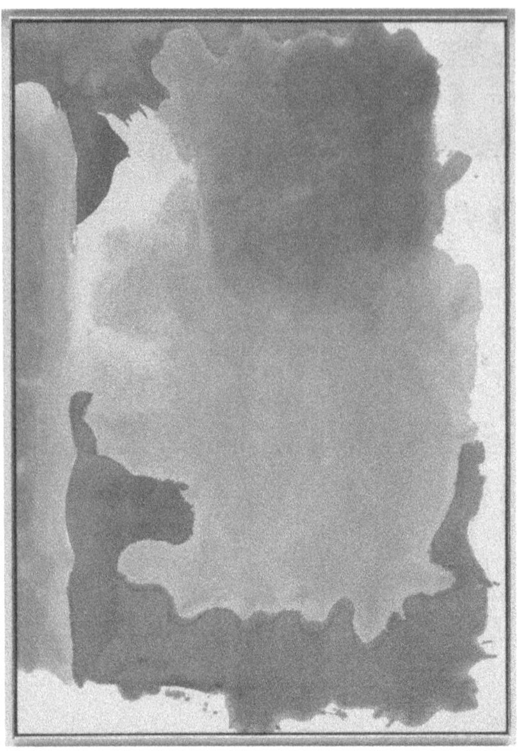

17. Helen Frankenthaler, *Canal*, 1963, acrylic on canvas, 81 x 57 ½ in. (205.7 x 146 cm). Solomon R. Guggenheim Museum, New York. Purchased with the aid of funds from the National Endowment for the Arts, in Washington, DC, a federal agency; matching funds contributed by Evelyn Sharp, 1976, 76.2225. © 2011 Helen Frankenthaler/Licensed by Artists Rights Society (ARS), New York, NY.

Indeed, the dynamic spatial ambiguity and subtle movement produced by the older artist's colour modulations and staining technique, as well as the fact that Frankenthaler also used buckets and worked on her large canvases on the floor, provide more striking and immediate precedents for Benglis's pours than do Pollock's webbed canvases and his use of brushes and sticks to manipulate his paint.[61] As such, Benglis's subtitle identities and affirms a connection given far less attention in narratives of her artistic process and inheritance. On the other hand, 'Hey Hey Frankenthaler' could refer to the older artist's subordinated place within the canon of postwar American painting, and to the fact that even though Frankenthaler received more professional opportunities than most women artists of her generation, she was frequently subject to unflattering, stereotypically gendered appraisals by leading artists and art critics.[62]

Such allusions, of course, counter the fact that Benglis's pour remains abstract, such that the title can only ever provide an equivocal answer to

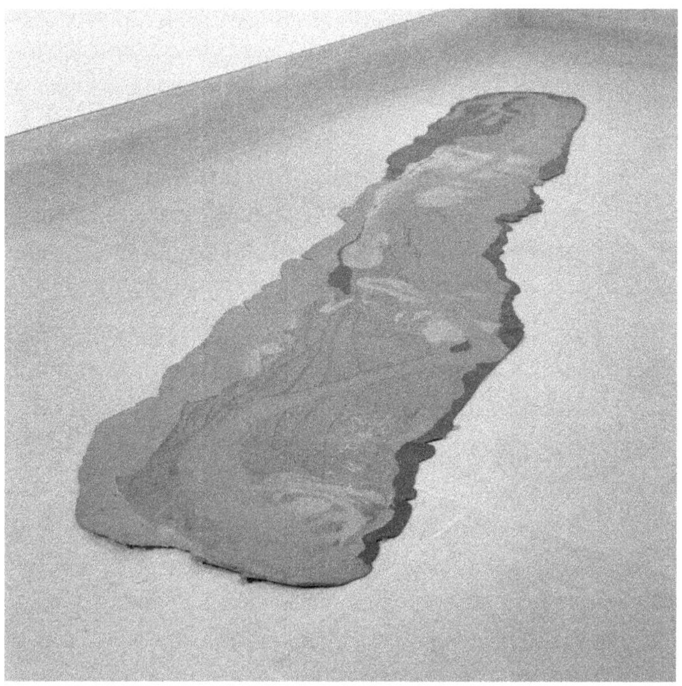

18. Lynda Benglis, *Odalisque (Hey Hey Frankenthaler)*, 1969, poured pigmented latex, 165 x 34 ½ in. (419.1 x 87.63 cm). Dallas Museum of Art, DMA/amfAR Benefit Auction Fund. © Lynda Benglis/Licensed by VAGA, New York, NY.

questions of influence, intention, or interpretation. Nonetheless, I find that Benglis's act of titling proves significant as a wry proposition about art world sexual politics, about who remains invisible and who does not, and about how visibility accrues gendered signification. In such a scenario, a woman artist's practice can never truly be 'totally at one' (to recall Davis's phrase) with advanced mainstream art. This is a point that the art historian Linda Nochlin would drive home in her groundbreaking essay 'Why Have There Been No Great Women Artists?' which was published in *Art News* in January 1971, and to which Benglis was invited to respond.

In this oft-cited essay, Nochlin cogently parsed the socio-historical conditions preventing women artists from entering the canons of Western art history. By identifying the external factors contributing to their subordination, the art historian demonstrated how the art world perpetually relegated women artists to the role of 'acknowledged outsider[s] and maverick[s]'.[63] The lack of 'great' women artists, Nochlin continued, is thus the result not of women's inherent inability to produce exceptional art but of the very value judgements driving the ideology of artistic creativity and genius. Instead of qualifying women's achievements separately from those of men, women needed to recognise and challenge the conventions that determined such cultural concepts as greatness and genius.

Nochlin's essay was accompanied by a set of responses by eight women, including Benglis. Forming an eclectic group of seven artists and one critic, the women varied in their opinions of Nochlin's article and its title question.[64] Some generational distinctions emerged: as one of the older and more established artists to reply, for example, Louise Nevelson bluntly rejected Nochlin's analysis. Calling it oversimplified, the artist countered it with the assertion that 'masculine-feminine' labels had little to do with individual artistic determination and development.[65] In contrast, the younger art critic Suzi Gablik saw her own experiences mirrored in Nochlin's account, thus leading her to reiterate the art historian's conclusion that greater awareness was needed in order to change a field 'saturated in assumptions, both conscious and unconscious, of male superiority'.[66] For Gablik, Nochlin's argument spoke to the years of isolation, rejection and harassment that women practitioners had endured at the hands of male colleagues and male-dominated institutions.

Benglis's response also echoed many of Nochlin's conclusions. 'I agree', the artist wrote, 'that the presence of few female artists in the past is very much a social condition, not an esthetic one'. However, in also offering her own rhetorical question – 'How am I to simplify the composite "female" and "artist" in words?' she asked – Benglis revealed her uneasiness with conflating these two aspects of her identity.[67] Uncertain as to how or even whether to relate the two, she held out the possibility that such distinctions were in fact unnecessary. Though she did not adhere to Nevelson's belief that individual fortitude transcended cultural and institutional biases, neither did Benglis envision her femaleness as singularly integral to her artistic practice. It was her ambition as an artist, ultimately, to have the appellation 'woman' signify nothing more or less than circumstantial fact. Her large, boundless latex pours and polyurethane installations tacitly indicate an artist who desired freedom from traditional artistic as well as social boundaries. Yet in concomitantly favouring organic forms expressive of bodily sensations, Benglis found her practice frequently dovetailed with broader conversations in the early 1970s about the possible existence of a distinctive female or feminine aesthetic, one integrally connected to the gendered body. The next chapter addresses this convergence through a consideration of the artist's encaustic relief paintings.

2 Flesh and Physicality

In addition to her poured latex and polyurethane projects, Benglis continued to produce small encaustic relief paintings in her studio. Around 1967 she embarked on a series she subsequently dubbed the 'two-brushstroke paintings', a body of work to which she would return intermittently through the early 1970s.[1] Like all her art from this period, the two-brushstroke paintings evidence Benglis's interest in utilising fluid materials. At the same time, they inspire sensuous bodily associations, their rich waxen surfaces provocatively skin-like, their softly rounded and bifurcated forms both labial and phallic. This dimorphism notwithstanding, the erotic character of the wax paintings has inspired claims for the gendered nature of Benglis's practice, and for situating the body in her work as specifically female.

In the historical moment of the early 1970s, establishing tangible connections among an artist, her sexed body, and her artwork held a certain level of urgency, with many female artists insisting on the specificities of their experiences as women. Not indifferent to the impact of gender on her artistic practice, Benglis nonetheless sought to express less resolved and more contradictory associations through her art. In examining the contexts in which the gendered readings of the encaustic paintings first emerged, this chapter follows the artist's lead in demonstrating how the work posits a different and more fluid conception of gender and bodily identifications. Since Benglis's use of encaustic is central to the erotic character of her two-brushstroke paintings, a brief consideration of the artist's labour-intensive technique is first in order.

working with wax

As a slow and often difficult technique, encaustic, or hot wax painting, was not widely employed by American artists in the 1960s. Curator Gail Stavitsky, in her catalogue essay for the 1999 exhibition *Waxing Poetics: Encaustic Art in America*, notes that while Jasper Johns gave it new prominence in the postwar era, the medium attracted relatively few practitioners until much later in the 1980s.[2] An important exception was Brice Marden, whose monochromatic oil-and-beeswax compositions were on view around New York in the fall of 1966 and were included in a show at Bykert Gallery when Benglis was employed there as an assistant. Marden's densely layered yet softly translucent paintings possess the kinds of sensuous surfaces that Benglis initially sought in her own work. Calling her earliest attempts a 'mummified version of painting', Benglis favoured the encaustic technique because it produced 'something buried with a dimension that isn't quite perceived upon first glance'.[3]

In addition to Marden's paintings, a limited edition serigraph by Barnett Newman provided another important visual stimulus for Benglis's experimentation with encaustic. Entitled *The Moment* (1966), Newman's print consists of a long and narrow ultramarine band flanked by two darker cobalt 'zips' printed on the back of a plexiglass support.[4] As seen through the transparent surface, the contrasting bands of colour resist a clear-cut figure-ground relation and appear suspended within the plastic. Newman's print, which the artist himself described as 'colour already in a frame and under glass', evidences the kind of spatial and physical ambiguities Benglis sought with the encaustic medium.[5]

The hot wax process also conjured childhood memories for Benglis. For instance, the artist recalls her fascination with smelling, touching, and tasting wax candies at Halloween and birthday parties. The ritualistic character of these festive occasions intrigued the artist, who infused her encaustic process with physical and metaphysical significance, even ascribing the term 'icon' to the work.[6] As 'icons', the encaustic paintings evidence a commingling of the material and the auratic, the serial and the unique, the pictorial and the tangible. More specifically, perhaps, the ritualistic overtures given by Benglis evince a popular and long-standing sentiment about the magical and even fetishistic appeal of encaustic as an artistic medium. Stavitsky sums up these qualities in *Waxing Poetic*: 'Transformed through fire/heat, encaustic is regarded as a mystical alchemical material, suggesting the metamorphosis of all matter. The embedding of images and memories is associated with the build up of layers and equated with geography, archaeology, the ritual accumulation and sealing of memories, and artistic impulses. Bearing the history of its creative process, encaustic is also prized as among the most permanent of mediums that simultaneously evokes and defies the vicissitudes of existence'.[7] Ultimately Benglis developed a technique that took full advantage of all these qualities of encaustic. After experimenting with different recipes and consistencies, she developed her own mixture of purified beeswax, damar resin crystals, and powdered pigment, which she carefully brushed onto a rectilinear Masonite support then fused with heat from a propane torch.[8] Early on, Benglis produced paintings with smooth surfaces and colours ranging from bold reds to subtle pastels. While their shape varied, the size of each of these early paintings was loosely derived from bodily dimensions: Benglis's height or the width of her arm, for instance.[9]

Around 1967, Benglis established a format and technique for what would become the two-brushstroke paintings. Using a lozenge-shaped piece of Masonite the approximate length and width of her arm, she built up a thick encrustation of wax using a brush of width equal to that of the underlying support. Adding layer after colourful encaustic layer, the artist worked on each painting as it rested horizontally on sawhorses or across a table, carefully tracing a bifurcated composition consisting of two brushstrokes: a single large stroke rippling upward, and another downward from a central line.

The resulting wax lozenges oscillate provocatively between painting and object. From a distance, the works appear to hover weightlessly against the wall; their irregular surfaces, soft edges, and translucent colours simultaneously absorb and reflect ambient light (plate 7). Defying a precise reading of space and depth, the waxen brushstrokes form a succession of ripples that ebb and flow both vertically and laterally across the wall. Closer inspection, however, reveals each work's softly bulging convex shape, the accumulation of encaustic three or more inches deep in some instances (plate 8). Here, the materiality of Benglis's paintings comes palpably into focus, their dense and craggy forms yielding colourful waxen strata; in some instances the softly modulated colours are built upon a substructure of Day-Glo fluorescence, the latter a surprising detail that connects the work, however tangentially, to the artist's brightly hued latex pours.

A side view also reveals the unruly nature of Benglis's chosen medium. Clinging precariously to the outer edges of the Masonite support, coagulated beads recall the medium's prior liquidity and the serendipitous forces of gravity acting on it. Pulling away and down from the frontal plane, the mercurial waxen drips underscore the impression of excessiveness generally conveyed by

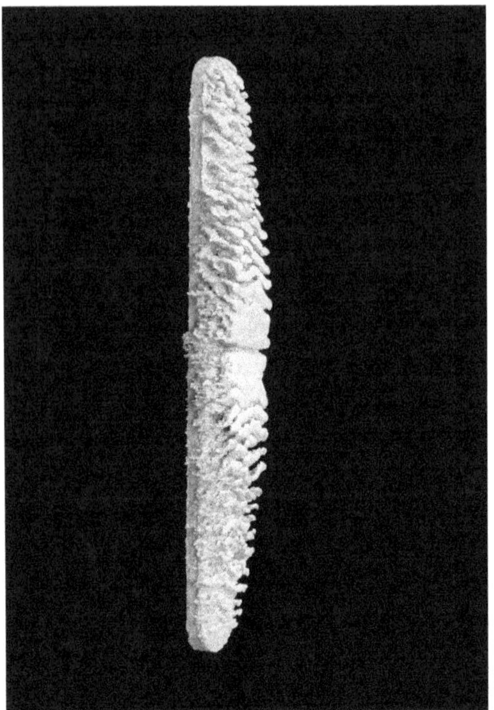

19. Lynda Benglis, *Excess*, 1971, purified and pigmented beeswax, damar resin, and gesso on Masonite, 36 x 5 x 4 in. (91.4 x 12.7 x 10.2 cm). Walker Art Center, Minneapolis; Art Center Acquisition Fund, 1972. © Lynda Benglis/Licensed by VAGA, New York, NY.

all the two-brushstroke paintings despite their compact size and uniform compositions. The aptly titled *Excess* (1971) bears out this impression of too much material contained on too small a support (fig. 19). At once image and object, fluid and dense, controlled and excessive, each of Benglis's two-brushstroke paintings produces what the art historian Helen Molesworth usefully calls 'a radical slippage of coordinates'.[10] This slippage not only makes it difficult to pin down the exact character of the work – its classification as painting or as sculptural object, for example – but also renders it dense with associations.

a slippage of coordinates

When I first encountered one of Benglis's works, I thought of miniature geological formations. Curator Susan Krane has also invoked landscape metaphors in her description of the paintings, in particular proposing that the central fissure constitutes a horizon line dividing earth from sky.[11] Art historian Philip Larson, on the other hand, has compared Benglis's paintings to sea creatures, and the critic Miles Beller to cocoons and pinecones.[12] More often than not, however, the works' waxy translucence and softly curved forms have inspired corporeal projections. Klaus Kertess, an intimate acquaintance of the artist at the time, proffered the following description of a work entitled *Tulip*: 'pale, translucent red and blue done in the spring of 1968, [it] is clearly a painting about brushstrokes. It also evokes the waxy beauty of tulips or of lips (two lips, my lips)'.[13] Though he begins with a statement about the literal materiality of the work, Kertess eventually settles on a bodily metaphor ('two lips, my lips'), which he then reiterates when observing that the artist's practice as a whole is involved with 'flesh and physicality'. Reinforcing this description, wax lozenges with such titles as *Excess, Cocoon,* and *Embryo* suggest bodily protuberances and nascent life forms, while *Bundi* and *Plum* conjure up images of sweet-tasting treats passing over the tongue.[14]

In identifying the sensuous and erotic character of the wax lozenges, however, Kertess ultimately foregrounded it in *the artist's* sexed body, concluding that Benglis produced 'images that openly declare a very strong female sensuality'.[15] Thus the critic shifted from his own empathetic response to the two-brushstroke paintings to an overarching characterisation of the works' source in the artist's body, in her 'flesh and physicality'. That Benglis intended her encaustic relief paintings to bear a specific connection to the female body, or to female sensuality, remains less clear, however. On at least one occasion, the artist resisted such a reading: when pushed by journalist Karen Edwards in 1971 to account for a strong sensation of 'femaleness' in her encaustic work, Benglis adamantly declared: 'Whether I am presenting it as specifically erotic I would say no. The work is itself about being specific; it's not about anything'.[16]

Though Edwards did not use the term 'erotic', Benglis inferred as much from the allusion to 'femaleness' and refused to countenance its bodily connotation. Her invocation of the 'specific' character of the work instead drew on the more neutral art critical discourse of the day, in particular recalling Donald Judd's influential essay 'Specific Objects', published in 1965.[17] For Judd, specific objects constituted a new breed of abstraction that exploded traditional categorical distinctions between painting and sculpture. Encompassing works by artists as stylistically diverse as Yayoi Kusama, Lee Bontecou, Claes Oldenburg, Dan Flavin, and Robert Morris, Judd's term stressed the discrete nature of the art object and its non-allusive character, a sentiment echoed by Benglis when she claimed of her work: 'It's not about anything'. Yet even Judd was not immune to associative readings of 'specific objects'; his reviews of Bontecou, for example, reveal his appreciation for her work's emotive and often libidinal charge.[18]

By the mid-1960s, an increasing number of US artists and critics were turning their attention to the erotic appeal of soft sculptural objects. In 1966 the art critic Lucy Lippard coined the term 'eccentric abstraction' to account for what she believed was an important psychosexual dynamic in the work of many contemporary artists working in New York; she organised a group show under this title at Fischbach Gallery, which Benglis had occasion to see. Featuring pieces by Louise Bourgeois, Eva Hesse, and Bruce Nauman, among others, *Eccentric Abstraction* signalled an important shift away from the coolly reductive work associated with minimalism.[19] In her accompanying text for the exhibition, Lippard explained her use of terms: 'In eccentric abstraction, evocative qualities or specific organic associations are kept at a subliminal level, without the benefit of Freudian clergy'.[20] Lippard recognised the bodily connotations in the work but, like Judd, believed they manifested not through mimesis but rather through choices of pliable materials and abstract configurations. As she would go on to explain in a follow-up essay for *Art International*, the erotic effect was the result of a formal 'reconciliation of distant realities', which the viewer inferred through a 'mindless, near-visceral identification'.[21] Thus, Lippard continued, 'a bag remains a bag and does not become a uterus, a tube is a tube and not a phallic symbol. Too much free association on the viewer's part is combated by formal understatement'.[22] The critic's characterisation, which reflected renewed interest in surrealism as a formal option for artists during the 1960s, intentionally kept open the range of non-figurative sensuous evocations that the artwork solicited from viewers. The latex and plaster objects of Bourgeois, the oldest artist included in *Eccentric Abstraction*, exemplified the anthropomorphism Lippard described, their lumpy and syrupy forms remaining 'undecidable as to sex', as art historian Mignon Nixon has more recently asserted (fig. 20).[23]

Benglis began the first of her two-brushstroke paintings not long after Lippard's *Eccentric Abstraction* exhibition, and the work possesses a similar kind of formal understatement expressed through seemingly contradictory effects; in short, it has a palpable, or 'eccentric', bodiliness that is difficult to pin down to identifiable image content. And yet pinning it down is precisely what the art critical language of the early 1970s would often demand of the

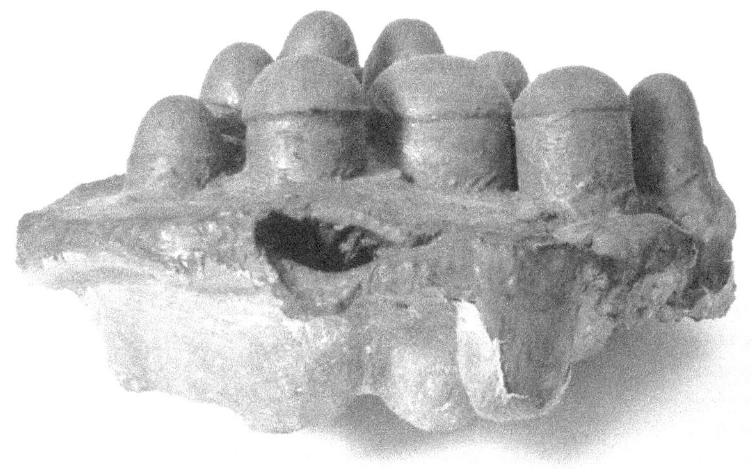

20. Louise Bourgeois, *Double Negative*, 1963, latex over plaster, 19⅜ x 37 ½ x 31⅜ in. (49.2 x 95.3 x 94.9 cm). Kröller-Müller Museum, Otterlo. Photograph by Peter Bellamy. © Louise Bourgeois Trust/Licensed by VAGA, New York, NY.

work, and of the woman artist producing it. It was a demand that Lippard would eventually make as the critic's growing commitment to feminist politics inspired her to focus specifically on female artistic production. In an essay of 1975 in which she reflected on the impact of the women's art movement, the critic revealed a shift in perspective, famously retracting her earlier pronouncement that a lot of women's artwork simply demanded that critics 'call a semisphere a breast if we know damn well that's what it suggests, instead of suppressing the association and negating an area of experience that has been dormant except in the work of a small number of artists, many of them women'.[24] Lippard was rarely one to force such readings when they did not apply, yet she also became a vocal advocate of women artists who were utilising both veiled and more explicit bodily iconography. As one of the few art critics entirely committed to evaluating and promoting women's practices, and notably women's abstraction, Lippard, in her writings from this period, provides an important contextual barometer for understanding Benglis's work. Therefore I want to linger a bit on the critic's shift in priorities.

At first resistant to the notion that women produced art reflective of their difference from men, Lippard had by 1973 come around to the idea, inspired as she was by Judy Chicago and Miriam Schapiro's vocal promotion of female imagery and their formulation of a theory that connected said imagery to a distinctive female sensibility.[25] For both artists, the intertwined concepts of female imagery and female sensibility constituted a strategic feminist reclamation of an unconscious tendency already present in women's art; the history of art demonstrated that women gravitated towards centralised, or 'central core', motifs, which in turn had a biological basis (fig. 21).[26] Lippard agreed, though she also identified an artist's choice of materials and her artistic processes as sites through which deeper perceptual differences manifested in women's art. Whether biologically or socially determined, the critic claimed, a woman's experience was 'simply not like that of a man', and her artwork needed to acknowledge that difference.[27]

Lippard's critical focus during the early 1970s indicated a pressing need for women to assert female artistic agency, and to establish both an artistic and

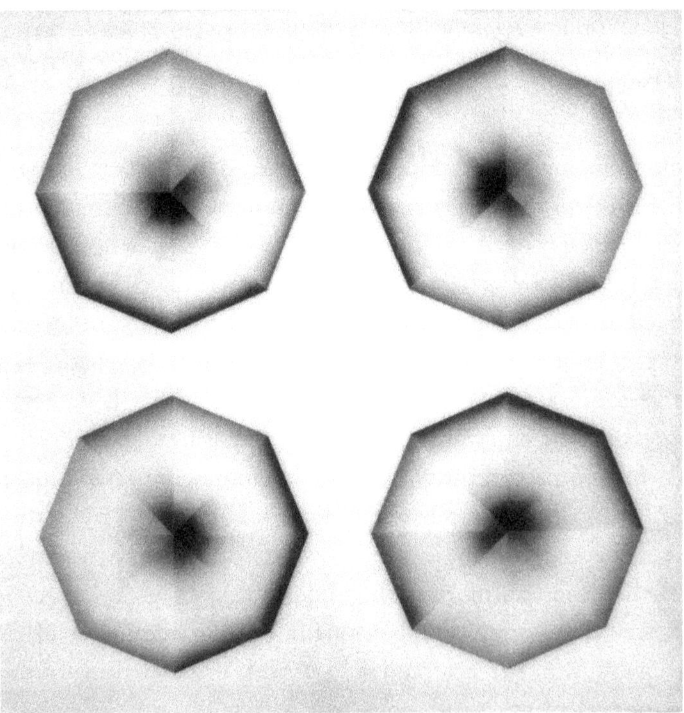

21. Judy Chicago, *Pasadena Lifesaver Red Series # 5*, 1969–70, sprayed acrylic on acrylic, 60 x 60 in. (152.4 x 152.4 cm). National Museum of Women in the Arts, Washington, DC; gift of Elyse and Stanley Grinstein. © 2011 Judy Chicago/ Licensed by Artists Rights Society (ARS), New York, NY. Photo © Donald Woodman.

critical language through which to give voice to their gender experiences.[28] Karen Edwards's question to Benglis regarding the 'femaleness' inherent in the wax paintings gives some sense of the currency such concepts held. With the rising tide of feminist politics, the very question of how the sexed body informed artistic practices came to bear considerable ideological weight through the decade of the 1970s. Ultimately, it required a level of commitment to a set of identities that were undergoing constant definition and redefinition. How was a woman artist to understand herself and the work she produced? Was her art an equivalent to the male perspective? Or did she need to attune herself to a different reality, one that would allow her to nurture more profound perceptual differences in her art? How should the body and its representation factor in aesthetic expression? These broad questions, which encompass myriad others, gave rise to fruitful debates about the discursive and phenomenological framing of gender in the US art world of the 1960s and 1970s.

Benglis was sensitive to the prevailing sexual politics of the era, if not openly committed to any one specific feminist agenda. While her response is most evident in the artist's 1974 self-promotional sexual mockeries as well as in her video work from the period, which I discuss in the next chapter, hints of it also surface in the context of her encaustic paintings. For instance, though Benglis balked at the journalist's question about the expression of femaleness in her work, to the art historian and critic Robert Pincus-Witten, she was less decorous, declaring in 1974 that her encaustic technique was 'like masturbating in the studio'.[29] The analogy is provocative – and fitting – for work that literally results from the artist repetitively stroking on the layers of wax. By extension, the skin-like materiality and bifurcated composition of each painting also recalls the touching of flesh on flesh in an autoerotic gesture.[30]

Since Benglis's blunt description to Pincus-Witten seems pointedly at odds with the artist's previous denial of the erotic content of her work, however, we might be cautious in lending too much weight to passing utterances made to interviewers. At the very least, we might heed the art historian Griselda Pollock's assertion that a work of art always exceeds the self-understanding that generated it, or Amelia Jones's claim that an artist is 'never fully coherent in his or her intentionality'.[31] We might also recall that artistic intention is itself an organic entity, prone to shifts and turnarounds even long after the ostensible completion of the work of art, and often in correlation to different critical receptions. The timing of Benglis's comment to Pincus-Witten is certainly significant, occurring as it did in tandem with the creation of the artist's infamous dildo self-image of 1974, and its planned appearance in the same issue of *Artforum* in which Pincus-Witten's article was to appear. Likewise, Benglis's previous aversion to the *Herald* journalist's reading of her work turned on the highly charged reference to 'femaleness' and its tacit association with concepts of female difference gaining momentum at the time. By interpreting – or, better yet, misinterpreting – the reference, Benglis headed off what may have been perceived as a reductive conflation of her own gendered identity and disposition with the content of her artwork.

Though her subsequent description of masturbation would seem to perform a similar conflation, suggesting as it does that the origin of the artwork lies in the artist's sexed body, Benglis's trope is ultimately given a different shade of meaning by the artist, one that potentially unhinges it from a singular reading of gender. The encaustic paintings, she continued to Pincus-Witten immediately after likening their production to 'masturbating in the studio', are 'nutshell paintings dealing with male/female symbols, the split and the coming together. They are both oral and genital. But I don't want to get Freudian; they're also Jungian, Ying-Yang [*sic*]'.[32] What Benglis seems to be proposing here is that the two-brushstroke paintings are sexually indeterminate: symbolising both male and female forms, their compositions represent the 'split and the coming together' that Jungian psychology posits as the fundamental duality of the androgynous psyche. Recalling her interest in 'prehistoric' feelings and sensations, which I discussed in chapter 1, Benglis's recourse to archetypes posits a similar idea, namely, that certain forms may be known or felt even if they are not immediately recognisable.[33]

Significantly, the artist's tropes of masturbation and androgyny have an historical context and as such are revealing of Benglis's negotiation of her critical reception and of the perceived relation between her art and her identity as a woman artist during the early 1970s. Rather than claim them as statements of intention per se, however, I believe that Benglis's descriptions give voice (perhaps intuitively) to the provocative 'slippage of coordinates' that Helen Molesworth would later associate with her artwork. To that end, Benglis's twin tropes parallel the defining logic of the two-brushstroke paintings and the nature of the body that they solicit.

the pleasure in one

When Benglis characterised her artistic process as masturbatory, she ultimately marshalled a popular and early second-wave feminist trope equating women's sexual and social liberation. Picking up on the rhetoric of sexual autonomy and true selfhood first enacted by the 1960s counterculture and theorised by such writers as Norman O. Brown and Herbert Marcuse, early radical feminists came to regard sexual satisfaction as an important step towards freedom from patriarchal oppression. That such pursuits were formulated alongside the explicit knowledge of the ways in which culture denigrated or denied women's sexual agency did not lessen the imperative to discover what this might look like or mean for women. As the anthropologist and feminist writer Paula Webster observed, the practice of female masturbation 'became the logical reconciliation of our bodies and our lives, and a necessary foundation for knowing what was erotically satisfying'.[34]

A similar strategy quickly developed in women's artistic practices, often through the rhetorical coupling of artistic and sexual agency. The New York-based painter Joan Semmel, who once claimed, 'I'm using sex to hang my art on', was a leading figure in the burgeoning genre of women's erotica in the United States.[35] Known primarily for her large-scale photo-realistic renderings of heterosexual couples engaged in lovemaking, Semmel also produced a handful of erotic self-portraits, including *Me without Mirrors* (1974, plate 9). In an analysis of this work, the art historian Marsha Meskimmon opines that Semmel pointedly abandoned the use of a mirror in order to resist collusion with conventional representations of the female nude in Western art. The artist effectively replaced the male artist's painterly touch with that of the woman artist, who is pleasurably serving as both subject and object of her own work.[36] Building on Meskimmon's analysis, the concept of being 'without mirrors' also recalls the context of feminist consciousness-raising sessions in the 1970s, which afforded many women an opportunity to explore the intimate details of their own bodies, often with the guidance of a mirror. In her self-portrait, Semmel, as an accomplished artist and a sexually confident woman, has no need for a mirror. Though the artist is not depicted in the act of self-stimulation, the pink cloth swirling around and under her body potentially symbolizes masturbation, mimicking not only the swollen appearance of aroused labia but also the 'blood-rushing' sensation of orgasm.

On the surface, Semmel's photo-realist painting appears to have little in common with Benglis's waxen abstractions, yet I believe they similarly (albeit tacitly) conjoin autoerotic pleasure with an assertion of female artistic agency; they were not alone in doing so. Judy Chicago famously utilised similar rhetoric in characterising both her imagery and the artistic process by which she produced it. In 1969, the artist embarked on a series of paintings entitled *Pasadena Lifesavers*, which feature brightly coloured circular forms built up from thin layers of acrylic paint sprayed onto the back of plexiglass supports (fig. 21). Despite their abstractness, Chicago felt these forms were symbolically expressive of her newly discovered ability to achieve multiple orgasms. In a 1973 interview with Lucy Lippard, the artist discussed this aspect of the work, as well as the difficulty of her technique: 'The solvent for the paint was the same as for the plastic. If I made a mistake, I couldn't take the paint off or I'd lose the plastic too'. The process of fixing mistakes, she continued, became both physically and emotionally difficult, as the paintings seemed 'somehow like my own skin'. Building on this analogy, Chicago then alluded to its pleasurable aspects: 'There's something fantastic, though, about the process, about playing on that edge; you can just push it and lose it. It's so tempting, because it's trying to pursue perfection, like the perfect orgasm, perfect pleasure, and you know you always have to stop just before it's perfect'.[37] That Chicago ultimately aligned her paintings with her central-core theories marks an important distinction between her work and that of Benglis, and yet her description of delicately working the surface/skin of her acrylic paintings pointedly linked the acquisition of difficult artistic techniques to sexual satisfaction in much the same way that I believe Benglis's more blunt reference to masturbation in the studio did.

Thus for each of these artists – Semmel, Chicago, and Benglis – the alignment of artistic process with the intimate pleasuring of the body rendered both activities an inevitable and highly satisfactory accomplishment. Although these three artists were not engaged in direct conversation with each other, their acts of eroticising their artistic processes similarly challenged the hierarchies of power and domination subtending the ostensible neutrality of modern artistic production. Whether explicitly or not, by assuming the very power to conceive of both artistic and sexual identity as tropes (as rhetorical devices through which to assert a subject position conventionally denied by modernist discourse), the artists strategically intervened in a long-standing tradition of regarding the studio as a site of masculine virility, onanistic reverie, and self-begetting creativity. In this regard, they commonly understood the institutional and discursive limitations they faced as women, even if ultimately Semmel, Chicago, and Benglis used that information to pursue different aims with their art.

For Benglis, the perception that artistic production was an inherently masculine endeavour was a critical subtext to the persistent coupling of her practice with Jackson Pollock's legacy. As much as she admired the older painter's formal innovations, she once tartly deemed his legacy 'a big macho game, a big, heroic, Abstract Expressionist, macho, sexist game. It's all about territory. How big?'[38] Benglis's *entendre* – her tacit conflation of anatomical size with the large scale of the paintings and the brash personality behind them – echoed popular perceptions of postwar American painting as aggressively and unapologetically virile. Though her comments were arguably reductive, Benglis expressed a not uncommon opinion at the time. Fuelled by critical reviews as well as anecdotal knowledge of the artists' private lives, the notion that a brutal and hyperbolic masculinity subtended their artwork constituted a popular and prevailing mythology for many of the male abstract expressionist painters.[39] As Roland Barthes tells us, the rhetorical operation of myth does not eliminate meaning so much as it impoverishes it to a pure signifying function; it seizes on incomplete pictures, 'where the meaning is already relieved of its fat'.[40]

Such myths were not limited to the New York school painters. Leading artists associated with the minimalist generation of the 1960s also inspired a set of gendered tropes. The art historian Julia Bryan-Wilson points out, for example, that Robert Morris intentionally affiliated his artistic practice with notions of blue-collar manliness and working-class masculine labour.[41] She goes on to observe that critics picked up on this rhetoric and even gave it a sexualised charge: for instance in a 1970 review, Peter Plagens characterised Morris, along with Richard Serra, as a 'penis' penetrating and roughing up the vaginal spaces of the museum with his large industrial-looking sculptural installations.[42] Though intended ironically, Plagens's assessment revealed the degree to which artistic practices were popularly understood to be masculine endeavours enacted on the passive and feminised canvas, stone, museum space, or spectator.

As a form of mythic speech, however, such tropes were neither absolute nor stable, and in the early 1970s, both male and female artists took advantage of this instability to create a space for alternative subjectivities and relationships to flourish. As the art historian Amelia Jones notes, the increased visibility of the artist's body in postwar American art, notably but not exclusively through the performance genre, helped give lie to the fragile myth of male artistic autonomy and mythic transcendence. Drawing insightfully on Judith Butler's theory of gender performativity and Merleau-Ponty's phenomenological account of embodiment, Jones argues that artists such as Benglis, Hannah Wilke, Yayoi Kusama, and Vito Acconci appropriated and reworked the 'entire mythology of creation as ejaculation' by performing a paradigmatically postmodern subjectivity that was at once contingent, dispersed, embodied, and intersubjective.[43] Even Acconci's notorious 1972 performance of *Seedbed*, in which the artist secreted himself beneath a false floor in New York's Sonnabend Gallery and masturbated to the sounds of visitors moving above him, stemmed from an impulse to relinquish artistic control and sexual power to viewers. Though rarely read as such at the time, Acconci intended his sexualised performance to call into question the notion of art as a solipsistic masculine endeavour, specifically by rendering himself vulnerable to the spectator's control – in essence, by assuming a passive position conventionally associated with feminine subjectivity.[44] For Jones, *Seedbed* proves similar to women's body art projects of the era insofar as it unhinges the privilege that conventionally accrues to the male artist and thereby enables a 'communicative exchange between desiring subjects'.[45]

In aligning Acconci's masturbatory performance with women's sexualised artistic practices, Jones's analysis of the postmodern artistic subject pointedly diverges from the rhetoric of self-determination, autonomy, agency, and empowerment initially espoused by women artists in the 1970s and expressed through such tropes as self-pleasuring. Benglis's claim that producing her encaustic paintings was akin to masturbation, for instance, seems at first blush to connote not a relinquishment of artistic privilege but rather an assertive claim for its possession. Nonetheless, it is possible to locate common ground and to understand how these various practices communicate an 'exchange between desiring subjects', as Jones concludes.

The scholar Patricia Waugh's work on women's fictional writing from this period provides some insights. She concedes that while women have been historically denied the experience of a 'whole' or 'unitary' subjectivity, and thus their 'desire to become subjects ... is likely to be stronger than the desire to deconstruct, decentre, or fragment subjectivity', such efforts on the part of women writers to redefine female subjectivity result not in the production of an isolated or transcendent self but rather in a self formed in terms of relationship and dispersal: 'What many of these texts suggest is that it is possible to experience oneself as a strong and coherent agent in the world, at the same time as understanding the extent to which identity and gender are socially constructed and represented'.[46] Waugh's account, which posits a subjectivity that is neither traditionally humanist nor radically deconstructed, nonetheless overlaps with Jones's claim that an important lesson of phenomenology and psychoanalysis is 'that the subject "means" always in relationship to others'.[47] I believe this notion of intersubjectivity has bearing on the second of Benglis's tropes, namely, her proposal that the two-brushstroke paintings evoke an androgynous 'splitting and coming together', to paraphrase the artist's aforementioned description to Pincus-Witten. Without forgoing the empowerment associated with sexual self-pleasuring, the trope of androgyny suggests how the quest for a 'whole self' opens out to a mode of intersubjectivity. To be certain, neither Waugh nor Jones cites androgyny as a possible model for postmodern intersubjectivity; indeed, androgyny is a concept that many scholars have dismissed as yet another iteration of an autonomous masculine subjectivity. Yet an alternative view of androgyny sees it offering a dynamic and open-ended structure of the self, one that potentially complements Waugh's account of the subject, who is by turns pleasurably whole and relational. Before I offer an androgynous reading of Benglis's work, it is useful to examine briefly the discourse on androgyny that flourished during the period in which the artist produced her two-brushstroke paintings. In the late 1960s and early 1970s, androgyny held sway as a powerful alternative to polarised gender thinking. Harbouring a deconstructive edge that carried a concomitant promise of a more equitable and expansive reconstruction of both male and female subjectivities, it was an especially appealing solution to the continual dissolution of female subjectivity in modern discourse.

the two in the one

In its most basic sense, 'androgyny' refers to the perceived blending of masculine and feminine psychological attributes in an individual, popularly characterised in Jungian thought as the principle of the 'two in the one'.[48] Yet the concept proves more protean than this description would suggest, as historically androgyny has encompassed a range of similar but not necessarily synonymous concepts that variously bind together gender and sexuality, including bisexuality, homosexuality, polymorphism, cross-dressing, and hermaphroditism. Indeed, as the scholar Tracy Hargreaves points out in her recent study of androgyny in modern literature, it can be a problematic signifier insofar as its meaning shifts depending on the context in which it is mobilised.[49] Also inflecting its signification are the two classical myths of the origins of androgyny in the Western tradition.

The first origin story appears in Plato's *Symposium*, with the playwright Aristophanes' recounting of the first humans. In the beginning there were three types of beings: one consisted of two male halves, another of two female halves, and the third of a male half and a female half. Overcome by wilfulness and hubris, however, the three beings were eventually split in half by Zeus and thus forever destined to seek the unity they once possessed.[50] The second classical source for the myth of androgyny is associated with the story of Hermaphroditus in book 2 of Ovid's *Metamorphoses*. As the child of Hermes and Aphrodite, Hermaphroditus attracted the unwanted attentions of the nymph Salmacis, whose desire for him was so intense that she begged the gods to make them one creature possessing dual anatomy.[51] Thus while Aristophanes details a cleaving of an original union, Ovid describes an opposite process, a union born out of two separate beings merging together.[52]

In parsing the significance of these mythic origins, the scholar Marjorie Garber usefully aligns them with two forms of modern androgyny: a 'good' Platonic kind, which pertains to the spiritual, perceptual, or psychological union of masculine and feminine traits, and a 'bad' Ovidean kind, which produces an erotically and corporeally indeterminate form of androgyny. The former, she opines, largely informs Jungian psychoanalysis and its promotion of a healthy androgynous psyche through the harmonious balance of the anima (the feminine principle within the male unconscious) and animus (the masculine within the female unconscious), Jung's favoured archetypes of the collective unconscious.[53] Conversely, a bad form of androgyny is manifest in what are perceived as alternative lifestyles and non-normative sexual and gender identities. Bad androgyny, Garber writes, is the physical, sexy, and disruptive version of the Platonic ideal.

Benglis's description of the androgynous character of her two-brushstroke paintings suggests some familiarity with Jungian thought, though to what degree is less clear. By the early 1970s, the proliferation of clinical, academic, and popular writings on androgyny enjoyed a level of cultural currency that made it difficult to ignore, let alone to pin down to a single source. For a number of intellectuals, the Jungian 'marriage' of masculine and feminine principles was a potential cure for a fractured and ailing society. In her widely read *Toward a Recognition of Androgyny* of 1973, the literary scholar Carolyn Heilbrun proposed that androgyny could ameliorate the imbalance wrought by the military aggression abroad and the violent civil unrest at home. Heilbrun deemed androgyny 'a spectrum upon which human beings choose their places without regard to propriety or custom'. She believed that as a means of achieving equality between the sexes, it afforded 'a full range of experience ... to individuals who may, as women, be aggressive, as men, tender'.[54]

In positing androgyny as an alternative way of thinking about gender relations, Heilbrun nonetheless had recourse to fairly conventional notions of sex differences. Her definition risked reasserting rather than transcending gender stereotypes, yet its initial logic stemmed from a radical sense of female entitlement. The notion that a woman could be both assertive and tender, for instance, not only reflected belief in her ability to refashion the identity imposed on her by society – and, by extension, refashion society itself – but also involved the presumption that androgyny harmonised only the positive attributes of each gender in the production of a more complete self.

In contrast to Heilbrun's concept of androgyny as an ideal psychic and emotional union, a number of radical thinkers, including Shulamith Firestone, Andrea Dworkin, and Gayle Rubin, advocated it as part of an even greater biological and social revolution, whereby women would be freed from their reproductive responsibilities, traditional family units would be dissolved, and society as a whole would embrace sexual experimentation. The radical feminist articulation of an androgynous society involved the total dissolution of gender as a meaningful identity category, and the proliferation of erotic desires beyond the confines of the heteronormative model privileged under patriarchy. As Rubin avowed, an androgynous society is 'genderless (though not sexless)' and 'one's sexual anatomy [becomes] irrelevant to who one is, what one does and with whom one makes love'.[55]

In the early and mid-1970s, a number of artists explored androgynous imagery and personae, and while such pursuits cannot be reduced to a singular intention, in many instances they stemmed from a desire to articulate a non-repressive and expansive concept of self. Paralleling these artistic practices, critics and art historians usefully examined its contemporary, historical, and mythical significance, citing everything from Plato's *Symposium* to alchemy, surrealism, psychoanalysis, and Indian tantric traditions as sources of inspiration for androgyny's contemporary artistic reiteration.[56] Many likewise espoused a popular modern Romantic conception of the imaginative mind as inherently androgynous: as the artist Michael Bonesteel averred in a 1979 article, creativity constitutes a 'symbolic and simultaneous mothering and fathering as well as a figuratively auto-erotic experience'.[57] But how did artists express such concepts visually?

For contemporary practitioners working both in abstraction and in figuration, formal techniques such as doubling, splitting, and juxtaposition

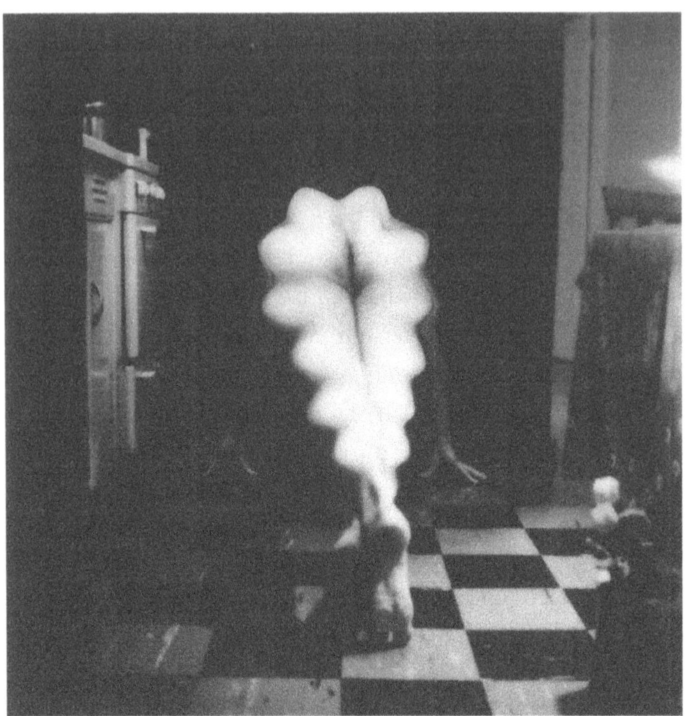

22. Lucas Samaras, *Photo-Transformation*, July 29, 1976, SX-70 Polaroid photograph, 3 x 3 in. (7.6 x 7.6 cm). Courtesy of the artist and The Pace Gallery, New York. © Lucas Samaras.

effectively evoked androgyny's fusion of dualities, as did more literal images of two-headed figures, or two figures merging together. Exemplary in this regard are Lucas Samaras's self-eroticising 'Auto-Polaroids' (1969–73) and 'Photo-Transformations' (1973–6), two series of self-portraits in which the artist manipulated the emulsion surface of Polaroid images in order to transform himself into phantasmagorical and androgynous-looking figures. In this particular image, the artist's legs and buttocks morph into an ambiguous form that is by turns phallic and vaginal-looking (fig. 22).

On occasion, artist Hannah Wilke produced sculptural forms bearing androgynous characteristics. Like Benglis, she favoured malleable materials and by the early 1970s had established a reputation for folding, kneading, and pressing clay, latex, erasers, and chewing gum into provocative bodily configurations (fig. 23). In terms reminiscent of Benglis's description of her artistic process as masturbatory, Wilke once exclaimed to an interviewer that making her work inspired 'metaphysical feelings related to orgasmic ecstasy'.[58]

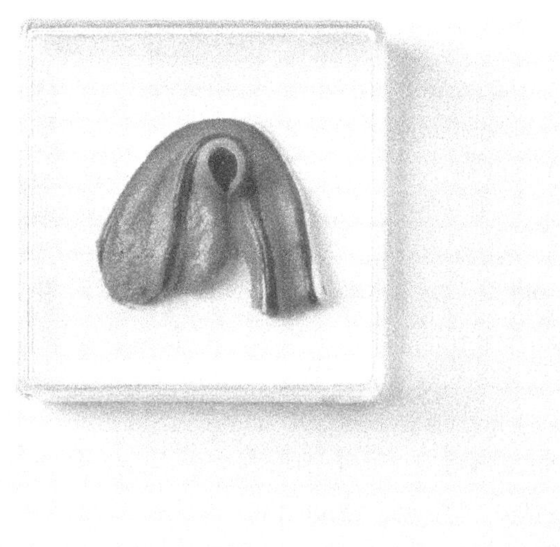

23. Hannah Wilke, *Untitled*, 1979, chewing gum sculpture in Plexiglas box, 2 ½ x 2 ½ x 1 ⅛ in. (6.4 x 6.4 x 2.9 cm). Hannah Wilke Collection & Archive, Los Angeles. © Marsie, Emanuelle, Damon, and Andrew Scharlatt/Licensed by VAGA, New York, NY.

At the same time, however, the artist appreciated how the sexual character of her work shifted depending on the viewer's relative position. As Wilke described, the folded forms 'can be seen as male or female, just as the head of a cock looks very much like a vagina' when viewed from a certain angle.[59] In parsing the artist's homology, the art historian Saundra Goldman has read it – rightly so, I believe – as an indication of a desire for gender equality that Wilke felt was pointedly lacking in the art world. The trope of anatomical androgyny was Wilke's way of inviting reciprocity and respect without forgoing the full expression of her female self, though as Goldman and others have noted, the artist eventually concentrated on the production of female genital forms and often insisted on the primacy of vaginal symbolism in her practice.[60] Nonetheless, Wilke's characterisation of the androgynous nature of her sculptures tacitly acknowledged the importance of the viewer's perspective and, by extension, pointed up the difficulty of ascribing fixed differences based on visual distinctions, a topic to which I return later in this chapter.

Cross-dressing performances constituted yet another manifestation of androgyny's allure, the adoption of public personae of the opposite sex recalling Duchamp's female alter ego of the 1920s, Rrose Sélavy, as well as more contemporary expressions of bad androgyny in 1960s subcultures. For many women artists, androgyny was a significant subtext to the exploration of alternative forms of female selfhood. The California-based performance artist Eleanor Antin, who developed a series of male and female performative personalities in the 1970s, usefully voiced this sentiment in an essay from 1974: 'My sense is that [my self-definitions] had to be permanent and mobile, not immutable or fixed, repetitive, like the parts of the Freudian allegory. I needed core images, something like Jungian archetypes that could couple, uncouple, and transform'.[61] Antin's description is not unlike Benglis's characterisation of her wax paintings to Pincus-Witten. In both instances, the artists articulate a desire to express something fundamental yet mutable about their respective identities through their artwork. Here, androgyny connotes a process of transformation and a potential for personal and social change in which sex differences are neither incommensurable nor static.

As feminists of different persuasions rehearsed its possibilities through the early 1970s, many found that androgyny simply failed to overcome patriarchal sex-role conditioning and, in the end, continued to subordinate female subjectivity to a masculine ideal of origination and selfhood. As a largely utopian concept, the espousal of gender eradication to which the expression of androgyny was often directed failed to materialise in any lasting way beyond the sartorial and sexual experimentations of youth cultures. Though widely read, Heilbrun's account sparked considerable disagreement and inspired a collection of articles published in 1974 as a special issue of *Women's Studies* entitled 'The Androgyny Papers'. Among the detractors, Barbara Charlesworth Gelpi cautioned that androgyny represented a male fantasy of union, its appropriation of feminised traits always figuring them as secondary to masculine intelligence and spirituality; similarly, Cynthia Secor opined that Heilbrun's reliance on conventional sex stereotypes reified the very divisions that her terms purported to transcend.[62] Daniel Harris likewise warned that psychological androgyny remained a 'sexist myth in disguise' with no positive value for women, and Catharine Stimpson took issue with its heterosexual biases and with Heilbrun's insistence on tethering her concept to conventional notions of marriage and the family.[63] In another context, the feminist theologian Mary Daly voiced her concern that the androgynous ideal constituted a pseudo-wholeness that effaced women's subjectivity and continued to privilege an all-too-familiar image of masculine self-sufficiency. For Daly, an early supporter turned detractor of the concept, androgyny was 'something more like a hole than a whole' in its denial of the specificity of the sexed female body, and along with female sensibility proponents she called for greater attention to the female perspective.[64]

In short, the concept of androgyny had reached a theoretical impasse by the mid-1970s, even as it continued to serve as a viable trope for artistic production.[65] A concept that began as irresolute, transitional, and spacious devolved into something fixed, conventional, and limiting. With this in mind, I believe that the *desire* for androgyny still remains a useful conceit for understanding the erotic character of much of the artwork discussed here, particularly Benglis's two-brushstroke paintings. What Garber identifies as a bad form of androgyny is illuminating in this regard. In contrast to an androgyny that denotes psychic wholeness or union, bad androgyny is transgressively 'double-signed', she writes, which is to say that it retains gender and sexual ambiguity at both the visual and discursive levels.[66] Tracy Hargreaves reaches a similar conclusion: though she concedes that it has tended to codify into an idealised and transcendent concept, she finds compelling instances in modern literature in which androgyny retains its dialectical force, when it 'circulate[s] rather than settle[s]: as image, in and out of culture, as sexuality, as embodiment and as sensibility'.[67] Here Hargreaves alludes to the scholar Francette Pacteau's psychoanalytic characterisation of the androgyne as a figure that can only ever solicit 'a *searching* look'. A flashpoint for the viewer's desire, the indeterminately sexed androgyne cannot be fixed by the gaze but must always remain 'an impossible referent'. As such, Pacteau continues, 'when the other is not identifiable, my own position wavers'.[68]

Pacteau's account of the androgyne recalls Helen Molesworth's description of the 'slippage of coordinates' generated by Benglis's two-brushstroke paintings. The works' bifurcated compositions produce two similar but not identical parts, each of which erupts into further subdivisions yielding to yet smaller and increasingly multiple structural details, from individual layers of colour to single drips of wax, and eventually back again to the lozenge whole (plate 10). As Molesworth writes of Benglis's paintings, 'every return to their visual and tactile field is rewarded by a propagation of small details that continually serve to scatter one's perception across the visual field'. Significantly, this effect is heightened when the encaustic works are displayed as a series, as 'the repetition of the lozenges mitigates against the notion of shock. Instead, one experiences a kind of shattering as the reverberations between the dualistic poles continue over and over again'.[69]

Molesworth's excellent account begins to indicate how and where the body factors in Benglis's two-brushstroke paintings. To a large extent, she echoes the conclusions reached by Anne Wagner in her consideration of the corporeality of Eva Hesse's artwork in her 1996 book *Three Artists (Three Women)*. Wagner's analysis, which is intended to free Hesse's work from reductive biographical readings and essentialist interpretations of its gender origins, is worth quoting at length, as it makes an important distinction between the various bodies in question and their implication for the viewing experience:

> The animation of [Hesse's] work – her use of materials and shapes that might be said to grant her objects the status of substitute bodies – always occurs in a formal context assertive enough to remove the work (if it is considered seriously) from a purely personal range of meanings.... The body in question is likewise not so importantly Hesse's as the viewer's, in that the presence of the sculpture summons from the viewer such bodily analogies as his or her personal experience and mentality will allow. And the body is also that of the sculpture itself.... The sculpture is literal about the body, we could say, at the same time as it explodes the whole notion of literalness. It insists on its language-like character – its structures of repetition and transformation – at the same time as it maps those properties onto evocations of a carnal world. The body is there somewhere, at the intersection of structure and reference. Though that somewhere may seem close, Hesse's art insists that it is permanently out of reach.[70]

The notion that Hesse's art solicits but also denies access to the body it materially summons leads Wagner to reject a facile reading of gender difference. Though she does not dismiss every account that takes the artist's gender identity as its starting point, the art historian is concerned to complicate the matter as it pertains to the critical reception of the woman artist. In a work such as *Tori* (1969), for instance, the repetition and similitude of the nine pod-like fibreglass forms structure an experience in which viewers are summoned as 'embodied and sensate in ways more profoundly similar than different' (fig. 24).[71]

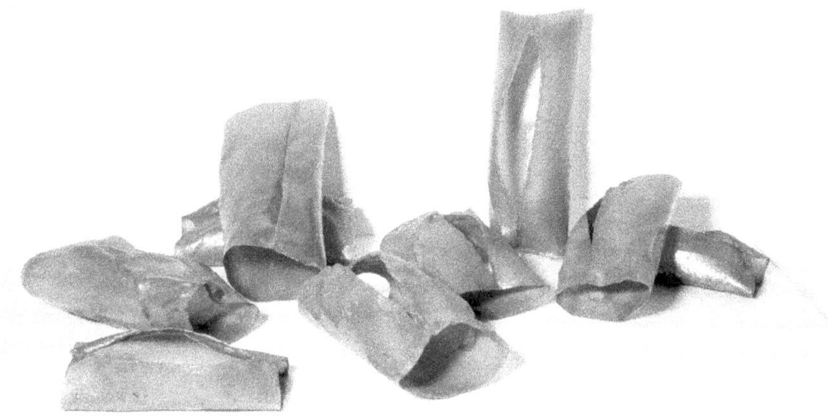

24. Eva Hesse, *Tori*, 1969, fiberglass, polyester resin, wire-mesh, installation variable, approx 90 x 160 in. (235 x 410 cm), nine units. Philadelphia Museum of Art, 1990. © The Estate of Eva Hesse. Courtesy Galerie Hauser & Wirth, Zurich. Photo: Eric Pollitzer.

In following Wagner's reasoning, the conditions through which the body manifests in Benglis's two-brushstroke paintings are equally contingent on a perceiving and embodied viewer. This is, perhaps, how we might understand the artist's various descriptions of the work. For instance, when she refers to her two-brushstroke paintings as 'specific', Benglis seems to deny their referentiality, and yet her word choice may also serve as a reminder to look *specifically* at the art, rather than at the artist's identity, for what it might say about the body and embodied experiences. The artist's masturbatory comment, which as I have already indicated is a pointed riposte to the modern myth of masculine artistic creativity, equally functions as a characterisation of the viewer's bodily response to the rippled layers of encaustic. Notably, it conjures up an image of sexual energy held in perpetual tension by the work's formal schema; this tension in turn manifests as an ambiguously androgynous form, one that never settles into a fixed position but instead remains relational and transformative.[72] As such, Benglis's recourse to androgyny undercuts the solipsism invoked by the image of the solitary artist at work in her studio and, just as importantly, indicates some of the ways in which the two-brushstroke paintings invite a pleasurable duality that does not perceive of differences as incommensurable or immutable. Rather than devolve into a trite or bland ideal of a lost primordial union, Benglis's two-brushstroke paintings invoke a dynamic androgyny; thus if the sexual or gendered body is there somewhere, its significance arises only through a continual process of splitting and coming together.[73]

The remarks Benglis made in response to Linda Nochlin's 1971 essay 'Why Have There Been No Great Women Artists?' which I discussed in chapter 1, afford a final overlap with early feminist articulations of androgyny's potential to transform structures of gender and sexual differences. In particular, to recall Gayle Rubin's account, androgyny is cast not as a prescribed mixture of masculine and feminine traits but as the total elimination of difference as a meaningful category. This fantasy is implicit in Benglis's expressed desire to have the label 'woman' be nothing more than circumstantial fact. Again this is a question not of Benglis's familiarity with specific theoretical positions or of her outright dismissal of gender inequities, but of her awareness, however intuitive, that a popularised concept such as androgyny potentially mirrored her own perspective. As she would claim in a 1976 interview, '[It] really depends on our culture, on our associations. How we are going to group it finally, we don't know enough about psychology to say of a body whether it is male or female in terms of physicality, or whether it is male or female in terms of psychology, maybe we will never know enough to say so. I think that's what art is about, describing those areas of feelings that have to do with bodily sensations, bodily feelings but it's also a total response, all art is about total responses'.[74] Benglis's conception of a 'total response' finds a correlative in the trope of androgyny. Similarly, Benglis intended her infamous 1974 *Artforum* project to serve as a 'total response'. The image of the nubile artist wielding the double-headed phallus against her naked and oiled body constituted a critique of the sexual politics of the art world, the resulting self-portrait as hermaphrodite purposely offering up ambivalence and contradiction in the face of gender and sexual absolutes. Less a statement about the artist's own gender identity or sexual disposition, however, Benglis's *Artforum* ad constituted a deliberate refusal of binary categories and their application to her artistic practice. Benglis considered the hermaphrodite 'ideal', for as she told an interviewer, the 'condition is a contradiction in itself. You embody the perfect contradiction in a neither/nor state'.[75] However, the visual facts of Benglis's photographic self-representation – the oversized rubber phallus mapped onto the clearly female body – expose how difficult the 'neither/nor' state is to inhabit, let alone accept, in the figure of the artist. Conversely, the two-brushstroke paintings offer up the ideal contradiction that the *Artforum* image simply could not; rather than an illusion of perfect union, Benglis's works retain the exploratory fantasy of a dynamic, excessive, and imperfect state of embodiment.

The topic of the next chapter, Benglis's videos from the 1970s also address issues of embodiment and agency. However, while the erotics of making are a central conceit in many instances, Benglis's videos also engage more emphatically than her encaustic paintings in a critique of the sexual politics of female self-representation and visual pleasure. Broaching questions about the reception of the body in technologically mediated forms, these works demonstrate how the artist often gauged the relevancy of her own practice within and against dominant artistic and cultural discourses, at times participating through strategically ambivalent visual gestures.

3 Video Input and Output

Between 1972 and 1977, Benglis produced thirteen videos, two in collaboration with the US filmmaker Stanton Kaye. They are all single-channel productions and from the outset were incorporated into exhibitions of the artist's sculptural work, as well as into museum and gallery surveys dedicated specifically to video and film. Benglis's works were, for instance, screened at Paula Cooper Gallery in New York (1973), the Contemporary Arts Museum in Houston (1973), New York's Museum of Modern Art (1974), the Kitchen in New York (1975), and Long Beach Museum of Art in California; the final two institutions were particularly committed to video programming throughout the 1970s. As a consequence of this exposure, Benglis's productions are frequently mentioned in early essays and reviews of video art. As critics and writers attempted to grapple with the theoretical implications of early video technology, her output was a significant reference point.

Of her use of video, Benglis once noted that the medium was 'no more or less' than one of several that she employed that dealt with 'the layering of time and space'.[1] This statement typifies the way in which many artists perceived video during this period, as the technological medium was regarded as a logical extension of other material and performance-based practices concerned with issues of simultaneity, duration, liveness, or process. Yet for Benglis, as indeed for many artists, the fact that video was well disposed to capturing subject matter made it an important tool for directly investigating the intersection of self and media technology. In providing an in-depth look at approximately half of Benglis's video productions, this chapter establishes the artist's stylistic and conceptual concerns with the medium while also conveying the tenor of works that may be difficult for viewers today to access in person.[2] What may seem at first blush to consist of random, pointless, or prolonged moments of experimentation with the camera eventually yields a more complicated body of work in which a tension between structure and content, visual pleasure and un-pleasure, is paramount.

For a number of women practitioners, Benglis included, video represented a new mode of visual production/perception that was not yet territorialised by male artists.[3] At the same time, however, its affinity with a number of other media, including television and film, on the one hand, and performance and the visual arts, on the other, meant that video could effectively engage with existing cultural and artistic conventions concerning gender identity and the body as well as address connections between representations of sexuality and sexual politics. These are concerns that Benglis would ultimately take up in two of her better-known videos, *Now* and *Female Sensibility*; thus I devote a significant portion of this chapter to analysing these works. The chapter concludes with an examination of the two works done in collaboration with Kaye, which Benglis crafted as pointed responses to the critical fallout from the 1974 publication of her dildo ad in *Artforum*.

a small image on a small box

Benglis's introduction to the video medium occurred around 1970, while she was teaching at the University of Rochester in upstate New York. Recognising how comfortable her students were with television and with the conceptual nature of a 'small image on a small box', Benglis assigned class projects that entailed exploring the formal syntax of video and its feedback mechanism.[4] This spirit of experimentation pervades the artist's own work, the content of which is often mediated by crude technical distortions and taping effects. In two of her earliest productions, *Noise* and *Home Tape Revised* (both 1972), Benglis established certain techniques and themes to which she would repeatedly return in her video works. Though gender and sexuality are not dominant themes here, each of these earlier works is simultaneously concerned with the seemingly mundane surface of daily life and the experience of the body through the video camera's subjective vision.

Noise has an informal cast consisting of Benglis and five of her friends in her studio (fig. 25). It opens with the artist writing the video's title across the

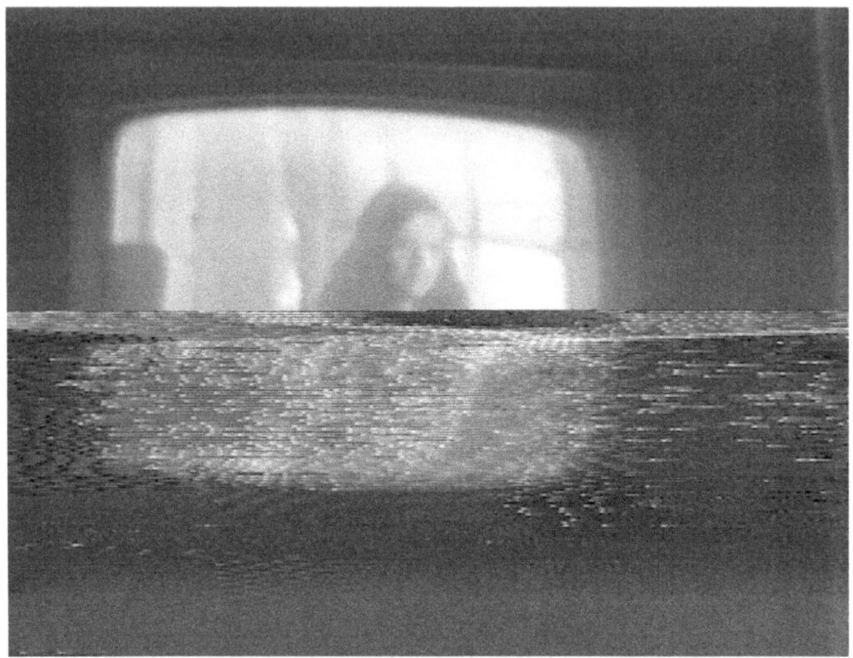

25. Lynda Benglis, *Noise*, 1972, black-and-white video, 7:15 min. © Lynda Benglis. Courtesy of Video Data Bank, www.vdb.org.

surface of a monitor, on which plays a tape of her performing the same action. The entire scene briefly shifts to static, after which the artist Richard Tuttle appears on screen. He engages in a barely audible conversation with Benglis, who remains out of sight, presumably behind the camera. A soundtrack of street noise is amplified to a jarring level, drowning out the dialogue between the two. Tuttle's closely cropped face is framed by a monitor behind him, on which plays a tape of another monitor playing a tape of a monitor. The multiple generations, produced by retaping material playing on a monitor, become increasingly grainy and distorted with each remove and are reduced in many instances to mere noise – a visual analogue to the soundtrack. After Tuttle disappears, static again briefly fills the screen, after which the other individuals come into view one-by-one to converse with the offscreen Benglis, their dialogues equally muffled by the amplified street noise.[5]

Taxing the viewer's patience and pleasure, *Noise* evidences Benglis's interest in generating abstract audio and visual effects that paradoxically counter video's more straightforward documentary function. The retaping of imagery from the monitor, which produces a telescoping effect of 'internal windows',

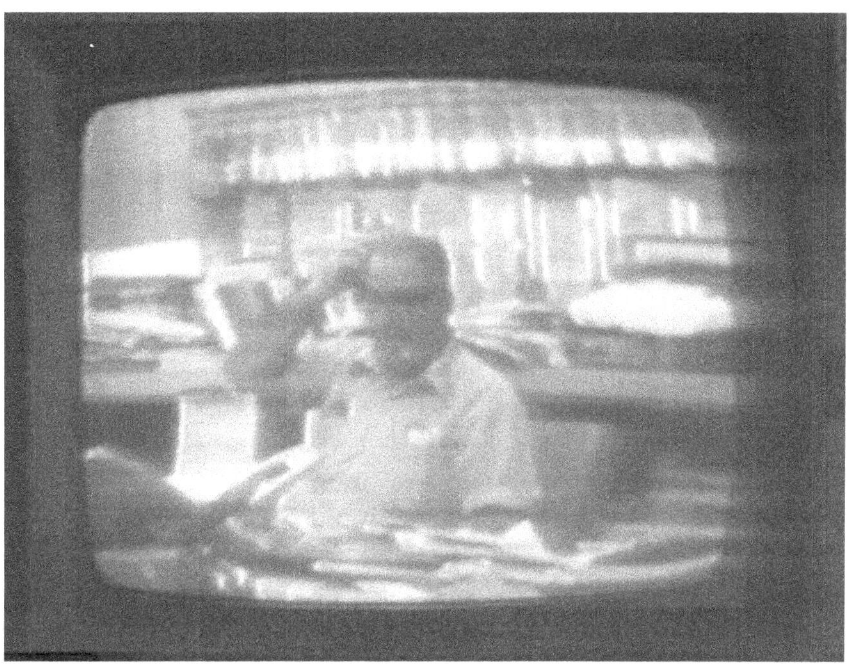

26. Lynda Benglis, *Home Tape Revised*, 1972, black-and-white video, 25:00 min. © Lynda Benglis. Courtesy of Video Data Bank, www.vdb.org.

is a technique she would frequently employ in her work, as it enabled Benglis to create spatiotemporal layers without the use of expensive editing equipment. More significantly, the layering thwarts the viewer's access to the interpersonal relations taking place within the work, as each embedded generation of taped material becomes increasingly removed in space and time.

In her second video, *Home Tape Revised*, Benglis continued to employ the technique of retaping from the monitor. This work is a travelogue of sorts, its material mainly derived from a trip Benglis took to visit her family in the southeastern region of the United States (fig. 26). However, the video opens with a short scene of a man seated at a typewriter in the artist's Baxter Street studio; though his identity is not revealed, the man is Klaus Kertess. The tape then quickly cuts to shots of Benglis visiting her family in Lake Charles, Louisiana, and Petal, Mississippi. Although the viewer sees various family members, their homes, their pets, and the family business, initially there is little information given about the people or what they are doing. Interspersed with these moments of straightforward documentation are shots of the same scenes retaped from and now playing on a television monitor; at this point, Benglis provides a voiceover narration of her trip. As viewers watch the internal monitors playing the home tape footage, several scenes of which are repeated and repeatedly distorted through the retaping procedure, the artist also acknowledges the viewing process. At one point, for example, she refers to the disruptive noise created by an air conditioner in her studio; at another moment, she admits, 'I said that before'. This back-and-forth narration about the family visit and the present conditions in the studio is both spatially and temporally disorienting and, like *Noise*, calls into question the different levels of reality embedded in the videotape. That Benglis alludes to spaces and events not directly pictured or heard further belies the absoluteness of the information portrayed on screen; as though to underscore this disjuncture, *Home Tape Revised* ends with another shot of Kertess reading from the paper inserted in his typewriter: 'Read to counteract the now of video time. Read to be more or less self-conscious. Read now. Now. Now I will read some ends. The end of my last short story', he concludes (fig. 27).

Despite its autobiographical content, *Home Tape Revised* is resolutely unemotional. Calling it 'precisely controlled' in a 1973 review, the art critic Bruce Kurtz notes how the tape is tempered by the intervention of the camera and monitor, the artist's monotone voiceover, and the emphasis on factual

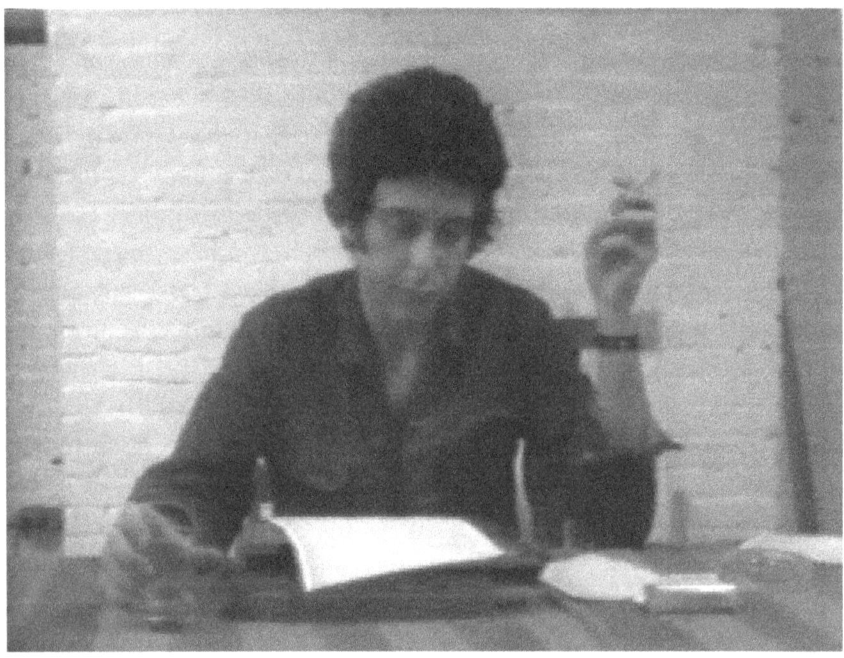

27. Lynda Benglis, *Home Tape Revised*, 1972, black-and-white video, 25:00 min. © Lynda Benglis. Courtesy of Video Data Bank, www.vdb.org.

description.[6] This studied neutrality in turn calls attention to the *revision* process indicated in the work's title, which undercuts not only the presumption of video's direct mode of access and address but, by extension, the reliability of any memory or storytelling moment. Kertess's monologue at the end of *Home Tape Revised* likewise casts doubt on the absoluteness of the narrative, for even though the footage and the voiceover belong to Benglis, there remains the question of whose story the video actually tells or who even has the authority to tell it.[7] In offering a glimpse into the artist's personal family life, *Home Tape Revised* continually circumscribes an intimate or confessional mode of address. Kurtz finds that Benglis's video epitomises the 'one to one relationship between the viewer and the monitor which distinguishes video so much from film, resulting in the feeling of shared experience'.[8] Indeed, the ordinariness of Benglis's family scenes could, by extension, speak to any number of mundane family scenarios or personal home movies. However, I find that the resulting video calls into question the very mode of perception through which the work enables a shared experience.

Television forms a significant subtext to both *Noise* and *Home Tape Revised*. The embedded monitors in Benglis's works implicitly evoke the culturally ubiquitous television screen and the expectations attending the conditions of watching TV. Kurtz discusses this connection in his review: for the critic, the relationship between video and television hinges on their shared audio-tactile sensations. Drawing on Marshall McLuhan's theory that the 'cool' medium of television downplays the visual in favour of a reintegration of sense perceptions, Kurtz focuses on video's ability to generate an immersive, tactile experience.[9] The 'surface' of the monitor becomes analogous to the viewer's skin. More recently, a number of scholars have usefully described this relationship between the video screen and the spectator's body/skin in terms of 'haptic looking'. A potentially erotic experience, haptic looking is understood to generate an intersubjectivity premised on mutual embodiment.[10] Such an analysis indicates some of the ways in which Benglis's videos align with her other artwork, notably the highly tactile two-brushstroke paintings, as well as her immersive large-scale polyurethane installations. At the same time, however, the artist's videos tend to work against this sense of mutual embodiment, or at the very least, to render its points of virtual contact more tenuous.

Indeed, and for the most part, early video discourse adopted a critical stance towards the capacity for the televisual screen to establish embodied interpersonal relations. As a dominant topic of much early video art, the medium's critical position *vis-à-vis* TV was commonly regarded as one of decentring and disrupting the flow of televisual information. For the artist and writer David Antin, TV watching is premised on the assertion of uninterrupted real time, and on the belief that 'it can and is providing an adequate representation of reality, while everyone's experience denies it'.[11] More recently, media scholar Samuel Weber has noted of the technology of television that it 'deprives distance as well as proximity of their traditional stability'.[12] As a result of this 'seeing-at-a-distance', television watching splits 'the unity of place and with it the unity of everything that defines its identity with respect to place: events, bodies, subjects'.[13] This ambiguous condition of being both 'here' and 'there' that is fundamental to TV watching is also examined by Antin, who cogently articulates how the broadcasting industry attempts to restore a sense of stability and wholeness through carefully timed and scripted programming. In contrast, Antin continues, much early video art purposely fails to represent a facsimile of televisual reality: by reworking the conventions of time associated with industry standards, or by calling attention to the actual taping process, it attempts to disrupt the seamless flow of media spectatorship. Thus, the time it takes to view a video work can feel surprisingly abbreviated or painfully protracted, regardless of its actual length. Indeed, critical commentaries on early video art often stress an inevitable sense of boredom and discomfort as the viewing process is thrown into relief, and the information presented on screen called into doubt.[14]

Writing on this topic more recently, art historian Anne Wagner suggests that in many instances it was the aim of early video artists to summon you 'as an audience, and sometimes, under selected circumstances, to make you all-too-conscious of that fact' through a refusal of 'the public pleasures of television, which, like the offers of advertising, center on illusions of presence, intimacy, and belonging'.[15] Both *Noise* and *Home Tape Revised* make this summoning gesture as they simultaneously defer the illusion of intimacy, accessibility, and shared embodiment afforded by video technology. This deferral is further instantiated in Benglis's video work in which self-representation becomes a primary conceit.

images of self

As Benglis continued to work with video, she increasingly turned the camera on herself. This was both a practical solution, as she was her most accessible subject, and a conceptual decision to explore the self-image dynamic in more depth. *Document* (1972) is an early and noteworthy example. This video features the artist's face in close-up as she moves her head back and forth in front of a monitor on which static is being transmitted. From off camera, a man (Benglis's technical assistant, Nathan Rabin) issues directions to Benglis to turn her head, centre her face, move forward and back, and so forth. At one point, he and the artist discuss the need to eliminate a 'hot spot' produced by the external video lighting reflecting off the monitor behind her head. Benglis eventually shifts her body so that her profile blocks out the reflected light, a move that asserts her physicality even as the artist is simultaneously dematerialized into an electronic video image. Benglis then issues her own directive – 'Tape it and take a photo' – before moving entirely offscreen.

The next scene in *Document* opens with the static-filled video monitor again, this time with a still photograph taped to it: presumably from the scene we just witnessed, it depicts Benglis's profile positioned in front of a monitor on which the artist's face also appears. As the viewer contemplates the still photograph, the 'live' Benglis steps back into the frame, at which point she begins to write the video's title on the monitor above the photograph, a move that establishes the 'tactile' surface of the screen (fig. 28). The artist retraces the word and adds a copyright notice below it. In a

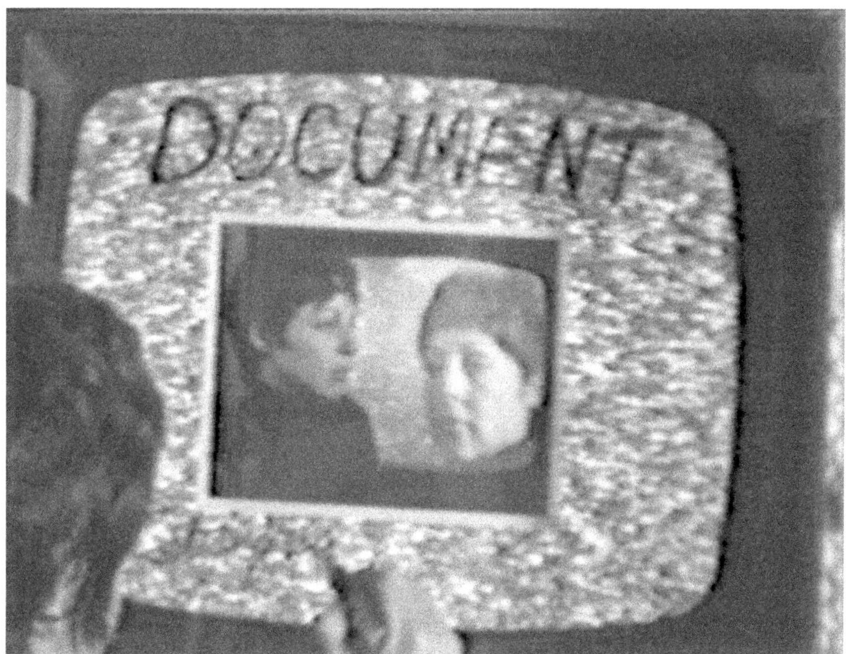

28. Lynda Benglis, *Document*, 1972, black-and-white video, 6:08 min. © Lynda Benglis. Courtesy of Video Data Bank, www.vdb.org.

Duchampian move, she then draws a moustache on the faces in the photograph, retracing them and the copyright notice.[16] As she repeats these gestures, the camera zooms in on the photograph and then out again to its original position. Benglis repeats her actions in virtual silence, which is broken at the end only by the sound of a telephone ringing.

Although Benglis's act of writing the copyright asserts her ownership of the work, there are several elements in *Document* that pointedly thwart a clear-cut notion of originality and authorship: the directives issued by the man off-screen, the multiple video and photographic reproductions of Benglis's face, and the artist's own repetitive gestures challenge the viewer's ability to discern an authentic source 'document'. If copyrighting implies the existence of a specific author and an original creation, *Document* purposely obscures its own point of authorial, spatial, and temporal origination. In bestowing masculine traits upon her own image, Benglis also playfully indicates how gender and originality are traditionally – repeatedly – understood to intersect through the figure of the male rather than female artist. Here Benglis's repetitive gesture of copyrighting her own work is coupled with her symbolic act of going 'in disguise' in order to legitimate her actions.

Throughout *Document*, questions of gender power, control, and subjectivity are tacitly posed yet never resolved. In subsequent videos, Benglis continued to explore similar tensions, specifically through the creation of erotic scenarios. Notably, in *Now* (1973), the artist utilised pre-taped images of her face to elicit the impression that she is kissing and tonguing her own image (plate 11). Colour, a new element in the artist's video repertoire, is central to this production: a predominantly pink-red and blue-green palette, comparable in intensity to the Day-Glo colours Benglis favoured in her sculptural work at the time, underscores both the sensuous and the contrived aspects of the autoerotic content.

As the scene unfolds in *Now*, Benglis can be heard issuing a series of commands and questions about the taping process. 'Start recording. I said, start recording', she asserts at the beginning. She then follows up this directive with and repeats in various sequences throughout the middle portion of the tape: 'Do you wish to direct me? Okay. Now! Okay. Now? Start recording. We are recording. Let's see how it is'. Occasionally, the artist also emits a loud 'ahhhhhhh' as her multiple faces appear to kiss and tongue on screen. At one point, laughter can be heard; at another, an unidentified man off-screen (Benglis's assistant, Tony Vlatkovich) interjects with the instruction to back up, to which one of the on-screen Benglises replies, 'Back? Back?' as she simultaneously does so. The video continues in this fashion for just over twelve minutes, its eroticism tempered by a strong dose of playfulness.

In acting as both subject and object of her own erotic encounter, Benglis created a visual counterpart to the masturbatory analogy she would proffer the following year to Robert Pincus-Witten concerning the process of making her two-brushstroke paintings, a topic I discussed in chapter 2. However, while the onanistic content of *Now* was not lost on early reviewers, most, including Rosalind Krauss in her oft-cited 1976 essay 'Video: The Aesthetics of Narcissism', assessed Benglis's video in terms of its narcissistic preoccupations. *Now* is one of several early works that inspired Krauss to formulate the theory that video technology, specifically its capacity to record and transmit simultaneously, inherently replicates the psychological condition of narcissism by which the self becomes trapped in an atemporal state of repetition. The technology of instant replay, the art historian claims, produces a narcissistic self that has 'no past, and as well, no connection with any objects that are external to it. For the double that appears on the monitor cannot be called a true external object'.[17] In *Now*, she concludes, Benglis reinforces the psychic structure of the narcissist through her continual articulation of the word 'now'.

In 'Video: The Aesthetics of Narcissism', Krauss takes issue with video narcissism for its failure to generate a self-reflexive work of art. If reflexivity entails a critical analysis of the aesthetic and historical conditions giving rise to a specific medium, much early video instead settles for mere reflection, according to Krauss. Significantly, she foregrounds her characterisation of narcissism solely on the 'bracketing' effect produced by the electronic feedback of video technology, not on the erotic presence of the artist in front of the camera per se; therefore the deeper implications of Benglis's narcissistic self-representation are not pursued in this seminal article. Only in passing does Krauss concede that the accelerated pace of modern mass communication in post-1960s culture compelled many artists to respond through video self-representations: 'The demand for instant replay in the media', she posits, 'finds its obvious correlative in an aesthetic mode by which the self is created through the electronic device of feedback'.[18] Here, video technology is understood unproblematically to serve the demands of commerce rather than the avant-garde.

Elsewhere in the literature on early video art, however, the question of female narcissism was subject to specific critical attention. Though scholars including Amelia Jones have more recently argued for recuperating female narcissism as a critical feminist strategy, contemporaneous perceptions of this thematic proved more equivocal, not least because it exposed the woman artist to criticism 'on a personal as well as on an artistic level', as the feminist art critic Lucy Lippard opined in 1976, which is to say it often entailed a problematic conflation of the artist and her artwork.[19] The use of video by women to generate self-images was particularly susceptible to reprobation because the medium, with its instant-feedback capabilities, functioned much like an actual mirror. Along with the attendant perception of female vanity associated with the mirror, authors also drew out the psychoanalytical repercussions of female narcissism. For example, in his 1976 article 'Video Art, the Imaginary, and the Parole Vide', Stuart Marshall proffered an account not unlike Krauss's when he deemed video art a regressive preoccupation akin to the mirror stage of development in Lacanian psychoanalysis. Like a child caught in the mirror phrase, the video artist never resolves the distinction between self and other that marks a healthy resolution of the oedipal phase. Not insignificantly, Marshall singles out the work of three women – Benglis, Joan Jonas, and Hermine Freed – as indicative of this regressive engagement with the self and self-representation.[20]

A perceived similarity to pornographic films was yet another factor contributing to the equivocal reception of women's video self-representations in the 1970s. In exploring this connection in a 1976 article entitled 'The Ins and Outs of Video', *Artforum* critic Jeff Perrone submitted that the 'sexuality of video and pornography is obvious and evident. The formal similarities are just as obvious, though we tend to disregard them. Both have characteristically low-definition images, grainy, close-range photography, and are crudely edited'.[21] Perrone was more intrigued by than critical of the comparison, and his essay usefully indicates how film pornography afforded early video artists a subversive, lowbrow genre from which to appropriate taboo themes. Nonetheless, the critic also acknowledged certain limitations when it came to work by women artists: 'That Benglis and Eleanor Antin, two women, come to mind', he concluded, 'immediately says as much about our propensity to objectify women's sexuality as it does about the inherent sexuality of video "structure"'.[22]

Here Perrone touches on an issue that Lucy Lippard simultaneously addressed in a 1976 essay entitled 'The Pains and Pleasures of Rebirth: European and American Women's Body Art'. In an oft-cited passage, she cautioned: 'A woman using her own face and body has a right to do what she will with them, but it is a subtle abyss that separates men's use of women for sexual titillation from women's use of women to expose that insult'.[23] Lippard's concern that a woman might collude in her own sexual objectification was not insignificant, particularly when the issue of pornography was also on the table. Indeed, the blatant orientation of porn to a male heterosexual audience led many women to condemn as patently inauthentic and denigrating its representation of female sexuality. As a leading figure in the production of female erotica, for example, the artist Joan Semmel drew clear distinctions between her explicit figurative paintings of heterosexual couples and mainstream pornographic imagery, suggesting that the former proved more palatable to a female audience because it affirmed the realities of women's lived experiences: 'Pornography titillates, eroticism stimulates. The erotic theme to me ... is one of communication – two people expressing their humanity to each other'.[24] Semmel's distinction was one commonly proposed as a means to ward off censorship and, just as significantly, to chart new erotic terrain from a female perspective. In attempting to expand the meaning of the 'erotic', however, such accounts foreclosed more ambiguous modes of sexual expression by women artists.

Thus Perrone's assessment that women's video self-images invited (whether intentionally or not) a level of sexual objectification would seem to point up the limitations of the medium for radicalising female self-representation. At the same time, however, Perrone's comparison between video and porn is a reminder that artists did not just operate against the grain of popular discourse but, to the contrary, often produced work that reflected, if not actively engaged with, existing experiences and perceptions. I find an awareness of this engagement permeates Benglis's *Now*. The artist's repetitive guttural noises ('ahhhhhhh') sound like parodies of pornographic pleasure. Likewise, Benglis's questions and invectives not only chart the taping process with the offscreen male voice but also address potential viewers: 'Do you wish to direct me?' and 'Let's run that through' become invitations for spectators to look, and to look again – and we do. This invitation, as Wagner avows, renders the viewer 'all-too-conscious' of the process and, in the case of *Now*, of the process of viewing a scene that is ambivalently erotic. Thus Benglis's solipsistic imagery may be said tacitly to articulate the problems attending the production, dissemination, *and* consumption of female sexuality. Rather than reifying female narcissism, as several authors have suggested, Benglis's video incisively probes the social and cultural relations contributing to its discursive formation.[25]

Though not crafted as a direct response, Benglis's *Now* is a provocative counterpart to sexualised video works produced by male artists at this time, notably, Vito Acconci's *Undertone* (1972, fig. 29). In this work, Acconci sits at the far end of a table under which, he informs the viewer, a girl is stimulating his penis. Interspersing his descriptions of her hidden actions, the artist occasionally addresses the camera directly. With comments such as 'I need to know you are there listening to me, tense and on edge', Acconci forces the spectator's complicity in, and perhaps even embarrassment over, the sexual activity ostensibly occurring on the tape. On one level, Benglis's *Now* echoes the sexual hierarchy of *Undertone*, insofar as the artist partially submits to the directives of the man offscreen while concomitantly presenting herself for the viewer's voyeuristic gaze. At the same time, however, the autoerotic content asserts a form of self-sufficient female sexual pleasure that mockingly deflates Acconci's overwrought psychosexual fantasies. Unlike Acconci, Benglis appears patently unconcerned with whether anyone else is watching – or as Krauss and Marshall contend, she remains narcissistically self-encapsulated. A similar lack of concern for the spectator seemingly pervades Benglis's *Female Sensibility*; however, it would be incorrect to accept this attitude at face value. The viewer's relationship to the work is an integral component of the video's erotic content and mode of address.

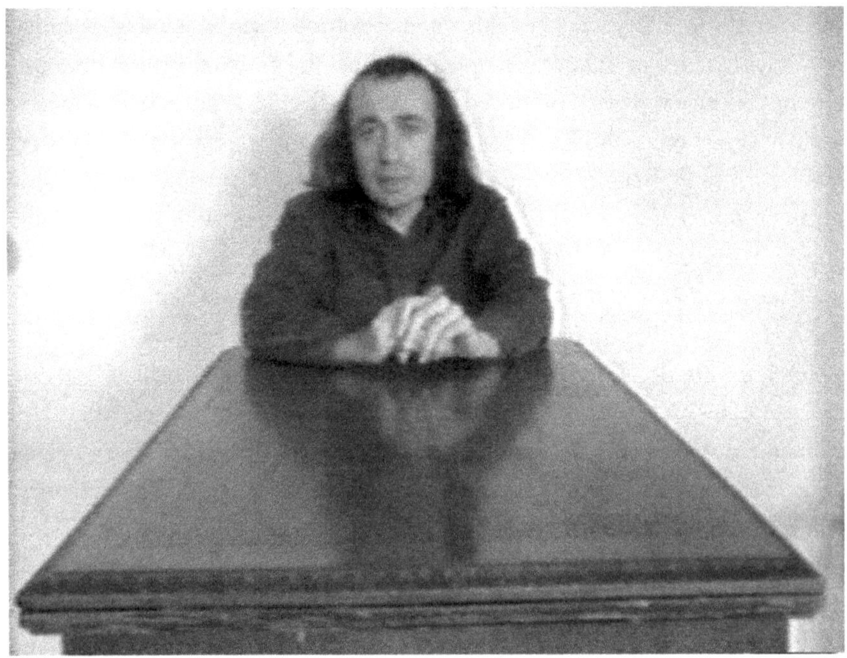

29. Vito Acconci, *Undertone*, 1972, black-and-white video, 37:20 min. © Vito Acconci. Courtesy of Video Data Bank, www.vdb.org.

picturing female pleasure

Female Sensibility (1973) builds on the structure and theme of *Now*. Instead of narcissistic imagery, however, this work entails a lesbian erotic scene, and instead of the layering effect, only one generation of tape is employed. The video opens with a close-up image of Benglis and her friend and colleague Marilyn Lenkowsky (fig. 30). Only their faces, necks, and hands are visible as the two women proceed to touch and kiss each other. Both wear lipstick – one frosty blue, the other dark red – and the intense colours focus attention on the engagement of mouths on flesh.[26] As the two women interact, an audio backdrop plays snippets of radio programmes taped from a California station. The sound forms a loud counterpoint to the intimate action on screen, but the women do not acknowledge it. Instead, and as the camera remains steadily focused on their faces and hands, the two continue to touch one another intimately for the duration of the fourteen-minute video.

The on-screen action in *Female Sensibility* appears to unfold in real time, with virtually indistinguishable stops and starts in the recording process. With the elimination of multiple spatial registers, it purports to addresses the viewer on a more direct and immediate level than Benglis's other videos.

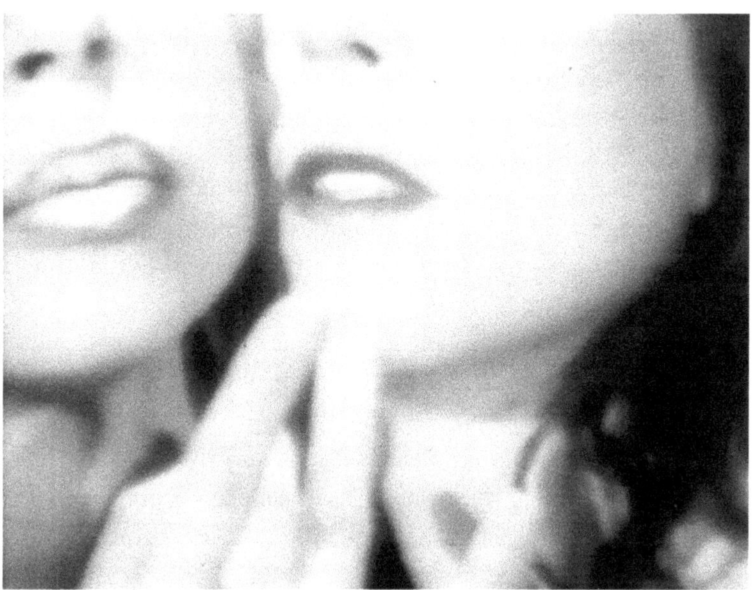

30. Lynda Benglis, *Female Sensibility*, 1973, colour video, 13:05 min. © Lynda Benglis. Courtesy of Video Data Bank, www.vdb.org.

However, if obvious manipulations drop out of the technical side of the work, they continue to manifest in the exaggerated and highly stylised nature of the on-screen sexual exchange. The depth-surface tension that Benglis exploited in earlier video projects through formal means is thus enfolded into the relationship the two women perform for the camera in *Female Sensibility*.

Although it is essentially non-narrative, Benglis and Lenkowsky's interaction can be loosely divided into three segments. In the first few minutes of the video, the women use their fingers to do little beyond touching each other's chin, all the while avoiding eye contact with one another. Significant pauses punctuate their gestures as the women variously shift their positions or move in and out of the camera's frame. Along with the exchange of nervous smiles and brief exchanges of inaudible dialogue, Benglis and Lenkowsky appear self-conscious and not entirely absorbed in their physical interaction. At several junctures, Benglis glances towards an offscreen monitor, an action that suggests that the artist is gauging the appearance of the women's performance on the tape.

In the second sequence, the women's touching evolves into kissing and intimate caressing. However, the exchange remains one-sided: as Benglis sucks and licks Lenkowsky's mouth, the latter stands immobile; in turn, Benglis fails to respond as Lenkowsky slowly licks the edge of her ear. The lack of reciprocity heightens the deliberation and control of the performance, even as the women's physical engagement becomes more erotically charged. In one particularly provocative moment, Benglis moves down and offscreen so that only her fingers are visible as they repeatedly caress Lenkowsky's lips. Lenkowsky arches her neck in response, and though Benglis remains out of view, one might imagine her kneeling down in front of her partner, perhaps touching her in other ways too. In the video's final sequence, the camera frames their faces as the two women exchange deep and penetrating kisses (fig. 31). However, Benglis and Lenkowsky continue in this fashion for only a minute or two, at which point the camera abruptly stops taping and the screen goes blank.

The raucous sound of radio segments accompanies the women's interaction throughout the video. The viewer hears snippets from 'Feminine Forum', a syndicated radio talk show hosted by Bill Ballance, banter by radio personality Dave 'Hullabalooer' Hull, an evangelical sermon, news reports about the price of gold, and refrains from country music songs. Most of the segments include specific references to women: the evangelical preacher

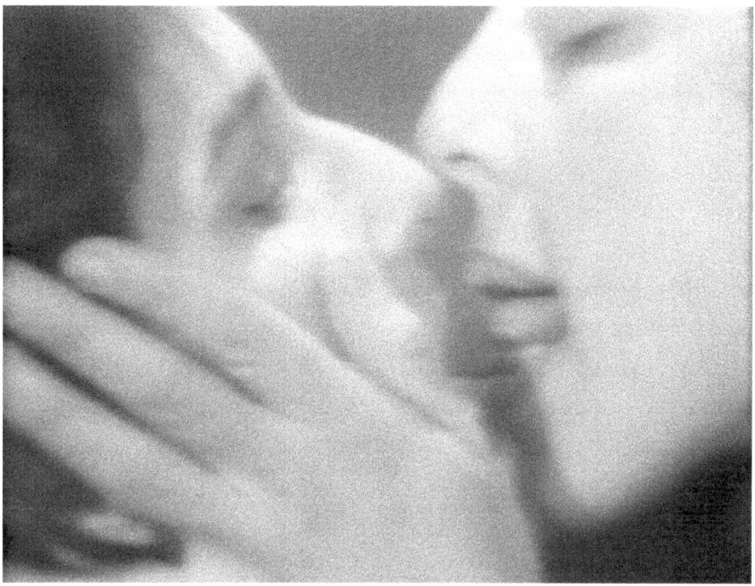

31. Lynda Benglis, *Female Sensibility*, 1973, colour video, 13:05 min. © Lynda Benglis. Courtesy of Video Data Bank, www.vdb.org.

evokes the sins of Eve, a musician croons 'When a Man Loves a Woman', a female caller shares unusual child-rearing tips with Ballance, and in one especially insidious clip, Hull incites a woman caller to tears after calling her 'muy chunko', to which he ruthlessly adds, 'Go ahead and cry if it'll take any weight off ya'.

For the film historian Chris Straayer, the radio sampling in *Female Sensibility* represents 'the prerogative of the male voice expressed through macho put-downs, moralistic exclusions and romantic and sexual clichés'.[27] She proposes that Benglis and Lenkowsky's lovemaking clearly operates outside this patriarchal framework and as such opens up a space of desire for viewers whose sexualities are generally denied by conventional modes of cinematic spectatorship.[28] Similarly, Amelia Jones proposes that Benglis's videos (both *Now* and *Female Sensibility*) serve as radical enactments of traditionally unacknowledged female desires in modernist art and art history: they invite a female viewer to become 'fully and pleasurably implicated in the process of determining meaning'.[29] However, while the women on screen appear impervious to the radio assault, the viewer of *Female Sensibility* cannot ignore it. The sound clips in fact induce their own set of visual images for the viewer, which at times interfere with and even obscure the action unfolding on screen. In other words, the video's components work in constant tension with one another as well as with the viewer, recalling Anne Wagner's suggestion that the paradigmatic effect of early video work is its refusal to be consumed straightforwardly. Instead, as the art historian notes, 'Abortive efforts at connection, whether with the self or another person, between men and women, between artist and viewer, are launched again and again', seemingly to little avail.[30]

The on-screen performance in *Female Sensibility* likewise contributes to this feeling of disengagement, as Benglis and Lenkowsky's pas de deux blends an odd mixture of passion and indifference. While its self-encapsulated and non-climatic structure may tacitly reinforce Straayer's conclusion that the video acknowledges alternative viewing pleasures, questions still arise: What am I looking at and listening to? And why? The title of Benglis's video provides one answer. In choosing *Female Sensibility*, the artist recognised how it would frame the work's reception in terms relevant to contemporaneous feminist debates over the existence of a distinctive 'female sensibility'.[31] More specifically, Benglis's video contributes to the debate in the form of an ironic parody. According to the literary theorist Linda Hutcheon, ironic parody draws on existing texts in order to create an 'extended repetition with critical distance'.[32] As a strategy of provocation, it generates a level of pleasure that spans a continuum characterised by the disdainful laugh at one end and the knowing smile at the other, depending on the degree of the viewer's engagement with a work's intertextual 'bouncing'.[33] As a multilayered form of expression, ironic parody complements Benglis's material and technical processes and as such indicates one way in which the artist continued to infuse *Female Sensibility* with complex signification even as she ostensibly simplified the video's formal construction.

The deliberate fashion in which Benglis and Lenkowsky touch each other calls to mind several of the elements upon which female sensibility theories were initially predicated. As the two women methodically kiss and caress one another on screen, their fingers and tongues appear to form, press, penetrate, and smooth out surfaces and crevices – in other words, they imply artistic activities. In a 'sculptural' fashion, the two women foreground the female body as both source and product of their creative gestures.[34] Although the viewer cannot see their entire bodies, he or she is afforded a clear picture of the two women delicately and deliberately using their tongues and fingers to penetrate each other's mouth and ears. These orifices become surrogates for the female body parts not visible on screen and provocatively allude to the 'female imagery' or vaginal symbology that some women advocated as the most direct manifestation of a female sensibility in the visual arts. What ultimately disrupts this reading, however, is the hesitant, even equivocal, manner in which Benglis and Lenkowsky interact. They proceed awkwardly as though the female imagery they are moulding is not inevitably rooted in their bodies or their female sensibilities. Consequently, ironically, the conflation of artist and sensibility, and of artist and artwork, is continually deferred in *Female Sensibility*.

In 1974, Benglis offered another response to the question of the existence of a female sensibility, one that has bearing on the video she produced in the preceding year. The artist was one of a handful of women invited by the editors of *Art-Rite*, a newsprint magazine published out of New York, to respond to the following questions: 'Is there a shared female sensibility in the work of female artists? And how would you describe or dismiss it?' The published results appeared under the title 'Unskirting the Issue'. The selection of respondents was wide ranging, yet the overall consensus leaned towards the rejection of a shared female sensibility; Judy Chicago provided the lone voice of assent, though even her response was tempered compared to statements she made elsewhere on the topic.[35]

On the surface, Benglis's response to the editorial questions appeared to affirm the existence of a shared sensibility, yet when she claimed, 'Yes, there is a shared female sensibility. Women want to please. Women are artists. Therefore, women make especially pleasing art. I, especially, like female art', her tone was intended ironically rather than earnestly.[36] By invoking the cliché that women want to please, she inferred that the female sensibility concept was equally premised on problematic clichés. Benglis's irony, in turn, matched the punning of the *Art-Rite* title, 'Unskirting the Issue', its implication of a candid reassessment of the issue (not 'skirting' around it, as the metaphor is conventionally employed) replete with the sexual innuendo of undressing a woman. Likewise, in preceding the responses with the pithy comment, 'The envelope please', the *Art-Rite* questionnaire framed the female sensibility concept as something of a sensational joke; invoking the drawn-out anticipation of a game show or beauty pageant, this phrase implied that the issue needed to be laid to rest rather than reexamined as a pressing art world concern. As such, Benglis's answer reads much like the banal response of a beauty pageant contestant.

Like Benglis's response to the *Art-Rite* questionnaire, *Female Sensibility* tackles some of the clichés, as well as the lacunae, the artist perceived to be informing the female sensibility debate. More specifically, its depiction of a lesbian scenario gives pause, as it is unusual for its time, and for having been produced by a mainstream professional artist such as Benglis. Outside underground subcultures, which did actively foster their own visual erotica, the production of explicitly lesbian-oriented art – for example, lesbian versions of the kind of imagery Joan Semmel was producing of straight couples – had minimal theoretical or visual presence within mainstream art communities in the United States until well into the 1980s. The pervasive heterosexism of the women's movement contributed to this absence; the lesbian artist Harmony Hammond, for example, recalls that during the early years of the feminist movement, women artists who were 'out' as lesbians tended to shy away from explicit sexual representations, preferring to utilise abstraction or highly coded imagery.[37]

Likewise, female sensibility proponents rarely articulated the possibility that a female viewer might derive sexual pleasure from viewing female body imagery. Choosing instead to frame the reception of such content in emotional, perceptual, or political terms, women artists believed they could avoid the kinds of female objectification associated with patriarchal culture. Even Judy Chicago, who linked her work to her own sexual awakening, never characterised its reception by other women in comparably erotic terms, and she was not alone in eliding this issue. In a 1974 article on the popularity of 'vaginal iconology' among women artists, the art historian and critic Barbara Rose opined that such art was 'designed to arouse women, but not sexually'.[38] Though not a specific apology for the existence of a distinctive female sensibility, Rose's account nonetheless proposes that cultural and political empowerment, not sexual pleasure, lay at the core of women's body imagery.

It seems insufficient, however, to claim that *Female Sensibility* radically advocates a sexual perspective generally occluded in women's art of the early 1970s or, conversely, that Benglis's lesbian scenario simply mocks 'what certain commentators have viewed as the *de rigeur* lesbian phase of an emerging feminist politicization', as Robert Pincus-Witten proposed in a 1975 catalogue essay.[39] Arguably, there is merit to both conclusions, yet I find that the lesbian eroticism in *Female Sexuality* also exceeds these surface readings. Specifically, I propose that Benglis's video draws on the contradictory status of gay identity in both feminist and popular visual discourses at the time. The scholar Katie King, in her analysis of lesbianism in the early US feminist movement, offers a useful way of thinking about this proposition. Calling lesbianism a 'magical sign', King contends that it constituted a privileged but shifting signifier through which feminist politics and identities were variously and at times tendentiously constructed during the early 1970s.[40]

The question of how to define the relationship between feminism and lesbianism dominated many early conversations about sexual identity in the women's movement. On one end, Betty Friedan's infamous condemnation of the 'lavender menace' captured the intolerance that some women's communities harboured towards lesbians. At the other end of the spectrum, advocates of 'Sapphic love' situated lesbian identity within both the feminist and gay liberation movements.[41] In this context, the liberation of lesbian sexual identity was a personal imperative that coincided with but was not entirely equal to the goals of the women's movement. Also widely promoted at the time, the term 'woman-identified woman' refigured lesbianism into a political identity available to all women seeking to cast off the shackles of patriarchal sex roles.[42] Unlike Sapphic lovers, women-identified women perceived lesbianism as foremost a political choice rather than a sexual preference. Couched in the rhetoric of female separatism, woman identification encouraged the adoption of a lesbian lifestyle as a form of feminist resistance.

Concepts such as 'lavender menace', 'Sapphic love', and 'woman-identified woman' proffered different versions of how to construe both the political and personal dimensions of lesbian identity within and around the women's movement. Benglis was alert to the significance of these issues in the art world; for example, she recalls that the topic of lesbianism was 'in the air' during the time, with well-known female artists openly pursuing same-sex relationships.[43] This statement tacitly captures the experimental atmosphere as well as the political timeliness of the issue of lesbianism. What remain unspoken, however, are Benglis's opinions about both the relationships and her own possible liaisons.[44]

In similarly ambiguous terms, the fits and starts of Benglis and Lenkowsky's erotic interaction in *Female Sensibility* prove difficult to pin down. Are the women offering up a representation of lesbianism as lavender menace, Sapphic lovers, or as women-identified women? More than just an issue of labels, such questions indicate the way in which Benglis's staging of a lesbian interaction draws on the status of lesbianism as an overdetermined yet mutable 'magical sign'. Located within competing and ever-evolving discursive structures in the early years of the women's movement, lesbianism bore multilayered and contradictory significations; tellingly, it also lost a point of origin. Without suggesting that Benglis was fully cognizant of these complexities, I do propose that on some level she recognised that the figure of the lesbian could perform certain operations in *Female Sensibility*. If the artist's earlier video projects subvert notions of an original or authentic self through obvious formal and technological manipulations, in *Female Sensibility* the lesbian scene performs that role.

If lesbianism was, to some degree, shorthand for feminist politicisation during the early 1970s, it was equally representative in the popular imagination of hard-core pornography. Indeed, to a large degree the circulation of lesbian imagery in pornography contributed to the instability of lesbian identity within feminist visual arts. With a long history of representation in underground stag films, 'girl-on-girl' acts exploded 'on scene' in the 1970s as a staple sex act in feature-length porn.[45] Stephen Ziplow's 1977 *The Film Maker's Guide to Pornography*, a popular how-to book for aspiring pornographers, cites the 'obligatory' lesbian scene as third in a set of recommended sexual acts, after female masturbation and straight sex. The guide goes on to assure would-be filmmakers that a lesbian number 'is a major turn-on to a large portion of your heterosexual audience' and thus integral to a successful porn production.[46]

When Benglis produced both *Now* and *Female Sensibility*, the pornographic industry was experiencing a brief cultural ascent due to the emergence of feature-length films. Most famously, the theatrical release of *Deep Throat* (dir. Gerard Damiano, 1972) initiated what the popular press touted as 'porno chic' among middle-class and urban intelligentsia.[47] Both men and women flocked to screenings in unprecedented numbers, and the film's legal problems merely fuelled its notoriety. Paradoxically, the inception of feature-length porn changed the dynamic of the heterosexual audience by thematising female sexual pleasure and spectatorship. Superficially, at least, the blatant orientation of hard-core porn to a male heterosexual audience yielded to story lines in which women actively sought and received sexual satisfaction.[48] The publicity for *Deep Throat* famously included posters featuring Linda Lovelace and the euphemistically phrased question: 'How far does a girl have to go to untangle her tingle?' Although the film's novel attention to female sexuality ultimately formed part of its appeal to masculine fantasies, *Deep Throat* established a precedent for a number of subsequent hard-core films, including *Behind the Green Door* (dir. Artie and Jim Mitchell, 1972) and *The Devil in Miss Jones* (dir. Gerard Damiano, 1973). Though not a prominent feature of *Deep Throat*, lesbian scenarios abound in these other films and helped secure the concept of 'girl-on-girl' action as a pornographic conceit. Consequently, any attempt to represent lesbian sexuality was problematic for many women artists and filmmakers.

As Linda Williams and other film scholars have observed, the actual method of depicting female sexual satisfaction initially challenged pornographers; close-up facial shots eventually became the most viable means of capturing evidence of female pleasure on film. A staple of mass media imagery, close-ups of women's faces serve to contain and fetishise female difference. Often the women in such images draw attention to their mouths through acts of eating, makeup application, or finger sucking, gestures that infantilise and also suggest phallic connotations. In porn, images of women's faces perform similar functions, with fellatio and cunnilingus offering more explicit representations of oral fixation or fetishisation. In fellatio scenes, moreover, a female performer's face may act as the receiving surface for male ejaculate, the ultimate sign of male sexual satisfaction in porn. However, the focus on a woman's facial expression also allows the viewer to account for female pleasure in other sex acts. Functioning as an equivalent of the 'money shot', the close-up of the woman's face purports to reveal her satisfaction in ways not captured by a shot of clitoral orgasm (fig. 32). While so-called beaver shots were crucial for detailing actions, only facial gestures could reveal female climax.

Several of Benglis's choices in her visual presentation of lesbianism in *Female Sensibility* recall popular pornographic conventions. Closely cropped by the camera, the two women's insistent oral fixation in the licking of earlobes and

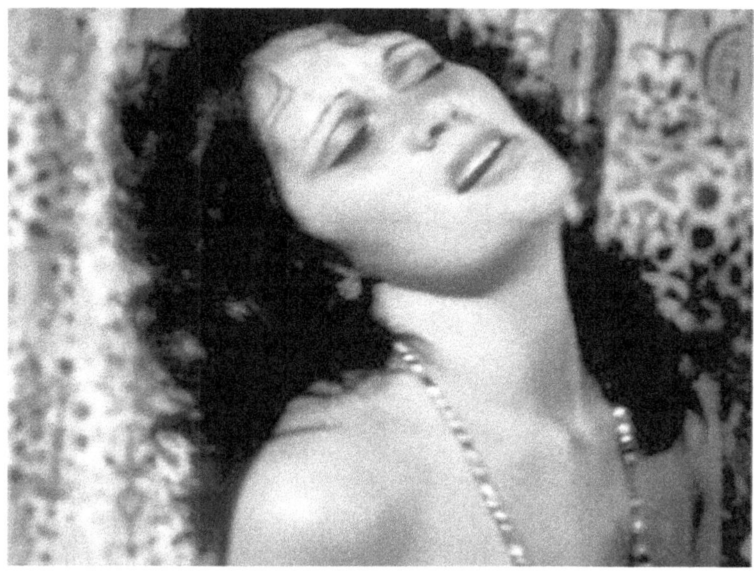

32. Linda Lovelace in *Deep Throat*, 1973, directed by Gerard Damiano.

the sucking of fingers playfully evokes associations to fellatio and cunnilingus, not to mention lesbian sex portrayed in heterosexual porn. Likewise, the persistent focus on their faces mimics the pornographic convention for displaying female pleasure albeit without the same degree of dramatic affect. Though lacking the explicitness of hard-core acts, the inference in *Female Sensibility* that such imagery is derived from pornographic codes potentially aligns it with the conventions of male heterosexual desire and its construction of female difference.[49]

Female Sensibility also alludes to the viewing conditions often attending porn (prior to the emergence of the home video market). From rudimentary stag loops to narrative feature-length films, porn demands a certain amount of work of any viewer to overcome certain limitations, whether it be the muffled sound or sound-image disjuncture of the film, the clumsy suturing of sex acts, the weak story line, the presence of other audience members, the constant feeding of a quarter machine in the sex arcade, or the furtive mechanics of masturbation itself. To a certain degree, *Female Sensibility* mirrors these difficulties through its own sound-image discrepancy and the somewhat monotonous progression of the women's lovemaking. Thus Benglis ironically challenges the viewer to partake of a complicated spectatorial process, one that may prove pleasurable, provocative, tedious, *and* anxiety-inducing – each response, arguably, is a component of the erotic, and each no more or less appropriate than the next. In the end, *Female Sensibility* unhinges the fixity of spectatorial desire and sexual identity by rendering their connection a product of a complicated, ambivalent, and open-ended process, one that occurs across multiple and overlapping visual discourses. In turn, the video alludes to but never resolves the question of personal content: the more Benglis appears to be 'on scene', the less certain the viewer becomes that autobiographical confession is at the heart of her video; instead, and as with the artist's more obviously manipulated video works, *Female Sensibility* continually defers its promise of accessibility, immediacy, and authenticity.

adventures of being human

After producing *Female Sensibility*, Benglis took a two-year hiatus from video, only returning to the medium in 1976 to produce two works in collaboration with Stanton Kaye.[50] In the interim, she continued her exploration into the sexual politics of self-representation through her notorious series of promotional 'sexual mockeries' of 1974 (see introduction). When Benglis teamed up with Kaye to make *How's Tricks* (1976) and *The Amazing Bow Wow* (1976–7), the *Artforum* controversy was not far from her mind. Consequently, both of these videos represent a response of sorts to that event, as each is a darkly humorous meditation on media spectacles, role-playing, and the crafting of public personae; the vulnerability of public exposure is also a dominant theme of each, as is the use of the media for duplicitous ends. Against the backdrop of the Watergate scandal and Richard Nixon's resignation in 1974, the particular plight of the artist in American society emerges as a significant subtext to both videos.

How's Tricks has a loose-jointed narrative consisting of informal but intimate conversations between Benglis and Kaye on the topic of art and illusion, a series of magic tricks and acts by Bobby Reynolds (a professional carnival performer), and bootlegged footage of President Nixon preparing for a State of the Union speech. Several of the scenes are acted out behind a scrim as dark silhouettes, including a closing shot of Benglis slowly rising out of a magician's trick box and striking the same pose she employed in the *Artforum* ad (fig. 33). The silhouetting, which recalls shadow plays and puppetry, carries associations to the carnivalesque; however, its shadowy effect

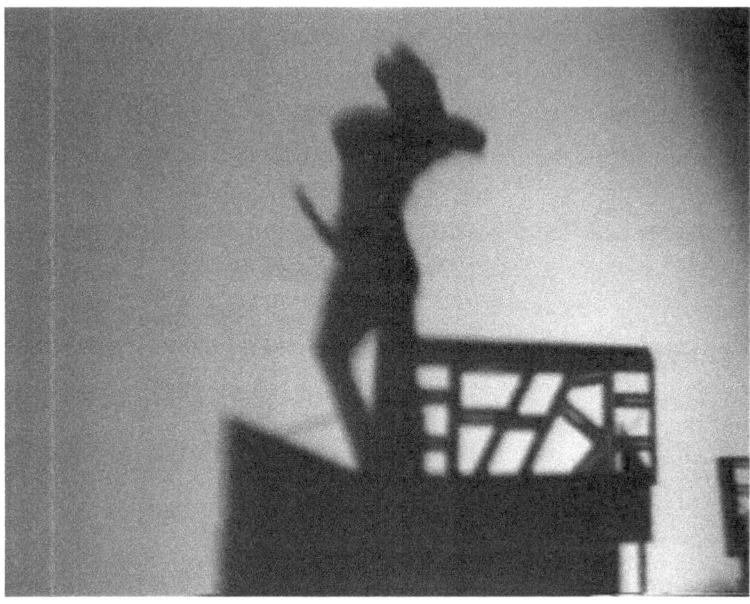

33. Lynda Benglis and Stanton Kaye, *How's Tricks*, 1976, colour video, 34:00 min. © Lynda Benglis. Courtesy of Video Data Bank, www.vdb.org.

has a more direct source in contemporary experimental film. The video's opening credits, which take the form of homemade signs propped up on a stuffed teddy bear, acknowledge the underground filmmaker Jack Smith – 'tribute to / Jack Smith / hi ya Smitty, how's tricks' (plate 12). Smith's playful but sexually explicit cult film about ambiguously gendered 'creatures', *Flaming Creatures* (1963), was notoriously confiscated by police during its New York premiere. Though *How's Tricks* contains no graphic sex scenes, its carnivalesque mix of the real and the fictive, the repetitive, and the overtly dramatic, is in homage to Smith's oeuvre, as is the intentionally crude quality of its filming and editing, the scenes blending into a seamless but nonsensical whole.

In their opening conversation, Benglis and Kaye reflect on their respective exposure as artists, the former admitting, 'I wish to go into disguise', to which the latter responds that his beard affords him 'protection'. At other moments, the two openly argue about the process of taping Reynolds's magic tricks, their annoyance with each other clearly visible. Further into the video, Benglis watches with exaggerated delight and awe while Reynolds performs a magic trick for the camera; later on, she serves as his assistant, allowing herself to be 'cut in half' inside the magician's box. Interspersed with the scenes of the magic tricks are clips from the bootlegged outtakes of Nixon preparing for his speech, the president coming across as uncomfortable and not quite 'in character' for the television cameras. As the curator Carrie Przybilla has noted, viewers of *How's Tricks* are compelled to draw inevitable connections between Reynolds's campy sleight-of-hand acts and the attempts of 'Tricky Dick' to spin the media after the Watergate scandal. Moreover, she continues, the 'glee and transparency with which the magic tricks are presented also points to the willingness by which a captive audience is misled'.[51] Similarly, *How's Tricks* inspires analogies between artistic processes and magic tricks, and by extension, between the audiences to which each is addressed. Darker in tone than Benglis's previous work, this video collaboration with Kaye weighs the desire to make art against the expectation that the results will both delight and confuse.

Benglis and Kaye revisited the themes of duplicity, gullibility, and miscomprehension in *The Amazing Bow Wow*, a work that runs just over thirty minutes. The majority of the tape was produced during a residency at Artpark in Lewiston, New York, in the summer of 1976, and it constitutes Benglis's only foray into fictional storytelling. The narrative features two carnival workers, Rexina (played by Benglis) and Babu (Kaye), who operate a seedy sideshow featuring a human-sized hermaphroditic dog named Bow Wow (Rena Small) given to them by a fellow sideshow barker (Bobby Reynolds).[52] The dog's unusual anatomy makes it a popular attraction, and Rexina and Babu dream of wealth (fig. 34). In the course of exploiting Bow Wow, Rexina discovers that the dog can also talk and sing, and that it is in fact quite intelligent and prone to philosophical ruminations: 'The human race will be better for my having been here. But when I compare myself to sculptures in books, I feel inadequate', sighs Bow Wow. Neither Rexina nor Babu is interested in the dog's intelligence, however, and they see opportunity only in displaying its hermaphroditic body for profit. Bow Wow, in turn, seems resigned to its plight as a sideshow freak.

Despite the fact that it is Bow Wow's hermaphroditic status that makes the dog a lucrative carnival attraction, neither Babu nor Rexina seems to acknowledge its sexual hybridity in their personal relationship with it: the dog is, from the start, female in Babu's eyes, while to Rexina, it is always a 'he'. As the story unfolds, the boundaries between maternal affection and incestuous attraction in the relationship between Rexina and Bow Wow begin to blur (fig. 35). Sensing this shift, and its perceived threat to his own paternal authority, Babu attempts in a fit of rage to castrate the dog but mistakenly

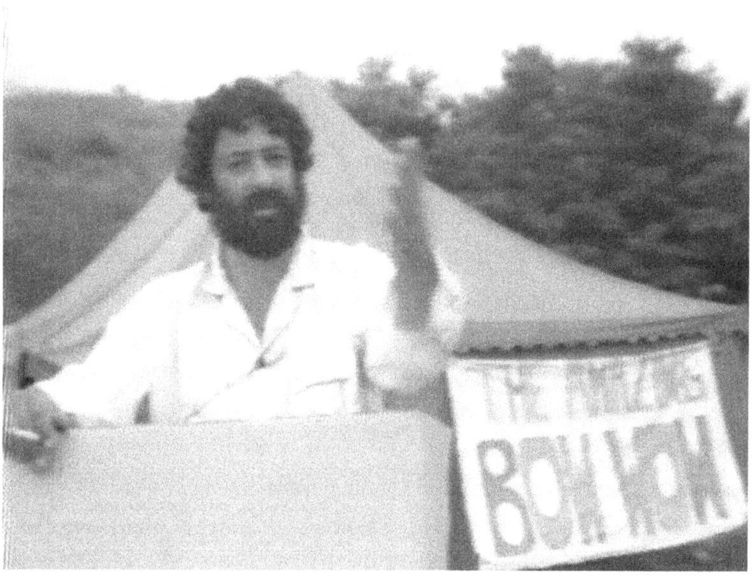

34. Lynda Benglis and Stanton Kaye, *The Amazing Bow Wow*, 1976–7, colour video, 30:07 min. © Lynda Benglis. Courtesy of Video Data Bank, www.vdb.org.

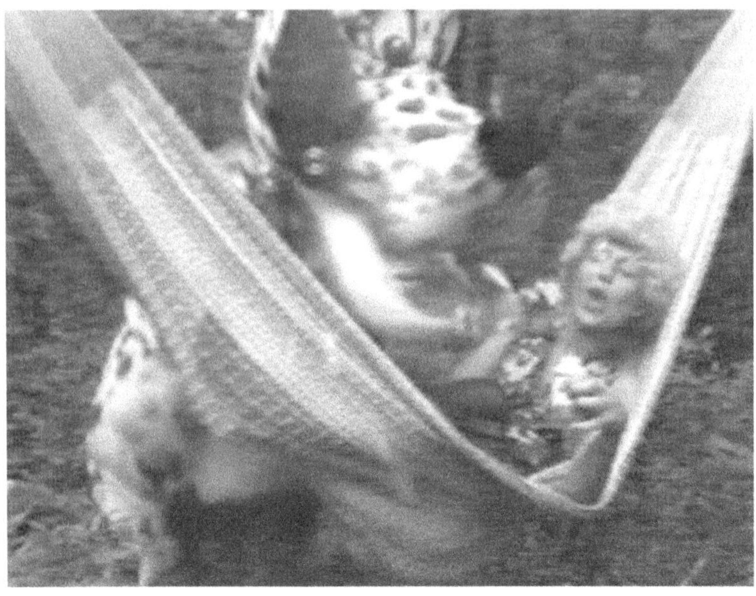

35. Lynda Benglis and Stanton Kaye, *The Amazing Bow Wow*, 1976–7, colour video, 30:07 min. © Lynda Benglis. Courtesy of Video Data Bank, www.vdb.org.

cuts out its tongue instead. No longer able to speak or sing, Bow Wow grows sick, its head shrivels up, and the carnival sideshow is ruined. In defence of his actions, Babu assures Rexina that 'it's for the good of humanity. She says she is a dog, but really she is a deformed human, a scientific joke. As a Good Samaritan, I meted out justice; I corrected a bad experiment'. Here, Babu's moralistic tone tacitly echoes the criticism meted out after the publication of Benglis's *Artforum* ad.

Playing freely on the Greek tragedy of Oedipus Rex and the psychic mechanisms of the oedipal complex, *The Amazing Bow Wow* moves from one set of tragic events to another as Rexina and Babu prove unable to accept responsibility for their respective actions towards Bow Wow. For Benglis, the narrative serves as a morality tale about human communication or, rather, the lack thereof. As she explains, 'humanism is the ability to see things of one particular context in relationship to other contextual situations. If the response was and is only a sexual one, then people have missed the point. The sexual iconography exists as a carrier to many other statements, to more complex statements'.[53] *The Amazing Bow Wow* thematises this repression of humanism and the policing of certain modes of self-expression in the early 1970s. As the fear and confusion over the dog's sexual identity escalate, all other conversations are silenced; while the literal muting of the dog's voice explicitly serves to analogise the situation, it is foreshadowed early on in the video when Benglis's character Rexina displays the dog to a carnival audience and asks, 'Does anyone have any important questions?' No one does.

In their joint statement for the Artpark catalogue, Benglis and Kaye indicate more specifically that Bow Wow's story is an allegory for the artist in society; when the artist's voice is silenced, it is to everyone's detriment.[54] Ideally (and there is an idealism that courses through Benglis and Kaye's video), the viewer retains what Rexina and Babu deny the dog, namely, a subjectivity that is odd and unclassifiable, but also insightful and relational.[55] That a certain refusal of fixed categories of knowledge and expression is posited here indicates the underlying political significance of *The Amazing Bow Wow* and, indeed, of Benglis's videos as a whole.[56]

The focus of the next chapter is a series of sculptural reliefs that Benglis produced in the early to mid-1970s. These sculptures are brash, colourful, and irreverent, and like Benglis's videos, they flirt with notions of artistic quality and rigor as well as viewing expectations and desires. More specifically, the artist's relief sculptures blur aesthetic boundaries in a manner that trenchantly exposes both the gendering and classing of 'taste' in contemporary visual discourse. While *How's Tricks* openly acknowledges its debt to the irreverent camp sensibility of Jack Smith and subcultural practices, Benglis's wall sculptures generate a subtler but no less provocative transgression of aesthetic and social propriety in a manner that may be also be deemed campy.

4 Questioning Taste

They are 'too garish to be pretty and too beautiful to be vulgar, although at first glance they are pretty vulgar', *Village Voice* critic John Perreault concluded in a 1974 review of Benglis's newest body of work, a series of relief sculptures based on a single motif: the knot.[1] These wall sculptures – known informally as the 'knots' – occupied the artist from 1972 to 1976, during which time she produced several distinct series. Marking a significant departure from Benglis's prior investigations into the fluid properties of a single medium, the knots are formed from long tubular pieces of aluminium screening covered with cotton bunting and plaster, which the artist then twisted and tied before adorning them with a variety of decorative materials (plate 14). As compelling studies in structural form and surface ornamentation, the knots are notable for demonstrating the artist's ongoing engagement with issues of artistic taste and value. Benglis well understands that 'taste is context', and with the knots she put this knowledge to the test, producing sculptures that openly flirt with different aesthetic sensibilities.[2] Ranging from the charmingly delicate to the grotesquely awkward, from the breathtakingly elegant to the unapologetically tawdry, these works ultimately position taste as something to be embraced and simultaneously challenged. Consequently, and as Perreault wittily noted, the majority of Benglis knots prove to be nothing short of 'pretty vulgar'.

Perreault's choice of words is telling: his pithy juxtaposition implies that the formal makeup of Benglis's knots is both contradictory ('pretty' but also 'vulgar') and excessive ('very vulgar'). Just as significantly, the critic's phrase carries tacit value judgements, his words indicating how gender and class connotations subtend aesthetic distinctions. In particular, and in utilising Perreault's description to frame an analysis of the knots, the following chapter is especially concerned with identifing the ways in which Benglis's work both explicitly and indirectly engages with cultural and artistic practices persistently coded as feminine and middle class. Though largely denigrated in modern discourse as conservative and non-self-reflexive categories, the feminine and the middle class (often conflated as 'feminine middlebrow') nonetheless consolidate a position that productively, and pleasurably, contradicts and thereby exceeds established cultural hierarchies of taste and artistic value.

In the 1970s, women artists in the United States and Europe actively challenged distinctions between 'high' and 'low' culture from a gendered point of view. A prominent strategy entailed utilising and revalorising so-called low craft and feminine decorative practices. This context is significant to Benglis's knots and their critical reception, yet at the same time, I argue that the artist's work requires more careful consideration of a middle ground of female production and consumption. While several scholars have usefully analysed the biases serving historically to relegate women's art to the realm of the low, few have considered the significance of the 'middle' as a gendered and classed category affecting contemporary women's cultural and artistic production. The introduction of the middle not only complicates the high-low binary but also potentially accounts for other interrelated aesthetic and cultural operations in women's art. It is here, in other words, that we might locate the radical nature of the 'pretty vulgar' effect of Benglis's knots.

striking poses

Benglis's earliest knots grew out of a small series of elongated 'totem' relief sculptures. Somewhat gawky looking, their forms clearly shaped by the artist's hand, these works represent the confluence of a number of stimuli, including Benglis's interest in African art, which she began to collect in the early 1970s, her knowledge of Barnett Newman's sculptural series *Here* (1950–62), which she had opportunity to see in the artist's home, and her admiration for the shaped and painted canvases of her friend Ron Gorchov.[3] These sources inspired Benglis to focus on the formal relationship between planes and edges, colour and structure, form and space. As their name implies, the totems also possess strong figurative allusions. Benglis emphasised these allusions by titling a pair *Hoofers I* and *II* (1971–2), after an American vernacular term for

36. Lynda Benglis, *Hoofer II*, 1971–2, glitter, acrylic, pigments, and gesso on plaster, cotton bunting, and aluminium screen, 102 x 4 ½ x 3 in. (259.1 x 11.4 x 7.6 cm). Courtesy of the artist and Cheim & Read Gallery, New York. © Lynda Benglis/ Licensed by VAGA, New York, NY.

percussive step dancers (fig. 36).[4] To exploit the dance analogy, Benglis also originally installed the totems low to the floor, such that they appeared to float like moving figures, their colourful and glittery surfaces reminiscent of the sparkling costuming integral to the hoofing spectacle.[5] The scholar Ann Daly, in writing about twentieth-century dance, has observed that through the early twentieth century, step routines typically operated in a 'pictorial mode', the (mainly female) dancers striking a series of poses intended to draw attention to their shapely legs and extravagant costuming; in the pictorial mode, distinctions between person and object became blurred.[6] Benglis's totems likewise appear to be striking poses against the wall, asking us to see them as both exotic figures and as richly embellished forms.[7] This figure-object oscillation subsequently becomes a central conceit of the knots.

It was not long before Benglis began to twist and tie the totems into knotted configurations, a decision that immediately shifted the works' figurative associations: no longer evocative of upright or dancing figures, the knots inspire comparisons to gesturing bodies, outflung limbs, twisted viscera, and elephantine heads. The knotted sculptures also possess a pneumatic quality: some appear to inflate, others to compress in a way that stresses the complex relation between interior and exterior, surface and form. In retrospection, Benglis has claimed that the work represents 'different states of being', a term that recalls the artist's prior exploration of proprioception as well as her ongoing interest in social gestures and conventions of behaviour.[8] In the knots, the tension between surface and form becomes a provocative metaphor for this notion of mediated embodiment and of the interplay between the physical and social body.

Over the next four years Benglis produced several series of knotted relief sculptures, experimenting with different formal configurations and surface treatments.[9] The earliest of these works, the 'sparkle knots' of 1972–3, sport colourfully painted and glitter-encrusted surfaces similar to those of *Hoofers I* and *II*. A notable example, *Zita* (1972) is a double-stranded, tightly looped knot with long unpainted ends stretching below a form liberally touched with paint and glitter (plate 13). Patches of magenta and green combine with glittery swatches of silver, pink, and gold placed atop dark grey and black passages. The colours follow the underlying form, emphasising the manner in which the knot twists and turns back in on itself. The effect proves markedly different from the softer tonalities and spatial play of Benglis's two-brushstroke paintings, which I examined in chapter 2, yet the metallic sparkles likewise tend to confuse a reading of spatial depth. As one early reviewer noted, the bold and glittery colours adorning the knots 'tend to lift off, visually, from the supporting structure even while their application carefully follows the convolutions and emphasizes the shapes'.[10] On the gallery wall, the sparkle knots become graceful balletic figures, their handicraft forms and the dime-store materials of which they are composed temporally obscured beneath the glimmer and sheen of light on sparkly surfaces.

In addition to the type of decorative treatment employed in *Zita*, Benglis developed a second approach with these early sparkle knots, one that she has playfully dubbed a form of 'Pollockizing'.[11] Even without the aid of this description, the allusion is evident in the brightly coloured *Omega* (1972, plate 14). With the exception of its short unpainted ends, the bulging surface of the knot is densely patterned with broad patches of bold and glittery hues overlaid with an intricate tracery of light blue, cherry red, and sunshine yellow paint. The colours and lines compete with each other as well as with the underlying knotted form, creating a dizzying sense of visual movement for which the untouched ends of the knot provide the only respite. The patterns are highly reminiscent of the colourful webbed surfaces of Pollock's signature 'drip' paintings, while the encrusted metal sparkles recall the older painter's penchant for aluminium paints. As long looping forms, the knot equally serves as a three-dimensional equivalent to Pollock's painted skeins, its material configuration indicating how Benglis continued to engage the abstract expressionist's legacy even as she ceased creating her poured latex works.

During a summer residency in Los Angeles in 1973, Benglis developed a different decorative treatment for her knots. Through the artist Robert Irwin, she met the fabricator and designer Jack Brogan, and the two began to experiment with his metalising gun, spraying liquid metals directly onto the plaster surfaces of the knots. In contrast to the vibrant and rhythmic patterns of colour and glitter adorning the sparkle knots, the monochromatic surface of each 'metalised knot' immobilises the twisted form and emphasises its tensile properties. Benglis experimented with different colourations and sheens, noting that she was drawn to the 'energy' that metals possess, and to the almost primal attraction that they inspire.[12] The cool lustre of *Victor* (1974), for instance, is the result of mixing zinc and tin, the subdued tonality well suited to the work's open and jaunty configuration (fig. 37).

Around 1974 Benglis also began to apply sculp-metal to the knots' surfaces. A hobbyist material popular since the 1950s, and subsequently used by artists in the 1960s and 1970s, sculp-metal can be painted onto a variety of materials and buffed to a smooth metallic sheen. Benglis occasionally combined the sculp-metal with other materials, including sparkles and fake gems. In the double-stranded knot *Omnicron* (1974), the individual gems placed along the contorted form are difficult to discern, their soft shapes and bright points of colour virtually overwhelmed by the dark metallic gleam of the sculp-metal; more obvious is the passage of purple sparkle stretching down along the knot's longest arm (plate 15). Despite its dime-store aesthetic, *Omnicron* is one of the more complex knots that Benglis produced, for the very fact that it is slow to yield the exact nature of its decorative elements to the viewer.

In 1974 Benglis developed yet another decorative approach: she added heavy-gauge aluminium foil to her material repertoire, using it to sheath the knotted forms in a stiff but malleable exterior, which she painted with bright enamel glazes. The crinkled exterior of *Peter* (1974), a long and gangly knot,

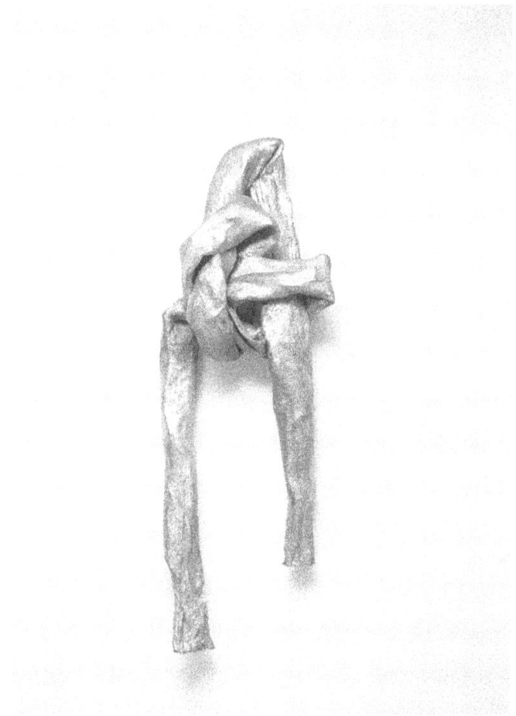

37. Lynda Benglis, *Victor*, 1974, sprayed zinc, tin, and steel on plaster, cotton bunting and aluminium screen, 66 7/8 x 20 1/2 x 13 1/8 in. (169.8 x 52 x 33.3 cm). Collection of the Museum of Modern Art, New York; purchased with the aid of funds from the National Endowment for the Arts and an anonymous donour. © Lynda Benglis/Licensed by VAGA, New York, NY. Photo Credit: Digital Image © The Museum of Modern Art/Licensed by SCALA/Art Resource, NY.

is liberally touched with patches of red, green, blue, and yellow (plate 16). In some areas the foil peels back to reveal the painted underside and the underlying wire mesh armature; elsewhere its hard exterior surface forms a pattern of angular and rounded planes that rustle and agitate across the knotted body. Of the three main decorative treatments Benglis employed with the knots, the use of the foil drew her work closest to the arena of mass cultural commodities.

Benglis's choice of titles deserves a brief mention: for the sparkle knots, the artist used Greek letters, and for the earlier metalised knots, the military phonetic alphabet. She employed names of friends and acquaintances for the foil knots, and compass points and numbers for several of the later series of metalised sculptures.[13] In the beginning, the artist modelled some of the knotted compositions after specific letters; however, as a whole the knots bear only oblique morphological similarities to their namesakes. Occasionally the relationship is premised on the sound that a particular letter evokes rather than its visual form.[14] Ultimately, Benglis's knots cannot be read or deciphered literally, and yet their titles, I believe, remain significant as reminders that the lived body is a function of different expressive conventions, learned modes of communication, and social codes. In this sense, the breathing, gesturing, or signalling quality of the knots is always mediated by their surface embellishments, as well as by the expectations and assumptions brought to the work by the viewer.

When Benglis first began to exhibit the knots in 1973–4, she employed different display strategies in order to inflect the viewing experience. For a solo show of foil and metalised knots at Paula Cooper Gallery in May 1974, she orchestrated two approaches, staggering the foil knots along the walls in a seemingly haphazard arrangement, and installing the metalised knots in even intervals at eye level (fig. 38). The juxtaposition clearly underscored the formal distinctions between the two series, and critics responded accordingly. John Perreault quipped with apparent relish: 'You can't be formal and neutral and colourless about the knots, for they themselves are not formal or neutral and at least half of them are very colourful indeed, operating just beyond the edge of good taste'.[15] For the critic, Benglis's work demanded that the viewer take a position, however ambivalently, relative to the work's aesthetic mash-up. In a similar vein, *New York Times* critic Peter Schjeldahl opined that Benglis's work ranged from 'relatively simple to Gordian, from flimsy-looking to imposing and from lyrically gestural and perhaps a little vulgar to dense and impassive'.[16] Ann-Sargent Wooster, writing for *Art in America*, declared the show 'schizophrenic'. She observed that while the metalised knots were clearly 'artistic', the foil knots were more 'gaudy', their colourful foil forms reminiscent of 'kandy-kolored tangerine-flake' and fast-food wrappers.[17] Significantly, all these reviewers were sympathetic to the work, and their assessments largely favourable. Yet Benglis's knots clearly resisted easy formal and conceptual positioning. If their status as art was never really in doubt, they nonetheless appeared to the critics to transgress at least one aesthetic boundary, if not more. But where were such boundaries understood to lie? How was Benglis breaching them? And why might the artist and some of her critics find pleasure in their transgressions?

The perception of vulgarity in Benglis's sculptural knots, even if grounds for pleasure, which I believe it is, indicates how taste standards continued to

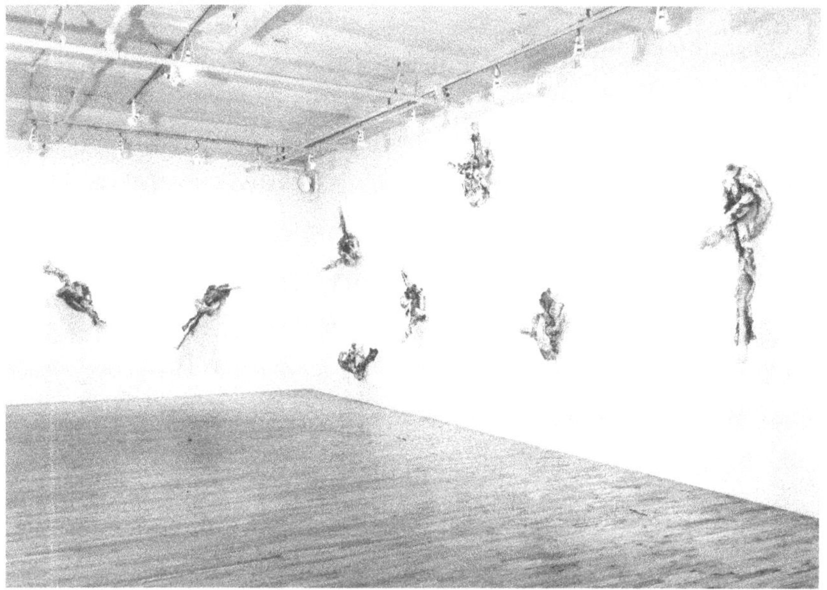

38. Installation view of *Lynda Benglis Presents Metallized Knots* at Paula Cooper Gallery, New York, May 1974. © Lynda Benglis/Licensed by VAGA, New York, NY.

hold sway in the pluralist landscape of 1970s art and culture. Without a doubt, the emergence of disparate artistic practices during the late 1960s and early 1970s exerted tremendous pressure on modernist standards of quality, taste, and artistic legitimacy. The expansion of popular culture and mass media outlets, the increased visibility of women and minority artists, the influx of non-Western traditions, and shifting patterns of consumerism all helped render taste a disputed concept. Indeed, it is more accurate to identify not one 'edge' along which aesthetic standards were simultaneously defined and transgressed, but rather several of them. Invoking a wide range of effects, Benglis's knots resisted but were not indifferent to these edges, or to the underlying assumptions central to their ongoing production and maintenance.

taste is context

For many reviewers, Benglis's different series of knots reflected entrenched and stereotypical geographical distinctions. For instance, Ann-Sargent Wooster intimated that the artist's 'gaudy' sensibility bore a specific relationship to the art and culture of Southern California, notably as popularly detailed in Tom Wolfe's 1963 essay on the custom car movement of that region, 'The Kandy-Kolored Tangerine-Flake Streamline Baby'.[18] Robert Pincus-Witten was even more explicit with this connection in his 1974 feature article for *Artforum*, 'Lynda Benglis: The Frozen Gesture', when noting that the artist's use of colours and materials evidenced 'the unapologetic, unrepentant range of California taste. [Benglis] chooses glinting metallic flecks and plastic substances like the automotive sheen of the art in Southern California, where she spends a good part of the year'.[19]

Like Wooster and Pincus-Witten, many New York-based critics perceived the Los Angeles art scene, notably as embodied in the pop-inflected 'finish-fetish' movement and the cool 'LA Look', as heavily dominated by artificial colours, slick surfaces, commercial materials, and illusionistic effects.[20] Reading the clean lines and surface perfections as signs of an absence of manual labour and a slackening conceptualism, they related the art to certain stereotypes about the West Coast lifestyle, including its rampant consumerism, casual work ethic, and uninhibited exhibitionism. As the art historian Francis Colpitt has more recently pointed out, the art coming out of Los Angeles in the 1960s was frequently perceived in sexual terms, with critics ascribing 'a hedonistic, unabashedly sexy emptiness' and 'pervasive immorality' to the finish-fetish artists and their studio practices.[21] In particular, the LA scene seemed permeated by a masculine eroticism peculiar to the Southern California lifestyle; as one critic opined, the surface sheen and visual illusionism of the art was not unlike the 'acres of tanning flesh and colonies of body builders' crowding the local beaches.[22]

Such characterisations of the Los Angeles art scene were exaggerated but not entirely misplaced. The male artists associated with Ferus Gallery, for instance, openly associated their art with their passion for surfing and custom cars, and they perpetuated an image of cool machismo by showing their work under the nickname 'The Studs' on at least one occasion.[23] Benglis was fascinated by the LA art scene and California car culture, just as she was cognizant of the overt machismo of both: her first sexual mockery, the so-called macharina portrait, constituted a pointed and playful response to this environment (fig. 2). In turn, many of the artist's knots convey a muscularity that verges on collapse or detumescence, such that their posturing appears no more real than a 'spray on tan'.[24] Not all negative, however, Benglis also appreciated the artistic sensibility she encountered on the West Coast and in particular has cited Billy Al Bengston's *Dentos* (1965–9), a series of lacquer and polyester resin paintings on dented and spindled squares of aluminium, as an important impetus for her turn to metal.[25] However, while the gleaming surfaces of both her metalised and foil knots are redolent of the finish-fetish aesthetic, Benglis's work retains a strong element of handicraft that ultimately distinguishes it from the industrial-like precision favoured by the Ferus Gallery artists.

If the perceptions of the Los Angeles art scene of the 1960s and 1970s provide one explanation for how Benglis's knots pushed 'the edge of good taste', the artist's Southern upbringing constituted another reference point, one frequently cited by both the artist and her reviewers. In particular, the abundance of sparkle and spangle in Benglis's knots seemed pointedly to recall the decorations and costumes integral to the Mardi Gras festivities of Louisiana, which functioned in turn as a metonym for the supposedly southern inflection of Benglis art more broadly. For instance, Pincus-Witten alluded to the Mardi Gras connection when opining that Benglis's practice as a whole evidences a kind of 'infantile and magical colouration that violates "adult" notions of taste and artistic decorum'.[26] This notion of violating 'adult' tastes conjures up the carnivalesque environment, with its temporary inversion of social hierarchies, aesthetics, and decorum, as well as a commingling of the ostentatious and the grotesque. Or as curator Jane Livingston has stated more bluntly, 'the slyly licentious, the festive and sometimes incipiently satanic esthetic elements which characterise her work derive directly from Benglis's early Louisiana background'.[27] Again, the account here is not necessarily dismissive but rather marks an attempt to come to terms with the artist's sensibility through its association with the cultural stereotypes of a geographical region.

Importantly, Benglis has not shied away from her Southern past, or from the aesthetic traditions for which it is renowned. In 1977, most notably, she produced a small series of relief sculptures she entitled *Lagniappes* after the Creole word for trinkets given away as small gifts. In many respects, these works derive from the knots that preceded them (plate 17). Consisting of short tubular forms coated in stripes of glitter, with iridescent polypropylene flounces attached to one end, or both, the *Lagniappes* are immodestly flamboyant. Conjuring the tawdry world of carnivalesque display and spectacle, they are phallic in form but decidedly 'feminine' in their material makeup, an ambiguity that likewise recalls the gender inversions of Mardi Gras culture. Beyond the carnival context, however, the heavy ornamentation employed in this work aligns with feminine creative labour and feminine self-fashioning more generally. Since Benglis actually produced these works while living in California, their glitter-encrusted and polypropylene-adorned forms equally recall the sparkling costuming and set decor of classic Hollywood cinema. *Lagniappe: Bayou Babe* (1977) conjures, if not strictly a female body, then a set of conventions and constraints typically inscribed on that body in popular culture. Thus for Susan Krane, Benglis's *Lagniappes* attest to the conflation of decoration with feminine subjectivity, which is to say, with the cultural delegation of women 'to positions of decoration – as pleasant, dolled-up accoutrements' not unlike nicely wrapped gifts.[28] This insight, which sees women both producing and embodying the decorative, is equally prevalent in Benglis's series of knots. The decorative aspects of this work, in turn, constitute another point of origin for the artist's breach of good taste.

feminine work

In a 1973 review of Benglis's sparkle knots, critic Thomas Albright vividly captured the gendered inflections of the artist's use of the decorative with the following description: 'Sometimes, the painting elements run wholly amuck, producing tightly-knotted encrustations of globs and goops that look like a Jackson Pollock canvas that got thrown in a washing machine with a sequin-covered gown'.[29] Albright's description has the knots traversing the realms of high art (Pollock), domesticity (washing machine) and self-adornment (the sequin gown); by extension, the critic's words rhetorically conflate the figures of the artist, the homemaker, and the female fashion plate. While the work itself solicited such connections, Benglis also utilised promotional imagery and installation techniques to underscore them further.

For the announcement for a 1973 exhibition of sparkle knots at Hansen Fuller Gallery in San Francisco, Benglis used a photograph that shows the artist interacting with her work. Standing against a white wall, she holds an undecorated sparkle knot in front of her face; two finished knots hang behind her (fig. 39). The juxtaposition emphasises the transformative effects of the decorative process: the bare knot in Benglis's hands literally pales in comparison to its paint- and glitter-encrusted counterparts. The artist's act of masking her own features behind the unfinished knot likewise echoes the 'masking' of forms that occurs once the knots are decorated.

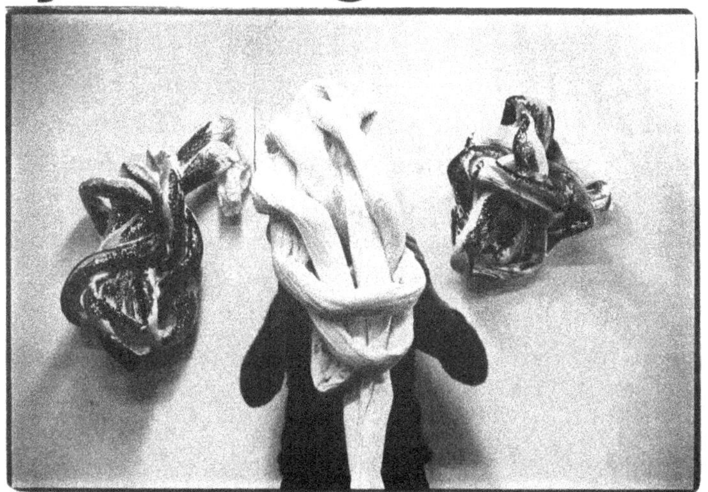

39. Lynda Benglis, invitation for *Lynda Benglis* at Hansen Fuller Gallery, San Francisco, California, May 1973. Courtesy of the artist and Cheim & Read Gallery, New York. © Lynda Benglis/Licensed by VAGA, New York, NY.

Redolent of Mardi Gras masks and masquerading, the Hansen Fuller announcement also speaks more broadly to feminine beautification rituals. More pointedly, Krane has observed that the visual contrast between the unadorned and adorned knots recalls the popular practice in women's magazines of presenting 'before-and-after' beauty shots.[30] A popular trick of the cosmetic industry, the juxtaposition is typically intended to dazzle readers with the transformation of the sitter's appearance while concomitantly imparting a series of learnable steps in correct cosmetic application. In looking at how the modern cosmetic industry has utilised the makeover process to attract female customers, the anthropologist Judith Goldstein compares it to the formulaic procedure of 'painting-by-numbers', which she notes 'is itself enough to deny makeup the classification of high art, to condemn it to the middle'.[31] Goldstein's analogy captures the wider cultural perception that makeup usage, as a form of women's art, promotes a superficial and decorative transformation, one that vulgarly melds high art standards of beauty with an assembly-line model of production. Neither strictly high nor low, the practice occupies a so-called middle ground, one to which modern aesthetic discourse consigns any number of feminine decorative activities.[32]

In December 1973, Benglis had a solo exhibition of sparkle knots at the Clocktower Gallery in New York.[33] As she would do the following year at Paula Cooper Gallery, Benglis carefully orchestrated the hanging of the show, installing her work at intermittent and seemingly random heights along the walls. She also looped strands of flashing holiday lights around the relief sculptures and along the handrail of a spiral staircase leading up to the next floor (fig. 40). Intended as an expression of disdain for President Richard Nixon's call on Americans to restrict their energy usage during a holiday season falling in the midst of the mid-1970s oil crisis, the lights also served to unify the series of artwork within the space of the gallery, thereby encouraging viewers to see the individual sculptures functioning as part of a larger visual environment.[34] In some instances, the light strands echoed the twists and turns of the knotted forms as well as the directional extension of their long arms; they rose and fell in cadence with the contours of the knots or

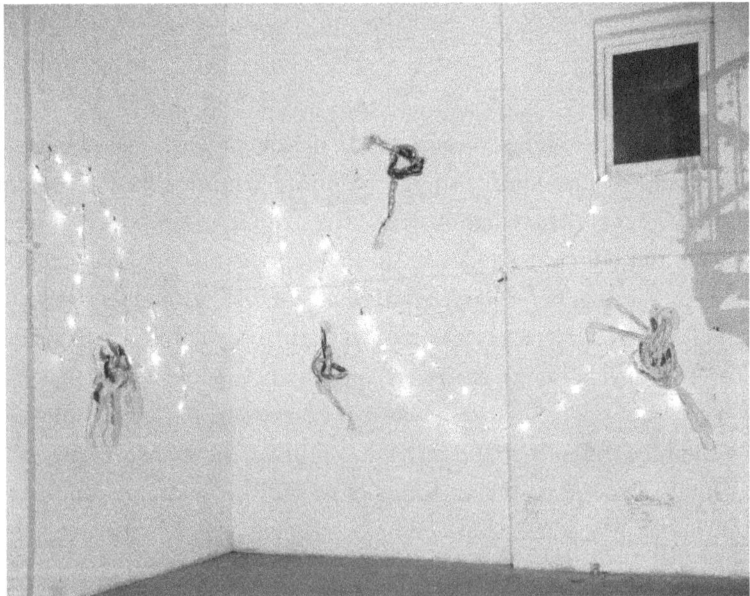

40. Installation view of *Lynda Benglis* at the Clocktower, New York, December 1973. Courtesy of the artist and Cheim & Read Gallery, New York. © Lynda Benglis/Licensed by VAGA, New York, NY.

mapped a sight line between two sculptures. In sensing this integral connection, the artist and critic Jeremy Gilbert-Rolfe praised the chromatic results. In finding that the holiday lights added to the expressive quality of Benglis's glittery knots and to the narrative continuity of the series as a whole, he concluded that the exhibition proved visually complex despite Benglis's choice of 'intrinsically banal' materials.[35]

Though Gilbert-Rolfe found complexity in banality, another way of seeing the inclusion of the lights in the Clocktower exhibition recognises the theatrical flair that they brought to Benglis's sparkle knots. Underscoring the work's latent exhibitionism, the lights added to the impression that each knot was striking a pose. It is perhaps no coincidence that Benglis subsequently used both her macharina and her pinup publicity images to advertise her exhibition of knots at Paula Cooper Gallery the following spring. Having closely studied the history of the pinup prior to making her own, Benglis no doubt learned that its original subjects were female dancers, whose onstage poses found a photographic equivalent in the pinup long before it became a staple for Hollywood starlets. With her series of promotional sexual mockeries, Benglis tacitly established photographic equivalents to the 'posing' sculptural knots in the gallery.

This reading of the Clocktower exhibition indicates how Benglis's recourse to decoration alluded to female adornment and masquerade, and to the cultural construction of the female body as a 'pleasant, dolled-up accoutrement', to recall Krane's phrase. Equally, however, the combination of the sparkling lights and the glittery knots at the Clocktower gestures towards the decorative's associations with other forms of women's work: specifically female handicraft and interior decorating. Where does one hang holiday lights, after all, but in the home?[36] And in 1970s US visual culture, knotted motifs were ubiquitous as a result of the hobbyist revival of macramé. Benglis has noted, however, that her use of the knot was inspired by her familiarity with Incan quipu ('knot' in the Quechua language) and Chinese knotting traditions, rather than macramé specifically, though she has also shared that her paternal grandmother taught her as a child how to crochet.[37] Such references generally reflect the resurgence of interest in global cultures and alternative artistic traditions during this period, of which fibre art was but one manifestation. If not a direct reference for the artist, I propose that women's decorative craft traditions, as epitomised through a practice like macramé, represented an important context for Benglis's knots and the perception of their aesthetic transgressions.[38]

For many US women artists, the craft revival constituted part of a larger agenda to legitimate female domestic creativity and to challenge presumptions that decoration and ornamentation lacked abiding aesthetic value. Miriam Schapiro's collages, or 'femmages', as the artist dubbed them, were paradigmatic in this regard. Openly indebted to both modern abstraction and traditional domestic handicraft, Schapiro's work presented paint and textiles as equally valid artistic mediums. Harmony Hammond likewise combined fabric and paint in her series of painted and braided rag-rug sculptures entitled *Floorpieces* (1973, fig. 41). Constituting a pointedly gendered response to Carl Andre's minimalist metal floor sculptures of the late 1960s, Hammond's work is infused with symbolic significance, the artist believing that it represented both an artistic and a sexual connection to other women.[39]

While Benglis's knots are not replete with such symbolism, they could be characterised as femmage insofar as they include fabric in their material makeup and possess forms that invoke sewing or knotting techniques.[40] Their serial installation, and the inclusion of the holiday lights at the Clocktower, also allows the associations to interior decor to gain foothold.[41] Like Schapiro and Hammond, then, Benglis understood how to parlay so-called feminine

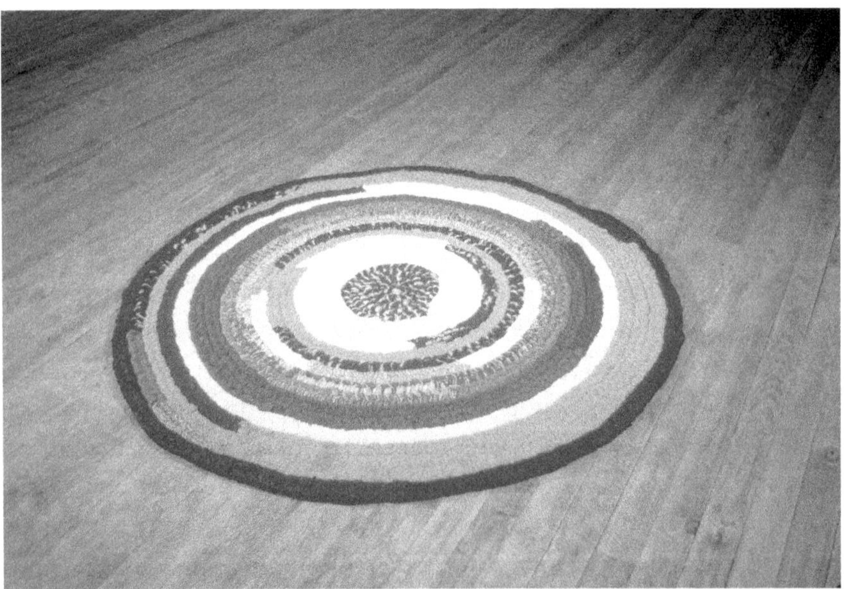

41. Harmony Hammond, *Floorpiece V*, 1973, cloth and acrylic, diameter approx 59 in. (150 cm). Courtesy of the artist. © Harmony Hammond/Licensed by VAGA, New York, NY.

materials and domestic decorative techniques into the artistic language of high abstraction. In each instance, the resulting works are brash, colourful, and exuberant blends of the high and the low.[42]

In following Judith Goldstein's lead, however, we might ask whether these works conjure a middle aesthetic ground. The middle, as Goldstein avers in her discussion of women's cosmetics, is sustained primarily by women and is at once a cultural and economic space, a set of tastes, and a series of activities 'lacking the virile authenticity of the low and the aristocratic cachet of the high'.[43] That the middle carries largely negative connotations proves significant for both women's professional and amateur artistic production in the early 1970s. The following section offers an overview of the development of the modern discourse on the middlebrow, before then considering the specific ways in which Benglis's knots relate to and rework it.

women in the middle

In modern aesthetic discourse, the 'middle' – often dubbed 'middlebrow' by critics – is said to constitute an impoverished cultural realm overwhelmingly associated with women's practices and so-called feminine tastes. The disdain for the middlebrow has its roots in early critiques of mass culture, which scholars such as Andreas Huyssen, Rita Felski, and Tania Modleski have thoroughly analysed for their gender biases. As Huyssen writes, 'The political, psychological, and aesthetic discourse around the turn of the century consistently and obsessively genders mass culture and the masses as feminine, while high culture, whether traditional or modern, clearly remains the privileged realm of male activities'.[44] Building on these insights, Modleski points out that women have also been held responsible for the lowering of cultural taste in the modern era, with critics regarding the female predilection for the decorative as something innate, inferior, and disruptive.[45]

In the postwar era, the threat of mass culture continued to hold the attention of cultural theorists; however, it was partially eclipsed by another menace: the burgeoning middle class and the spread of a so-called middlebrow taste sensibility. Through the 1950s and early 1960s, American critics such as Dwight Macdonald and Clement Greenberg excoriated the middlebrow for its parasitic relationship to high art. Even more troubling than mass culture kitsch, the middlebrow constituted a poisonous blend of 'the genuine and the spurious, the elevated and the vulgar', as Greenberg famously asserted in 1953.[46] For these critics, middlebrow art represented an inferior facsimile of an aesthetic experience, appealing to an audience that desired cultural edification but lacked the requisite cultural capital to be able to discern the difference; its travesty, in other words, lay in its misrecognition of its own lack of discerning taste.

Modern critics frequently associated the middlebrow with a middle-class feminine sensibility variously conceptualised as vapid, superficial, and excessive. As a number of contemporary scholars have usefully argued, the confluence of the feminine and the middlebrow is especially evident in literary criticism of women's novels and their readership.[47] For art critics, the association proved more tacit than not and was often conveyed through seemingly subtle language choices and textual digressions. Greenberg, for instance, lamented in 1947 that the middlebrow American was 'more knowing than cultivated … a compendium of what he or (more usually) she reads in certain knowing magazines – anxious to be right, correct, *au courant*, rather than wise and happy'. No better than a tourist with a guidebook, Greenberg continues, the middlebrow American voraciously consumes art magazines 'whose copy is supplied by permanent college girls, male and female'.[48] In both texts, Greenberg pictures middlebrow college-educated women as well meaning but naive in their cultural dilettantism, the results of which could only be an impoverished form of art. Such concerns echoed the critic's frequent recourse to the 'feminine' in his writings as a derisive term for art perceived to have no abiding aesthetic value; often linked with his dismissal of the decorative and the applied arts, Greenberg's feminine was not reserved solely for women's cultural practices, yet it accrued to them nonetheless.[49]

More recently, the art historian T. J. Clark has argued for the 'vulgarity' of much abstract expressionist painting in the 1950s in a way that also conjures up feminine connotations. As if anticipating its betrayal by 'those who by rights ought to be in the vanguard of good taste', Clark opines, postwar abstract painting increasingly aligned itself with the crass materialism and pseudo-intellectualism of the ascending petty bourgeois class. The art historian finds Hans Hofmann's work particularly emblematic of this 'vulgar' turn: 'A good Hofmann has to have a surface somewhere between ice cream, chocolate, stucco, and flock wallpaper. Its colours have to *reek* of Nature – of the worst kind of Woolworth forest-glade-with-waterfall-and-thunderstorm-brewing. … It is a picture of their "interiors", of the visceral-*cum*-spiritual upholstery of the rich. And above all it can have no illusions about its own status as part of that upholstery. It is made out of the materials it deploys'.[50] Clark's description of the overwrought expressiveness of Hofmann's canvas – one can virtually hear, taste, and smell its effects – aligns the art not only with a compromised notion of petty bourgeois individualism but, just as significantly, with specifically feminised spaces and activities: eating, home decor, and shopping. It is women's aspirations, Clark insinuates like Greenberg before him, that unwittingly 'vulgarise' both postwar masculine subjectivity and avant-garde art.

Clark's argument for the vulgarity of abstract expressionist painting affirms the cultural historian Janice Radway's assessment of the gendered connotations of middlebrow tastes and cultural practices in the twentieth century. In conceding that the majority of its constituents were indeed women, many of whom did not have alternative opportunities for cultural or artistic edification, she indicates how middlebrow culture's primary threat to cultural tastemakers occurred through its materialisation of subjects perceived to be vulgarly caught up in the particularities of shopping, cleaning, caretaking, and decorating. Critics shored up their differences from such subjects by establishing distance from the culturally devalued feminine subject. However, Radway also argues that middlebrow culture did not seek merely to imitate high culture, as Greenberg and others would have it, but instead drew upon a counter-discourse with values and tastes derived from middle-class consumerist routines and day-to-day domestic life.[51]

Significantly, the middlebrow counter-discourse came increasingly in the postwar era to include aesthetic tastes and values that were originally associated with working-class culture but which had, as a result of US economic prosperity and class advancement, migrated into middle-class lifestyles and tastes. In her study of American middle-class households and women's consumerism in the 1950s, for example, the historian Shelley Nickles convincingly argues that a distinctive working-class ethos of 'more is better' infused suburban domesticity, confounding cultural arbiters who expected middle-income housewives to develop more refined tastes reflective of their upward mobility and their desire to assimilate into a higher cultural stratum.[52] To the contrary, Nickles concludes, many housewives retained a taste for overly shiny finishes and flowery flourishes and eschewed the streamlined modern designs associated with the upper class.

While this disjunction between economic and cultural mobility attested to some degree to a democratisation of taste in the realm of interior design, it did little to lessen cultural perceptions that middle-class femininity remained vulgarly caught up in the troubling particularities of standardised consumerism and superficial decorative practices. Such perceptions changed little over the following decades: in the 1970s they not only continued to inflect critical perceptions of women's consumer practices but, as the art historian Helen Molesworth argues, likewise contributed to the ongoing invisibility of American women's painting practices, which were seen as emblematic of a lowering of standards of artistic quality.[53]

Indeed, a tainted air of dilettantism haunted women's artistic practices through the 1970s, not only in the context of painting but also in the feminist craft revival of the decade. The critical reception of Judy Chicago's *The Dinner Party* (1974–9), for instance, made the connection manifest. Comprising painted porcelain plates and elaborately embroidered textile runners, Chicago's ambitious project largely retained both the functionality and the technical precision of its domestic sources – in spirit if not in actuality, as *The Dinner Party* was a work of art and as such was never intended for use as a dining service (fig. 42). When Chicago's installation went on public view in 1979–80, however, most mainstream critics failed to appreciate its skilled handicraft. Instead, they found that Chicago's domestic trope reeked of an amateur hobbyist aesthetic. Thus, one critic compared its 'schlocky ceramic ware and stitchery' to the inconsequential contents of 'a "counter-culture" gift shop or an "alternative" school project'.[54] In a similar vein, another writer deemed the plates 'the Hummel figurines of the feminist movement', while a third concluded that *The Dinner Party* 'may well appeal to the taste of the middle-class housewife', but it also cleared the pathway for art that merely trafficked in 'trivial symbolism and knick-knacks'.[55] While some of this resistance to Chicago's project may have been inspired by the vulvic connotations of the dinner plate designs, or by the artist's own highly vocalised ambitions and self-promotion, it was mainly on (gendered) aesthetic grounds that critics deemed *The Dinner Party* a tasteless failure.[56]

The critical reception of *The Dinner Party* aptly illustrates what the feminist critic Lucy Lippard once noted about craft itself, namely, that 'there are "high" crafts and "low" ones', the distinctions of which are strictly regulated by class and gender systems. In her 1978 article 'Making Something from Nothing (Toward a Definition of Women's "Hobby Art")', Lippard set out to evaluate amateur hobbyism in the context of both the feminist craft revival and the modernist design movement. The upward mobility of certain domestic designs, as touted by the collecting practices of institutions like the

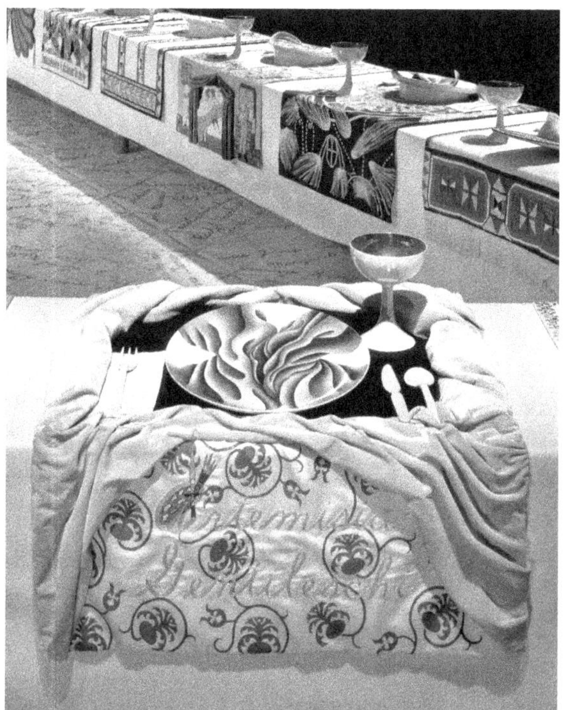

42. Judy Chicago, *The Dinner Party* 1974–9, mixed media, 48 x 42 x 3 feet (1463 x 1280 x 91.4 cm). The Brooklyn Museum, New York; gift of the Elizabeth A. Sackler Foundation. © 2011 Judy Chicago/Licensed by Artists Rights Society (ARS), New York, NY (detail: Artemisia Gentileschi place setting). Photo © Donald Woodman.

Museum of Modern Art, had by the 1970s made the ongoing devaluation of other forms of domestic craft equally apparent. Objects made by and of personal interest to women, Lippard observed, rarely entered the sanctioned realm of the museum; instead they languished in obscurity in the home, dismissed as signs of 'female fussiness or plain Bad Taste'.[57] This assessment lends credence to Nickles's subsequent account of the failed attempts to divest suburban women of their predilection for an overabundance of decoration.

The flourishing of the hobby arts and crafts industry in the postwar era did little to change the perception that women possessed inferior aesthetic tastes. By the early 1970s, the industry had blossomed into a highly profitable business, with companies like Mangelsen's, Herr's, and Hazel Pearson Handicrafts providing materials, kits, and how-to books for novices to enjoy at home. Large numbers of women hobbyists took up domestic craftwork, producing everything from macramé plant hangers to driftwood sculptures, bread dough jewellery, and tin-can sconces. No longer a by-product of necessity and thrift, domestic hobby arts and handicraft were pursued primarily for leisure and pleasure; as the scholar Glenn Adamson notes in his study of modern craft, hobbies are a product of 'surplus economy' and 'a culture of prosperous excess', from which the middlebrow were ideally situated to benefit.[58]

However, as Lippard argues, hobbies also represented one of the few creative outlets available to the average woman, leading the critic to believe that hobbyism might inspire an important form of visual consciousness-raising in the art world. As the art historian Julia Bryan-Wilson argues, Lippard did not necessarily endorse women's craft as a form of art but instead wanted to see women's art as a form of craft.[59] This conclusion is borne out in Lippard's essay. It was perhaps no coincidence, the critic concludes, that a lot of feminist art in the 1970s resembled the types of projects illustrated in the Handicrafts for Fun book *Feather Flowers and Arrangements* (1967), a publication that at first glance the critic was inclined to describe as 'sleazy' and 'garish' but which she ultimately seemed to admire for its obvious distance from dominant cultural standards of good taste (plate 18).[60]

If the feminist craft revival of the 1970s confronted head-on the modernist denigration of decoration and its association with an inferior feminine middlebrow aesthetic taste, few critics other than Lippard acknowledged the degree to which post-1960s domesticity was affected by shifting class relations and increased mass cultural consumerism. The hobby industry, conversely, fully exploited the connection, calling on aspiring hobbyists to utilise their newly acquired purchasing power and leisure time to indulge their tastes for decorative handicraft. Of course, not all hobbyists shared the same tastes, nor did the industry entirely ignore modernist design standards. Yet, as Lippard recognised, the art critical disdain for women's hobby crafts tended to cross class boundaries even as it relied on the perception that the average female hobbyist was white and middle class.

Though Benglis never explicitly aligned her work with women's hobbyism, her use of 'crafty' materials invites comparison to the types of projects illustrated in the Handicrafts for Fun series discussed by Lippard: for instance, the ornaments fashioned out of tin cans and deco-foil in *Fantasies of Foil and Metal* (1967). At the material level, the hobbyist activities of cutting metal, forming wire, and tying hemp were not unlike Benglis's artistic processes in creating the knots (figs. 43, 44). Likewise, the encouragement to decorate

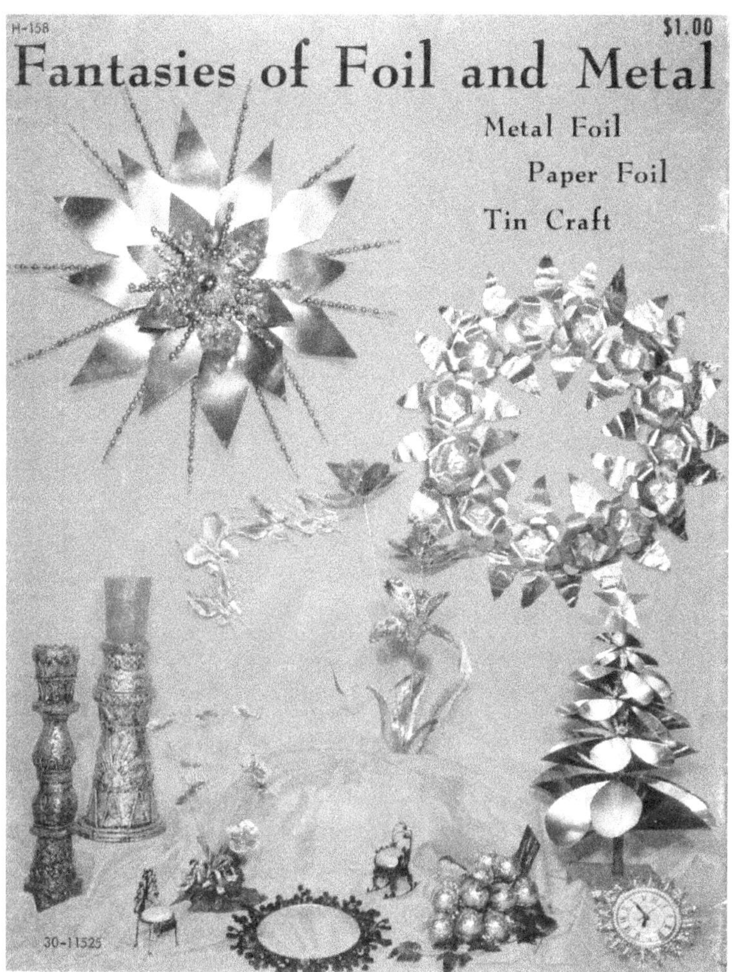

43. Cover, *Fantasies of Foil and Metal* (Temple City, CA: Craft Course Publishers, 1967). Printed permission by Tiffany Windsor, www.Cool2Craft.com.

everything profusely with colour and sparkle suggests another affinity with the artist's choice of decorative treatments. However, while the hobbyist may have taken earnestly the suggestion that these finishing touches lent 'that special touch' to any craft project, Benglis well understood how they connoted 'vulgarity' and 'bad taste' relative to modernist paradigms. Likewise, while Judy Chicago intended the painted china plates and embroidered tapestries in *The Dinner Party* to pay homage to the visual beauty of their historical and domestic sources, Benglis's knots challenged the very propriety of high art to which the former aspired.

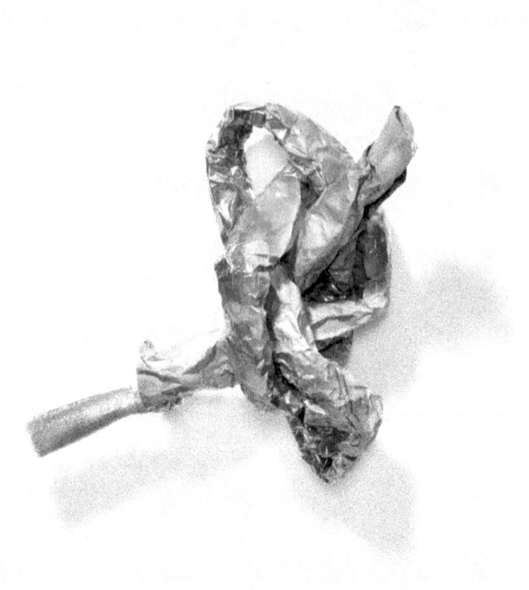

44. Lynda Benglis, *Roberta*, 1974, enamel, sculp-metal, and tinsel on aluminium foil and screening, 31 x 35 x 16 ¼ in. (79.1 x 89.1 x 41.3 cm). National Gallery of Australia, Canberra. Purchased 1975. © Lynda Benglis/Licensed by VAGA, New York, NY.

Simultaneous to the knots, in 1975 Benglis created a temporary installation that pointedly addressed issues of taste and artistic value. Produced in conjunction with a solo exhibition at Paula Cooper Gallery, the work was entitled *Primary Structures (Paula's Props)* and consisted of four small columnar pedestals – identically cast in plaster, lead, bronze, and aluminium – arranged on the floor with a length of dark blue velvet cloth, a ficus tree, an artificial houseplant, and a miniature toy Porsche cast in metal (fig. 45). Adding to the overt theatricality of the installation, one of the metal columns split during the casting process, yet Benglis chose to include it nonetheless, its broken parts dramatically displayed against the velvet like a kind of failed but nonetheless visually interesting artistic project.

Benglis's choice of title for her installation alluded to the exhibition survey *Primary Structures: Younger American and British Sculptors*, held at the Jewish Museum in New York in the spring of 1966. A critically acclaimed show, it featured works by a number of artists subsequently identified with minimalism, some of whom also exhibited regularly with Paula Cooper (serving

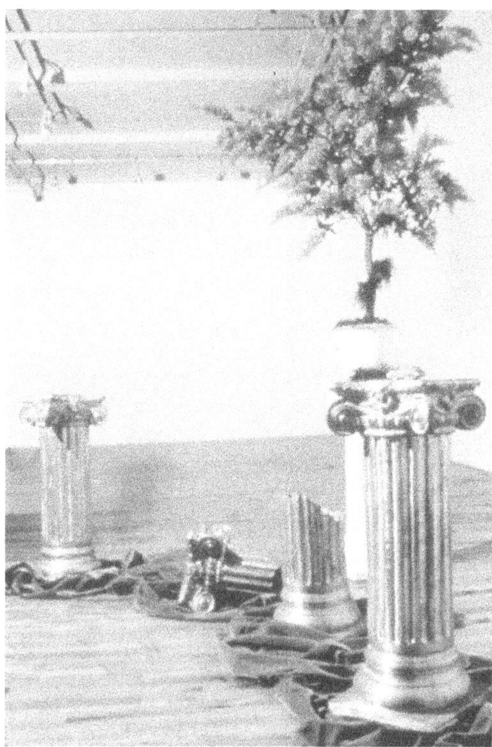

45. Lynda Benglis, *Primary Structures (Paula's Props)*, 1975, lead, aluminium, bronze, plaster, velvet, a plastic and a live plant, approx 97 x 99 x 63 in. (246.4 x 251.5 x 160 cm). Courtesy of the artist and Cheim & Read Gallery, New York. © Lynda Benglis/Licensed by VAGA, New York, NY.

perhaps as the 'props' of Benglis's subtitle). In retrospect, Benglis has elaborated on her choice of the main title: 'I chose to call it *Primary Structures* for two reasons: one was the idea of the minimal primary structure because this [her installation] was not minimal. The other was the idea of the structure, of object and pedestal. I was playing with the idea of what structure was. It was the pedestal that was also an architectonic structure, a primary structure that acted as a facade'.[61] Thus the choice of the small ionic column set into play a chain of associations reinforced by the other elements in Benglis's installation, each alluding to aspects central to the artist's own practice while simultaneously privileging everything that minimalism ostensibly denied: traditional metal casting, scattered forms, disparate textures, compositional variety, representational objects, and pointed cultural allusions. The broken column, in this respect, also imparted an air of non-functionality, and thus of visual elements included for the sake of visual interest, detail, or ornamentation.

What is additionally striking about Benglis's installation, however, is the manner in which its materials, scale, and layout are not dissimilar to the crafty tableaux featured on the covers of many of the Handicraft for Fun books, including the two reproduced here. While this is not to claim a direct source for *Primary Structures (Paula's Props)*, or to identify artistic intention, such a connection is a reminder of the ways in which certain tastes and practices serve to 'prop up' the value of others. Benglis's installation not only traced the nebulous line between high art and the realms of design, craft, and even kitsch but cannily exposed how institutional structures – including the gallery in which the artist exhibited – contribute to such hierarchies.[62]

In the end, however, neither *Primary Structures* nor Benglis's series of knots can ever really be mistaken for a hobbyist craft project. This case of mistaken identity, it would seem, was one of the downfalls of Chicago's *The Dinner Party* – its ceramic plates and textile runners *were* craft objects aspiring to be art, not abstract artworks alluding to feminine craft. In contrast, Benglis's knots importantly fail to meet certain craft standards of form: they do not have the simple geometric shapes and symmetrical compositions favoured by hobbyist projects, nor are they clearly figurative in the manner of a winking macramé owl or tin-can Santa Claus. Similarly, the juxtaposition of heavily coloured and glittered passages with patches of bare cotton bunting, and the occasional tattered thread or peeling foil, defies the hobbyist's quest for precision and perfection.

In Benglis's hands, the credo of 'more is better' is filtered through the innovative expressive language of gestural abstraction. As such, her work reflects a sensibility attuned as much to high art as to cosmetics, fashion, popular culture and middlebrow hobby crafts. This commingling is, perhaps, the type of 'middlebrow' art against which detractors fulminated. However, rather than regard this sensibility as marking a naive conflation of the genuine and the superficial, to echo Greenberg's critique of the middlebrow, another perspective sees it as a productive reworking of the possibilities each realm has to offer. This is not a simple inversion of taste, or an outright appropriation of the 'vulgar', but instead it is a pleasurable albeit unresolved encounter between different aesthetic registers. In this respect, it calls to mind an observation proffered by Susan Sontag in her 1964 essay 'Notes on Camp': 'One cheats oneself, as a human being', she writes, 'if one has *respect* only for the style of high culture, whatever else one may do or feel on the sly'.[63] This notion of a refusal to pick sides gives purchase on the contradictory effects of Benglis's knots, and in particular their commingling of the high, middle, and low in the production of an effect that I would dub 'campy'.

all that glitters

Susan Sontag did much to popularise camp when she outlined its main characteristics in her 1964 essay. While a number of scholars have subsequently offered important critiques of 'Notes on Camp', this initial account nonetheless remains useful for understanding the campiness of Benglis's knots.[64] In overcoming her expressed reluctance to pin it down too securely to a singular definition, Sontag noted from the outset that a camp sensibility entails a 'love of the unnatural: of artifice and exaggeration'. Thus 'to camp', she famously continued, is to perceive everything in quotation marks, to understand 'Being-as-Playing-a-Role' and life as a form of 'theater'. In capturing its aesthetic stance on questions of taste with the phrase 'It's good because it's awful', Sontag believed that pleasure, not judgement, informed a camp affection for Tiffany lamps, Aubrey Beardsley drawings, and Busby Berkeley musicals, to name but a few of the examples she cites.[65]

Building on Sontag's initial study of camp, the cultural historian Andrew Ross has indicated how the sensibility has generated a multitude of uses and meanings for the different groups for which it has historically served as an exercise in taste. Though long associated with gay subcultural practices, by the 1960s camp represented a sophisticated mode of cultural politics that appealed to practitioners of different persuasions.[66] While its indulgence in artifice and theatricality placed camp at odds with feminist theories in the 1970s that sought to politicise an authentic or so-called essentialist female difference, its subversive attraction to flamboyant forms of femininity and excessive cultural statements rendered camp equally appealing to women artists interested in reworking what Ross deems 'disempowered modes of production'.[67]

Many of Benglis's reviewers recognised how the artist's work flirted with camp, though none have followed through on the significance of this identification. The critic and art historian Donald Kuspit, for instance, noted in a 1979 review that the metalised knots possess a 'look-at-me, I'm-in-the-spotlight, don't-I-shine look of an abstract Liza Minnelli strutting her stuff'.[68]

Having made this fabulous claim, however, Kuspit sets it aside in order to redeem Benglis's knots as a form of decorative 'luxury art' that successfully transcends its own cheap cultural effects to produce an ineffable art experience. Like Gilbert-Rolfe in his account of Benglis's 1973 Clocktower show, Kuspit appreciates but does not necessarily find aesthetic value in the artist's material choices; it is only by claiming their 'cosmetic transcendence' into luxury art that the knots regain a secure artistic foothold for him.

The difference between my claim for the campiness of Benglis's knots and Kuspit's argument for their transcendence rests on the fact that the former finds value in the 'bad' while the latter does not; as camp, the work is comfortable with its inconsistencies, but as luxury art, it tries to cover them up. To deem the knots camp instead of luxury art would, I believe, better account for their lyrical sophistication but also their flamboyant decorative effects; it would capture the disjuncture between the encrustation of glitter, paint, or metal and the areas of bare cotton bunting and the occasional loose thread, crumpled foil, and awkwardly twisted forms (fig. 46).[69] It would, in the end, not attempt to reconcile these disparities but instead conceive of them as equal parts of a pleasurable whole. Or, as Sontag claims in a description that aptly applies here, 'Camp taste is a kind of love, love for human nature. It relishes, rather than judges, the little triumphs and awkward intensities of "character"'.[70] Thus when John Perreault deemed Benglis's knots 'pretty vulgar', he ascertained that they troubled both aesthetic and cultural assumptions of the time but, in so doing, did not necessarily level out taste hierarchies so much as cast them in stark relief.[71]

Just as importantly, I believe, reading Benglis's work as campy suggests one way in which to understand the cultural work of the feminine middlebrow.[72] What I am calling Kuspit's cover-up tacitly mirrors the cover-up that has occurred around the modern formulation of the feminine middlebrow. In many respects, this cover-up has made female cultural production unwittingly ripe for camp appropriation. As it has traditionally unfolded in both practice and academic discourse, this process of appropriation has elided rather than affirmed female agency and cultural work and as such is no different from the modernist denigration of feminine decoration and handicraft. Conversely, in looking at women's historical relationship to camp, the scholar Pamela Robertson makes a persuasive case for instances of women's agency.[73] She notes that while academics tend to regard female cultural activities in terms of either passive complicity in or active resistance to dominant paradigms, in the context of camp the two combine: camp inspires a form of pleasure for

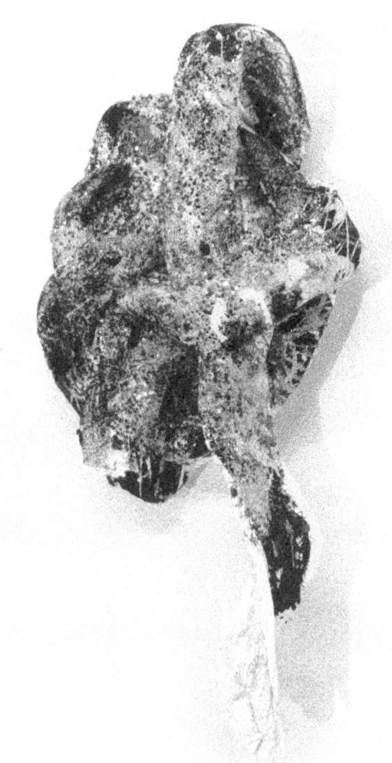

46. Lynda Benglis, *Chi*, 1973, enamel, silver paint, and sparkle on cotton bunting and aluminum screen, 27 x 13 ½ x 9 in. (68.6 x 34.3 x 22.9 cm). Courtesy of the artist and Cheim & Read Gallery, New York. © Lynda Benglis/Licensed by VAGA, New York, NY.

women that is both resistant to and complicit in dominant discourses. While the difference between resistance and compliance is often difficult to gauge, Benglis's knots may be said to hinge on precisely this difficulty.

Robertson's account of women's participation in the formulation of what she calls 'feminist camp' also challenges the perception that the sensibility is strictly an elitist activity understood only by the cognoscenti. Her own example of working-class women's fascination with film actresses raises interesting questions about the role of camp in the realm of the so-called middlebrow. The scholar Rita Felski offers some useful insights in this regard. In reflecting on her own lower middle-class background, she proposes that the middle is a transitional cultural space with no fixed or coherent identity. One neither embraces the status of the middle, particularly when it is the lower middle, nor sees it as an end point of identity formation. Instead it constitutes a kind of non-identity, one with little or nothing 'to declare', Felski writes.[74] Building on this notion of 'non-identity', I wonder, then, if the perceived middlebrow taste for the effulgent, the superficial, and the decorative is itself already a form of camp that tacitly acknowledges the nebulous positioning of the middle. Without suggesting that Benglis was fully cognizant of these operations, I do believe the artist was and remains sensitive to the negative construal of the decorative, the feminine, and the middlebrow in modern artistic discourse, and to the ways in which these terms have accrued to women's art and artistic identity. In this respect, there is a way in which her knots indicate that the middle does have something 'to declare'. At the very least, this body of work takes serious pleasure in the cultural ambiguities, contradictions, and excesses afforded by its 'pretty vulgar' effects.

5 Iterations and Expansions

The preceding chapters give considerable weight to the first decade of Benglis's career. For good or bad, this period of her practice continues to shape the artist's critical reception today. In tacitly acknowledging how the artist's early output still garners fascination, however, I have also wanted to complicate its future reception. In developing in-depth formal and contextual analyses of the artwork, I have not rejected prior critical assessments of Benglis's early career so much as expanded on them, drawn out their unspoken implications, and indicated what I propose are their wider historical and art historical interconnections. I continue this tactic here; however, while each of the previous chapters is organized around a discrete body of artwork, this last one takes a broader view of the artist's mature practice. It indicates, however briefly, a number of new directions in Benglis's work while also demonstrating the continuation of a core set of concerns. In looking broadly at the last thirty or so years of the artist's career, I do not posit overarching conclusions so much as identify potential topics for further examination.

north south east west

In the summer of 2009, a travelling retrospective of Benglis's work opened at the Van Abbemuseum in Eindhoven, the Netherlands. Organised by a group of European and American curators, and with several venues planned both in Europe and the United States, *Lynda Benglis* included work from virtually

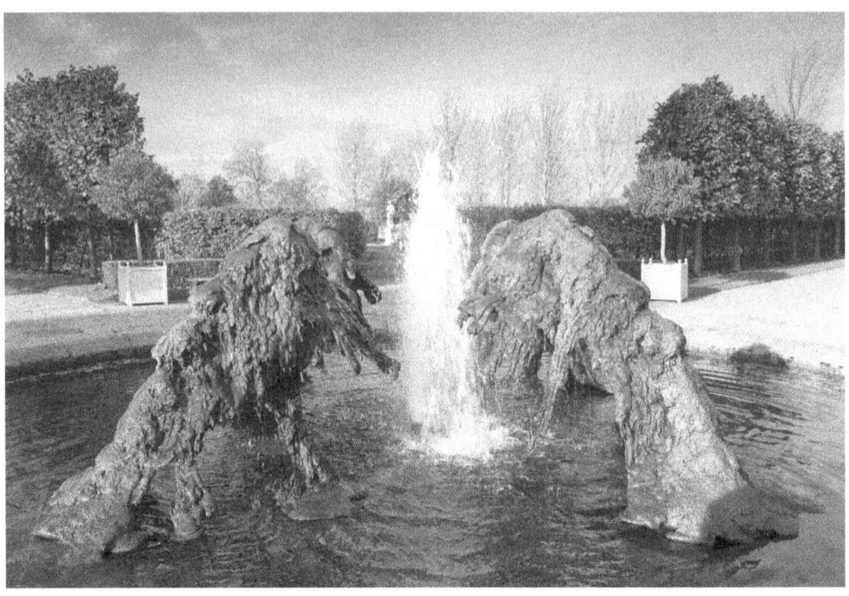

47. Lynda Benglis, *North South East West*, 2009, bronze and steel, 66 x 184 x 184 in. (167.6 x 467.4 x 467.4 cm). Irish Museum of Modern Art, Dublin. © Lynda Benglis/Licensed by VAGA, New York, NY.

every period of the artist's career including, in the Dublin instalment of the exhibition, a recently completed fountain project.[1] On permanent view in the formal gardens of the Irish Museum of Modern Art, *North South East West* (2009) consists of four wave-like cast-bronze forms that come together in the centre to form a column of shooting water (fig. 47). The fountain, or 'hydraulic sculpture' as the artist calls it, directly recalls Benglis's cantilevered polyurethane projects of 1971, of which the only extant version, the phosphorescent *Phantom*, was also re-purposed for the travelling exhibition.[2] In tandem, the fountain and the polyurethane installation demonstrated to museum visitors the artist's abiding interest in gestural and organic forms as well as the aesthetics of proprioceptive experiences.

In gesturing backwards to Benglis's early work, however, the Dublin fountain also points to important shifts that have occurred in the artist's practice since the late 1970s, some of which this chapter sets out to explicate. The first of these shifts, I propose, is a consequence of changes in Benglis's physical environment. Since the late 1970s, the artist has spent considerably more of her time outside New York City. Apart from a small loft/studio space she still maintains in the Bowery district of Manhattan, the artist now divides her time between Santa Fe, New Mexico; East Hampton, New York; Kastelorizo, Greece; and Ahmedabad, India. Along with continual references to her Louisiana roots, Benglis's immersion in these locations has had a tremendous impact on her material choices as well as on the appearance of her work. Likewise, she has on occasion closely consulted with local artists and craft artisans, an experience that has sustained her interest in global arts and cultures. The four elements of the Dublin fountain, for instance, symbolise the four quadrants of the world while concomitantly acknowledging the significance of the cardinal directions in visual cultures worldwide.[3] A not insignificant gesture on Benglis's part, this association reflects the artist's quiet refusal to prioritise a Western (let alone a New York-centric) perspective.

The peripatetic lifestyle has likewise fostered Benglis's interest in exploring new mediums and artistic techniques, including traditional craft production in clay and glass. While *North South East West* does not manifest this particular aspect of the artist's work directly, as a fountain it implicitly invokes the 'minor' categories of decorative and applied arts with which craft is often grouped. Along those lines, decoration has continued to play an important role in Benglis's sculptural practice, the artist giving increasing attention to sensual surface embellishments. Because the results have met with mixed reviews, the artist's output since the 1980s serves as a barometer of a kind of the art world's shifting allegiances to decorative and craft aesthetics.

Finally, *North South East West* illuminates the role that casting has played in Benglis's career. As a technique premised on permanence, mastery, and tradition, casting has entailed a distinct set of values for the artist to explore and, at times, subvert. Additionally, as a duplicative technique, it has enabled Benglis to serialise her forms in multiple materials, a process not unlike the different manifestations of the knots in the 1970s. To see an identical form rendered in lead, bronze, and even cast polyurethane necessarily focuses attention on subtle differences of texture, mass, and colouration, which in turn invites close viewing. Ultimately, if an overarching theme connects the various bodies of work Benglis has produced since the 1970s, it is this sustained inquiry into surface aesthetics. The artist's work in the arena of craft is a case in point.

material matters

In 1979 Benglis made the first of many trips to Greece and India. While the former constituted a return of sorts – the artist is part Greek on her father's side – the initial visit to India occurred at the encouragement of other US artists who had travelled there, including Robert Rauschenberg and Frank Stella.[4] A letter of invitation from Dr Anand Sarabhai, a member of a prominent textile family with a rich history of supporting cultural and artistic endeavours in Ahmedabad, provided further impetus. Benglis's initial visit to India entailed a month-long residency and was quickly followed by a longer stay in 1980.

On her second visit to India, Benglis undertook work on a commissioned project for Hartsfield (now Hartsfield-Jackson) Atlanta International Airport. The artist had originally planned to submit a series of relief sculptures but abandoned that idea in favour of a textile project. After conceiving a design consisting of colourful geometric and organic shapes floating against a patchwork background, Benglis consulted with local Indian artisans to translate it into a pair of silk-satin appliqué banners measuring ninety feet in length when hung side by side (fig. 48). Entitled *Patang*, the Hindi word for 'kite', Benglis's composition was inspired by Ahmedabad's annual kite flying festival, which takes place in mid-January to mark the solstice. The image of the kite-filled sky made a strong impression on the artist, who felt that it provided an apt theme for the airport commission.[5]

In further preparation for *Patang*, Benglis also studied Henri Matisse's paper cutouts from the 1940s and 1950s; this body of work, which enabled Matisse to simplify forms and reconcile colour with drawing, was influential

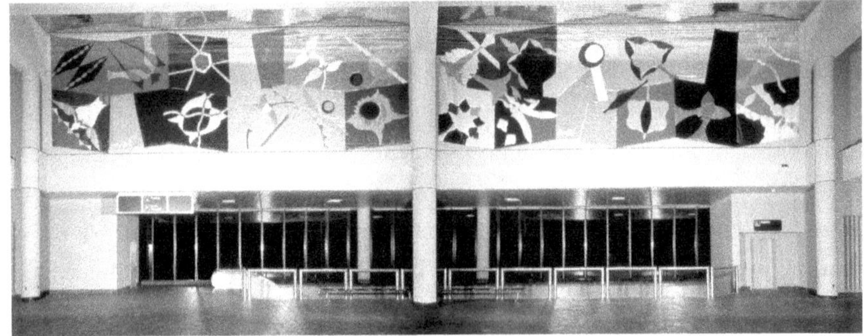

48. Lynda Benglis, *Patang*, 1980, silk-satin appliqué, 180 x 1080 in. (457.2 x 2743.2 cm). Hartsfield-Jackson Atlanta International Airport. © Lynda Benglis/ Licensed by VAGA, New York, NY.

in the 1970s for US artists associated with the Pattern and Decoration (P&D) movement. Though Benglis was never affiliated with P&D, her openness to decorative principles and cross-cultural sources represented significant parallels, as did her recourse to textile arts, a decorative craft tradition to which many P&D artists turned in the 1970s.[6] Indeed, *Patang* is a spectacular example of Benglis's move into realms traditionally associated with artisanal craft. Since the 1980s, the artist has increasingly worked with glass, clay, and, to a lesser degree, textiles, all of which have been historically classified as craft practices distinct from the realm of high art.

In a 2001 review of the artist's considerable body of work in glass for *Glass: The UrbanGlass Quarterly*, the critic Matthew Kangas reasonably asked: 'Is it time to recategorize Lynda Benglis as a closet craft artist?'[7] Such a question, arguably inflected by its context in a journal dedicated to contemporary glass practices, implicitly acknowledged the critical silence around the artist's craft-based work. From the outset, however, there are several factors indicating why Kangas's question has no easy answer. For one, the definition of 'craft' itself inspires little consensus: while the artist and writer Paula Owen concedes that laypeople often equate craft with 'hobby-level kitsch', the art historian Glenn Adamson points out that even among practitioners, it 'exists only in motion'.[8] Recently, the craft scholar M. Anna Fariello has proposed that the classification of craft has everything to do with 'an *approach*', which is to say, with a set of core values that practitioners bring to their materials.[9] Likewise, as the art historian Elissa Auther has adduced in her study of fibre art of the 1960s and 1970s, the contemporary divide between the realms of art and craft hinges less on differences in style, medium, or process than on the confluence of artistic intention, reception, and privileged institutional positioning.[10] In emphasising hands-on techniques and intense interactions with unconventional materials such as string and felt, the artists loosely associated with process art in the late 1960s, including Eva Hesse and Robert Morris, rarely if ever considered the resulting work to be *craft*, nor did the visual similarities of their work to that of leading weavers of the time lend artistic stature to the latter. Similarly, Benglis's turn to craft mediums followed on the artist's earlier immersion in the radical avant-garde art scenes of New York. Her critical alignment with Pollock's legacy and process-oriented practices, and against the waning authority of minimalist art, made her work relevant to the dominant sculptural and painting, rather than craft, discourses of the day. While her subsequent move by the 1980s to so-called craft materials troubles categorical distinctions between art and craft, it has not entailed a concomitant redefinition of artistic identity.[11]

Given the increasingly prominent place that ceramics and glass have played in Benglis's mature practice, however, Kangas's question remains compelling, if not easily laid to rest. As I discussed in chapter 4, the artist's series of knots from the mid-1970s openly flirted with amateur and dime-store hobby craft paradigms, utilising these aesthetic and cultural associations to push notions of good taste. Benglis's subsequent recourse to clay and glass approaches the hierarchical relationship somewhat differently, notably by bringing a sculptural idiom into the traditional realms of craft. While her work retains many of the values associated with craft – material integrity, technical skill, and visual brio, for instance – it also submits them to the same play of formal and conceptual ironies that inform Benglis's larger sculptural practice.

If the craft label is not an easy fit for Benglis, then that of the crossover artist proves more useful. In a recent anthology on the art–craft divide in the contemporary art world, Paula Owen offers up this description, observing that along with figures such as Ken Price, Anne Wilson, and Martin Puryear, Benglis has helped to bring artistic concepts to traditional handicraft practices.[12] The notion of crossing over productively acknowledges the artist's ties to the mainstream art world while concurrently accounting for her interest in maintaining a hands-on, studio-based approach with her practice. It also begins to indicate how Benglis simultaneously benefits from and contributes to the dissolution of certain boundaries between contemporary art and craft, such that her work resonates for practitioners working from both sides of the divide today. A brief consideration of the artist's work in ceramic and glass sheds light on this process of crossing over.

crossing over into craft

Benglis initially studied clay in the early 1960s as a student at the H. Sophie Newcomb Memorial College in New Orleans (an institution renowned in the United States for its history of ceramic production) but did not return to the medium until the early 1990s. Eschewing the potter's wheel, she began to build small-scale sculptures by stacking, gouging, and stretching extruded tubes and slabs of clay into both serpentine and architectonic forms; a not uncommon technique among ceramists, the use of extrusions introduced an industrial element into the artist's hand-building process. Over the years, writers have characterised Benglis's approach to clay as one of 'respectful irreverence' and as 'a kind of carnage'.[13] Such descriptions not only capture

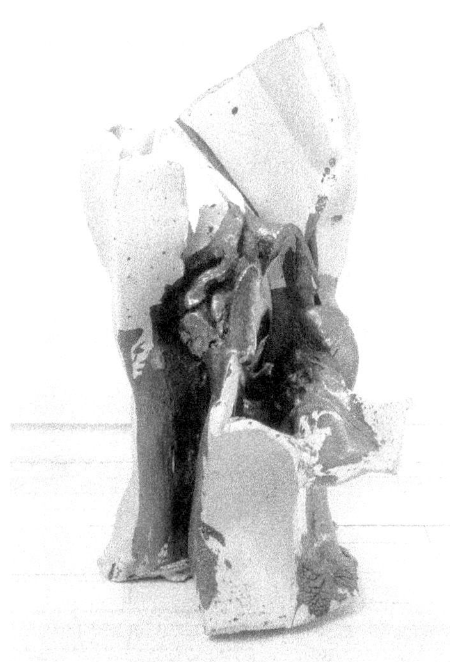

49. Lynda Benglis, *Winner (Warrior)*, 1993, glazed ceramic, 32 x 16 x 16 in. (81.3 x 40.6 x 40.6 cm). Courtesy of the artist and Cheim & Read Gallery, New York. © Lynda Benglis/Licensed by VAGA, New York, NY.

the physicality of her artistic process but also belie the stereotypical image of the ceramist carefully crafting a refined and functional form.

Winner (Warrior) (1993) exemplifies Benglis's muscular treatment of clay (fig. 49). A roughhewn stoneware sculpture, it comprises several hollow rectilinear extrusions that have been stacked, pulled, and mashed into an upright configuration that nonetheless appears to be on the verge of collapsing under its own weight. As though in response to the artist's aggressive handling, the sculpture spews forth a dark, earthen glaze from deep inside its interior, an alluvial flow that partially recalls the oozing character of Benglis's large-scale polyurethane forms of 1971. In the ceramic work, the downward pull of the earthen glaze is stemmed by the countermovement of vertical passages of bright matte blue running along the outer sides of the sculpture. The artist has elaborated on the kind of surface-form relationship she seeks with clay, indeed with all of her work, when noting how she 'play[s] with the idea that surface and texture can also describe form: we see the surface and the texture of things and we complete or feel the form'.[14] Though her forms are rarely figurative, they evoke a bodily or proprioceptive response, one felt as a series of oppositional movements that are revealed by the sculptures' surface conditions: the glazes in *Winner (Warrior)* for instance underscore the way in which the form appears simultaneously to rise up and slump downward, to collapse in and expand outward, to twist in on itself and turn outward to the viewer.

Winner (Warrior) retains a relatively clear formal configuration: one can see how it was put together, just as one can appreciate the interrelationship between the colourful skeins that compose Benglis's early latex pours. The same cannot be said, however, of *Untitled C* (1993), a diminutive sculpture of extruded clay that Benglis has twisted and kneaded into a wildly contorted hunchbacked form resting on two 'feet' (plate 19). Any clear sense of inside and outside is abandoned with this work, its form instead presenting a labyrinthine complexity. A lustre glaze dominated by bright yellow heightens the ambiguity of the underlying form. It also gives the sculpture the vitality of a mutating living organism and the glossy allure of a glitzy and inanimate objet d'art. Like *Winner (Warrior), Untitled C* announces its 'handcrafted' origins but diverges in the connotations to which it gives rise: while the former exemplifies a more candid approach to the medium, the latter teases out the fictitious and showy possibilities of a non-functional clay object. As if simultaneously aware of and indifferent to its potentially second-class status as a craft object, it self-consciously couples the organic and the kitschy. Further, whereas *Winner (Warrior)* illuminates Benglis's 'muscular' approach to clay, *Untitled C* is showy, perverse, and irreverent about its atypical form and lush glazing. Neither humble nor refined, it forms an important precedent for the equally self-conscious category-bending work of such contemporary artists as Nicole Cherubini, Sterling Ruby, and Rebecca Warren.

Like her ceramics, Benglis's work in glass evidences a similarly multifaceted approach that bridges craft, high art, and kitsch. The artist has worked with the protean medium since 1980, producing a body of small-scale sculptures ranging from expressively raw sand-casted forms to brightly coloured handblown and *pâte-de-verre* pieces. She has enjoyed residencies at leading glass workshops around the world and often responds to her specific environs through her formal and technical choices. Just as she has done with clay, from the outset Benglis eschewed the traditional functionality of glassware in favour of abstract configurations that invoke both natural and manmade forms. Above all, glass has enabled her to expand her investigation into the visual and material effects of light and colour.

Glassmaking entails prudent consideration of specific steps in order to ensure the intended design. As such, the care that goes into glass production seems anathema to an artist known for emphasising an extemporaneous approach to her materials, and yet just as Benglis's large-scale polyurethane pours required careful attention to structural details, so too do her glass pieces traverse a provocative line between gestural spontaneity and conceptual refinement, with inspiration coming from both nature and the glass studio environment.

Benglis was introduced in 1984 to the sand-casting technique by the Swedish artist Bertil Vallien while both were in residence at the Pilchuck Glass School in Washington State. She subsequently produced a series of twisted and semi-translucent sculptures softly coloured and textured with powdered glass, ceramic shards, and metal inclusions (fig. 50). The knotted morphology, arrived at through an intuitive engagement with the molten glass, recalls the artist's knotted relief sculptures of the 1970s. However, with their rough

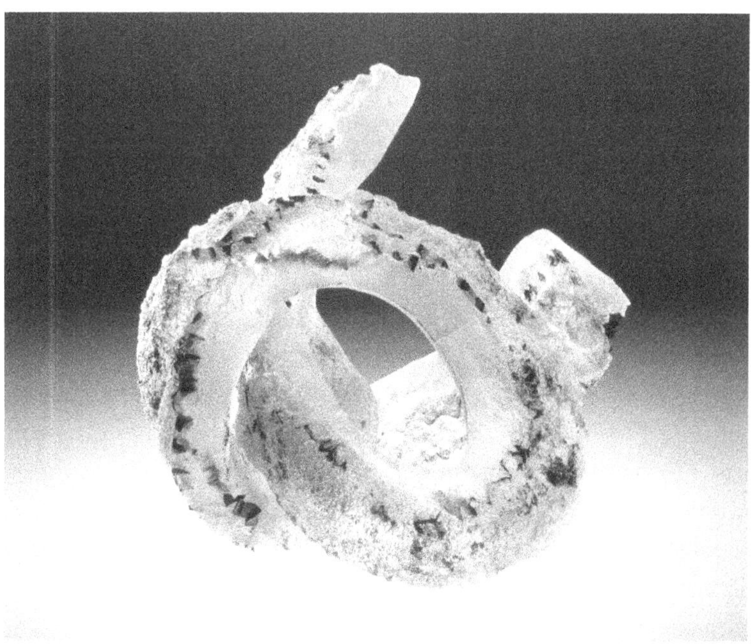

50. Lynda Benglis, *MI*, 1984, glass, sandcast, powdered; ceramic oxides, and metal inclusions, 13 ½ x 17 x 16 in. (34.3 x 43.2 x 40.6 cm). Los Angeles County Museum of Art, Los Angeles; gift of Daniel Greenberg and Susan Steinhauser (M.86.273.1). © Lynda Benglis/Licensed by VAGA, New York, NY. Photo Credit: Digital Image © 2011 Museum Associates/LACMA/Art Resource.

surfaces and sinuous curves, the glassworks are more primordial in their associations; they evoke fossilised reptiles and worms even as they retain a strongly abstract character. In 2006, examples of Benglis's sand-casted glass sculptures were included in *Glass: Material Matters*, an exhibition of contemporary glass production at the Los Angeles County Museum of Art. Displayed in a section of the show entitled 'Primal Nature', her work underscored the mercurial and metaphysical qualities of glass, and its romantic associations to generative forms, earthy substances, and enigmatic life forces.[15]

In contrast to the raw molten quality of her sand-casted work, Benglis has also produced several series of colourful handblown glass sculptures. One such work, *Blansko* (1996) was produced during a residency at the Ajeto Studio in the Czech Republic (plate 20). Composed of two elongated cylindrical forms joined in the centre with additional layers of glass formed over the blowholes at either end, the sculpture is vaguely functional looking without actually being functional; its smooth and rounded form begs to be handled, yet for reasons that escape logic. *Blansko*'s split composition is not unlike the artist's two-brushstroke paintings of the early 1970s (plate 10), or even the infamous double-ended dildo deployed in her 1974 *Artforum* ad (fig. 1). Conversely, Benglis has offered that the glass sculpture consists of 'double nipple forms', a description which, in undercutting the work's phallic connotations, nonetheless points up the latent bodily orientation of the work.[16] *Blansko* is in fact one of several glass sculptures through which Benglis has given colourful and decorative expression to similar phallic–breast ambiguities. As such, these oddly shaped glass sculptures are comically perverse: indulging the fetishistic character of the medium, their sensuous double-pronged forms playfully serve as an exaggerated compensatory mechanism for the inferior status frequently granted to glass handicraft by the mainstream art world.

The modern artistic perception of the lowly status of glass has much to do with the technical bravado and unapologetic visual beauty that traditionally attends glass production. Equally, and much like plastics, the history of glass as a substitution for more expensive materials (precious gems, for instance) has also contributed to its devaluation within modern and contemporary critical discourse.[17] Although this connection may not have been foremost in Benglis's mind when she initially took up glass, it plays into the artist's ongoing interest in questioning conventional notions of aesthetic and social value. As a twist on this, since 2006 she has produced several cast-polyurethane wall sculptures that emulate the delicate luminosity of glass; it is only upon closer scrutiny that the flat and 'flocculent' quality of the plastic comes across (plate 22).[18] The visual and conceptual seduction of this work, which I discuss in greater depth later in this chapter, lies in part in the initial uncertainty of its material makeup and demonstrates some of the ways in which Benglis's engagement with glass has carried over into her exploration into the physical properties and appearances of other mediums. In conceptualising the potential overlaps between materials, she questions our way of seeing and determining value, which in the end yields much more than a revalorization of the maligned category of craft concedes.

Closely related to craft traditions, the issue of functionality has recently entered Benglis's practice, notably in a series of paper lamps that the artist first executed in 2009.[19] Inspired by the traditional forms of Indian clay pots, the *Vessel Lamps* consist of interlocking individual components stacked into vertically hanging configurations (fig. 51). Recalling Isamu Noguchi's *Akari* light sculptures from the 1950s and 1960s, Benglis's works possess a

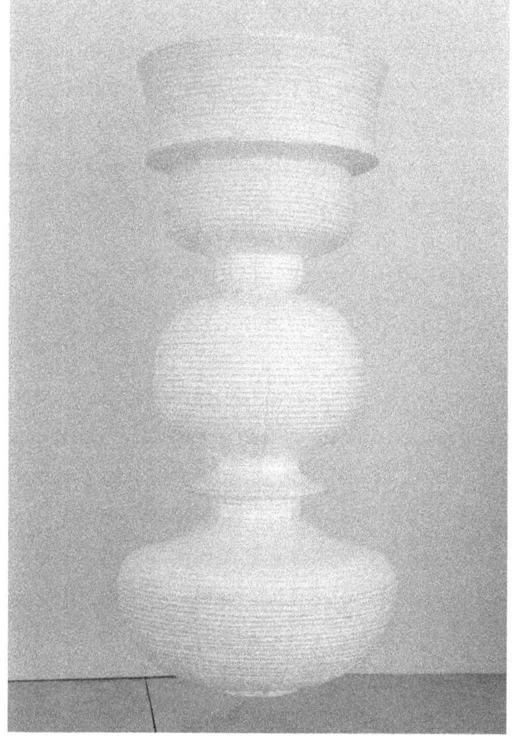

51. Lynda Benglis, *Manu Vessel Lamp #3*, 2009, paper, wood, electric bulbs, and wire, 72 x 36 x 36 in. (183 x 91.5 x 91.5 cm). Courtesy of the artist and Cheim & Read Gallery, New York. © Lynda Benglis/Licensed by VAGA, New York, NY.

dual and potentially ambiguous status as sculptures and as functional design objects, their uneasy interplay of hierarchies raising questions about conventions of artistic context, presentation, and perception. Related to the lamps, which have been exhibited in galleries and museums, Benglis has collaborated with the Ahmedabad-based design firm EATIT (Ecological Applications of Technology for International Trade) World to design smaller versions for retail.[20] This intersection of craft, functionality, and aesthetics finds parallels in the work of contemporary artists as stylistically diverse as Jorge Pardo and Pae White, who likewise utilise their position as artists with museum and gallery representation to broker the qualitative distinctions between home furnishing and sculpture, decorative and fine arts.

Whereas so-called functional art represents a relatively new aspect of Benglis's practice, the decorative has been integral to her oeuvre since the 1960s. Over the decades, the artist's work has grown increasingly involved with surface effects and embellishments, with details of colour, texture, and pattern. To a large degree, the decorative is a category closely aligned and even conflated with craft, yet as I touch on in the previous chapter, it is also negatively imbricated in the development of modern and contemporary abstraction. An examination of the critical reception of the decorative in Benglis's work since the late 1970s is revealing of this continuing trend, as well as of more recent countertrends aimed at recuperating the visual pleasure of the decorative under the rubric of a 'return to beauty'.

the decorative impulse

When Benglis embarked on a new series of wall sculptures around 1980, she took her cue from Greek art and architecture, specifically the palmette motif from an acroterion (architectural ornament) mounted on a funerary stele, which the artist had come across in an exhibition of Aegean art she first saw in Paris, and later again in New York.[21] Feeling that she had exhausted the knot motif, Benglis was inspired by the fan-shaped design of the palmette to begin pleating her wire screening sculptural armatures before then forming them into fanned configurations. Initially she finished these works with gold leaf, the lustrous quality of which accentuates the effects of light playing across the surface crinkles and folds (fig. 52). While this use of gold leaf brings to mind another connection to Greece, specifically the gilded icons of the Greek Orthodox tradition, the initial impulse for Benglis stemmed

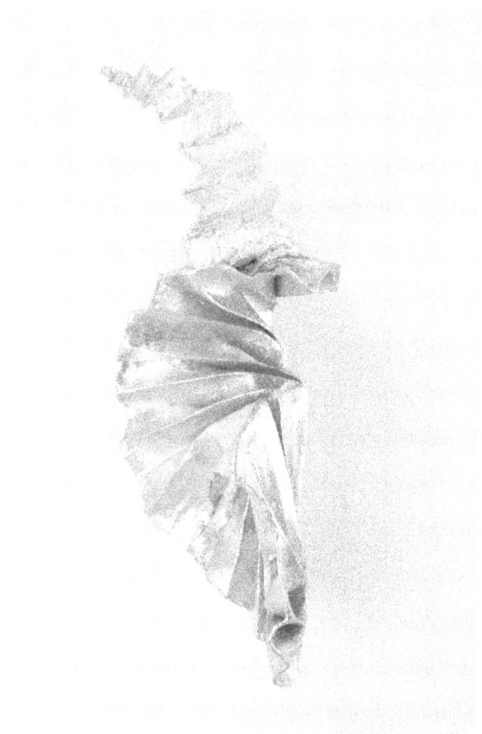

52. Lynda Benglis, *Kaudi*, 1980, gold leaf on hydrocal, 39 x 15 x 13 in. (99.1 x 38.1 x 33 cm). Courtesy of the artist and Cheim & Read Gallery, New York.

from different quarters, specifically the precarious world gold market of the 1970s.[22] As a product of global political and economic instability and pressures, the drastic inflation of gold prices during this period epitomised for the artist the volatility of other value systems serving to uphold cherished aesthetic and cultural binaries. With her extravagant use of gold leaf, Benglis playfully manipulated perceptions of both the literal and perceived preciousness of her sculptures.[23]

In 1982, Benglis began to spray coat the pleated and fanned sculptures with liquid metals, having determined with a fabricator how to do so without the use of an intermediary layer of cotton and plaster, which she previously employed with the knots. Over the next several years she continued to mine the formal potential of the pleated and fanned form, generating works evocative of wings, flowing drapery, and flowers. By the decade's end, the reliefs had evolved into elaborate and voluminous configurations, with flowing arabesque passages combined with twisted angular forms. As Susan Krane has noted, the larger-scale works are largely concerned with volume: 'The works are enlivened by a sense of sufflation, of biological expansion and contraction'.[24] Exemplary in this regard, *Eclat* (1990) swells across the wall in a series of pleated and gathered billows, the sculpture's shiny aluminium exterior intensifying the impression of movement and energy (plate 21). Up close, *Eclat*'s rippled surface reveals a variety of textures, with some areas polished to a mirror-like shine, others left rough and granular.

Like all of Benglis's works, the reliefs elude fixed readings of content. At times, the artist bestowed automotive names on them (*Passat* and *Diablo* for instance) in order to emphasise their industrial associations, and perhaps to draw tacit connections to John Chamberlain's sculptures of crushed car parts. In other instances she selected titles based on constellations. Yet, as Krane concedes in her catalogue essay for the 1991 retrospective *Lynda Benglis: Dual Natures*, it was mainly as images of feminine adornment that Benglis's pleated and metalized wall sculptures were received through the 1980s and early 1990s, the allusions to shiny bows, flounces, and scarves in turn inspiring concern about the essentially vacuous, decorative turn in the artist's practice.[25]

Critical reviews of the *Dual Natures* exhibition confirmed Krane's observation. Though openly admiring of Benglis's career as a whole, *Arts Magazine* critic Amy Jinkner-Lloyd admitted to some uneasiness in finding pleasure in works she worried might 'turn out to be merely decorative rather than profound'. Reflecting on this discomfort, she continued: 'It may be that the guilt that pleasure induces in [Benglis's] audience, because the response is not cerebral, makes her objects and objectives seem less important than those of her male contemporaries'.[26] From the pages of *Newsweek*, the arts critic Peter Plagens put it even more bluntly. Though claiming that Benglis possessed a 'nearly unerring sense of bayou beauty', the critic also believed her career to be 'marked with wrong turns: "If this, then why not this?" she seems to be constantly asking'. For Plagens, more specifically, the artist's wrong turns occurred when her work evidenced too much overt 'girlishness' or 'native craft', both characterisations tacitly pointing to the more decorative (and feminised) aspects of Benglis's art.[27]

The criticisms raised by Jinkner-Lloyd and Plagens recall many of the issues I examined in some depth in chapter 4 in relation to the critical reception of Benglis's knots. However, if such readings in the 1970s saw Benglis cutting provocatively and pleasurably across the significant stylistic and evaluative categories of the day, by 1991 her recourse to overt decorative effects was seen to be charting a more conventional aesthetic course. To be sure, Jinkner-Lloyd rightly intuited how the gender politics of contemporary visual pleasure rarely weighs in favour of the woman artist, who must always take into account the perception that her work will likely be regarded as 'less important' if it engages a decorative aesthetic. Nonetheless, and whether openly aligned with the more extreme critical positions of the day or not, both Jinkner-Lloyd's and Plagens's reviews appear to take as axiomatic the notion that the pleasure of the decorative is somehow empty or dissembling. No longer a question of good or bad taste, of campy subversion or crafty appropriation, overt aesthetic effects could only be 'merely decorative rather than profound' to recall Jinkner-Lloyd's words, or 'wrong turns', as Plagens would have it.

With the so-called 'anti-aesthetic' turn that followed in the 1980s and 1990s on the introduction of poststructuralist and psychoanalytic theories into contemporary artistic discourses, many critics and scholars rejected the decorative and the visual pleasure it potentially afforded because they perceived it to consolidate a conservative position against critical engagement and institutional change.[28] The cultural critic Fredric Jameson's 1984 article 'Postmodernism, or The Cultural Logic of Late Capitalism' (and subsequent book of the same title) was a flashpoint for arguments concerning the 'depthlessness' of visual arts and the reduction of aesthetic affect to the demands of consumer capitalism. In his 1995 essay 'Transformations of the Image in Postmodernity', Jameson revisited his initial critique, in particular singling out beauty and the decorative for reprobation: 'all beauty today is meretricious and the appeal to it by contemporary pseudo-aestheticism is an ideological manoeuvre and not a creative resource'.[29]

While anti-aesthetic positions, whether or not they followed Jameson's lead, launched invaluable attacks on the ideological biases and conservative interests of Enlightenment discourses, in their extreme forms they also acted to foreclose more measured analyses of the function and effect of the decorative in contemporary visual discourse. One consequence of this wholesale dismissal is that subsequent attempts since the 1990s to 'revive' an aesthetics of beauty have rushed to fill the gap, either through a simple inversion of values or by appealing to ahistorical notions of universal tastes.[30] Contributing to this discourse, Jeremy Gilbert-Rolfe has proffered one of the more nuanced arguments in favour of recuperating beauty and decoration in contemporary art, which he applied to Benglis's work on the occasion of a 2010 exhibition at Locks Gallery in Philadelphia. In particular, the critic singled out a cast-polyurethane relief entitled *Swinburne Egg I* (2009): a light-filled ovoid form with an effulgent pink colour and vermicular surface, the sculpture imparts a fragile beauty that immediately compelled Gilbert-Rolfe (plate 22). After pronouncing that it 'should live in a museum', he then offered that the 'decorative' constituted the work's very reason for being: it 'does not, as in the case of most of Benglis's sculpture, use the decorative to supplement and qualify the opposite of decoration. Instead it uses the decorative to intensify one's sense of decoration as the superfluous articulated, embodied and experienced as an end in itself, at least in so far as it is not there to give way to something that is not decorative'.[31]

Gilbert-Rolfe's enthusiastic assessment of *Swinburne Egg I* reflects ideas developed more fully in his book *Beauty and the Contemporary Sublime* (1999). Notably, his claim for the 'superfluous ... as an end in itself' echoes his broader contention that beauty proves significant for art simply because it requires no purpose and thus brokers no moral obligations. He writes: 'As such, beauty stands in opposition to the idea of productive thought and perhaps to the idea of production itself. ... [It] requires no explanation in the sense in which its completeness leaves nothing for the work of art to do except frame it'.[32] For Gilbert-Rolfe, the enjoyment of beauty and decoration becomes no more or less provocative or meaningful than a trip through Bloomingdale's, a conclusion that, in echoing Jameson's contention that the aesthetics of beauty has been thoroughly assimilated by market forces, nonetheless differs in finding something laudatory in this process.[33]

Gilbert-Rolfe, I believe, usefully identifies the centrality of the decorative in Benglis's sculpture. I am likewise compelled by his proposition that beauty need not be overtly productive. At the same however, this proposition effectively voids beauty of any deeper conceptual meaning or communicative function; in freeing it from the 'demands of duty',[34] and thus from any critical framework that seeks to denigrate it, the critic's transvaluation falls short of altering the hierarchical structure through which decoration is historically perceived as embodied rather than cerebral, sensual rather than intellectual, feminine rather than masculine, marginal rather than central. To be certain, Benglis's refusal of aesthetic restraint – her attraction to shiny surfaces, repetitive details, pretty colours, lush materials, and so forth – bears comparison to the commodity culture invoked by Gilbert-Rolfe's department store reference, and as I discussed in the preceding chapters, the artist has consistently engaged with popular cultural references and trends, either to raise issues of taste and vulgarity or simply because she *likes* these aesthetics. At the same time, however, Benglis does not relinquish beauty aesthetics entirely to the culture industry, as Gilbert-Rolfe does. Rather, with her work she continually explores aesthetics as an open-ended question of pleasure and displeasure, and thus as always entailing a perspective that is local, partial, and relational. Benglis's use of decorative effects is subjective, but in the sense in which the critic Dave Beech usefully characterises the possibilities of beauty: 'Beauty is political not despite the fact that it feels subjective but precisely because it feels subjective. Beauty enters us into a world of dispute, contention and conflict at the very moment when we feel ourselves to be at ease'.[35] Thinking through beauty, for Beech, occurs at the intersection of the individual and the social and, like gender or sexual identity, may be differently mobilised in ways that do not automatically presume a universalizing, naïve, or reactionary perspective.

The ovoid shape of *Swinburne Egg I* is one of three forms to which Benglis has repeatedly returned since the late 1990s, the others being hemispheres and torsos/human figures. The elemental iconicity of these forms contrasts with their intricately patterned surfaces, produced from casting moulds created by spraying coils of compressed urethane foam onto wire armatures. The formal properties of the interlaced surfaces shift depending on the material and colouration of the individual piece. While the urethane surface of *Swinburne Egg I* appears soft and congealed, that of the hemispherical cast-bronze *Pollen* (1999) looks gnarled and scarred, and the black patinated *Figure 4* (2009), flexible and velvety (fig. 53; plates 22, 23). These differences, subtle as they are, invite close looking, not least of which because they shift and transform under different ambient conditions: soft gives way to hard; rough yields to smooth; matte becomes shiny. In a 2001 review of a show at Toomey Tourell Fine Art in San Francisco, writer Kenneth Baker noted the following of Benglis: 'To activate the tension between our physical inertia and the mobility of our minds is one of her aims as a sculptor'.[36] This notion of shifting one's perceptual, imaginative, and perhaps metaphysical orientation has long been Benglis's goal. In her earliest latex and polyurethane pours, it was achieved through seemingly boundless forms and unconventional spatial orientations; in this more recent work, it occurs through a concentration of rich surface details.[37]

The relief sculptures also demonstrate how drawing has played a central role in Benglis's mature sculptural practice, but not as a preparatory step. While the modernist concept of 'drawing in space' is largely associated with the open-form, welded assemblages of Pablo Picasso, Julio Gonzales, and Anthony Caro, Benglis's approach deploys three-dimensional lines in order to activate the works' surfaces; instead of extending out into space, the lines become the skin or boundary containing the work and delimiting it from its surroundings. At the same time, however, these boundaries are permeable,

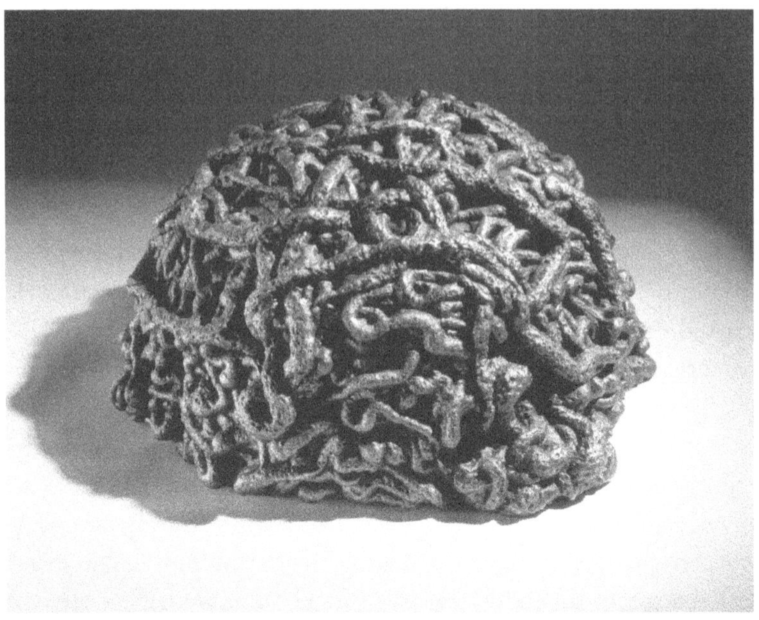

53. Lynda Benglis, *Pollen*, 1999, bronze, 11 x 5 in. (27.9 x 12.7 cm). Courtesy of the artist and Cheim & Read Gallery, New York. © Lynda Benglis/Licensed by VAGA, New York, NY.

irregular, and seemingly in constant flux. They alternately define the singularity of the form and the multiplicity of the surface. This is as much a result of the tangled coils and filaments produced by the compressed foam as it is of the fortuitous accidents of the foundry process. The topic of the following section, the passage of one medium to the next that is integral to the casting technique not only enables duplication and serial production but brings subtle changes to the surfaces of the artworks.

casting: surface processes

Metal casting has occupied a central place in Benglis's practice since the mid-1970s. One of the artist's earliest endeavours entailed five castings of the dildo used in the notorious 1974 *Artforum* ad, each implicitly dedicated but never formally given to one of the five associate editors responsible for the letter of condemnation against Benglis's ad. One of these, which the artist punningly entitled *Smile* (1974), subsequently appeared on a postcard announcing

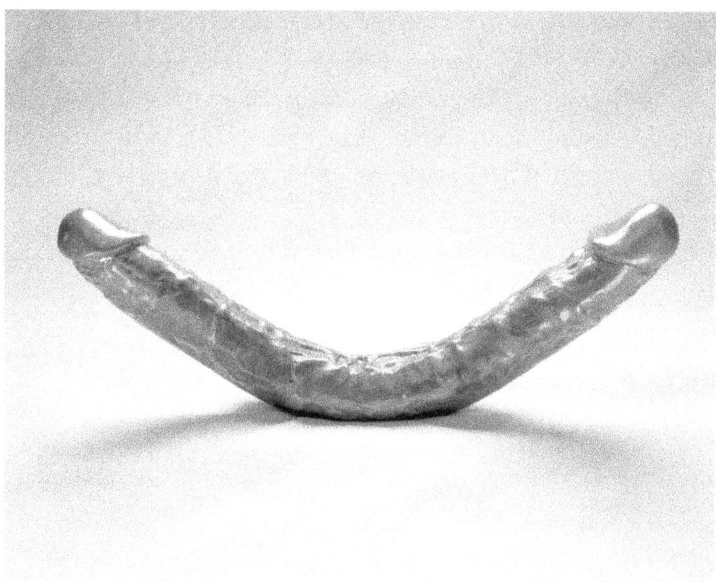

54. Lynda Benglis, *Smile*, 1974, cast bronze, 15 ½ x 6 ½ x 2 3⁄16 in. (39.4 x 16.5 x 5.7 cm). Courtesy of the artist and Cheim & Read Gallery, New York. © Lynda Benglis/Licensed by VAGA, New York, NY.

an exhibition of Benglis's knots at Texas Gallery in Houston (fig. 54). In recalling Jasper Johns's sculp-metal sculpture *The Critic Smiles* (1959), one of a group of works the older artist created in response to his negative experiences with smug critics, *Smile* reads simultaneously as the frozen, tight-lipped grimace of an annoyed critic and a coy wink and a smile by Benglis herself. Similarly, in the following year, Benglis enshrined two of the castings (in aluminium and lead) in a velvet-lined wooden box. She included the work, which she entitled *Parenthesis* (1975), in a solo exhibition at Paula Cooper Gallery along with *Primary Structures (Paula's Props).* Again playing on the curved shape of the phallic prop, *Parenthesis* seemed a significant gesture on Benglis's part, suggesting that the *Artforum* ad and its fallout were – or needed to be – relegated to a parenthetical aside in the artist's career.

In 1974–5, Benglis also cast several of her polyurethane pours, an endeavour for which a Guggenheim Memorial Foundation fellowship provided essential funding. This somewhat anachronistic turn to metal casting paralleled the work of some of her peers – Joel Shapiro's cast metal objects, for instance – while also marking an artistic engagement with the history of modern sculpture. Though many contemporary sculptors eschewed casting because of its traditional associations, artists such as Benglis and Shapiro saw in its very conventionality an opportunity to extend the working process with more lasting results. *Untitled (King of Flot)* (fig. 10), Benglis's homage to Robert Morris's process-oriented work from the late 1960s, became the lead-casted *Quartered Meteor* (1975), while several smaller unidentified pours formed the bases for two different versions each of *Modern Art Number 1*, *Eat Meat*, and *Come* (all 1969/74).

Transposing the polyurethane pours into such metals as bronze, lead, and aluminium imparted different formal qualities to the work, and as Benglis relayed to an interviewer, it made the illusion of weight in the foam pours 'literal'.[38] While the casting also gave greater permanence to the original polyurethane pieces, it did not arrest the impression of movement and flow inherent to the original poured forms, nor did it negate the work's corporeal connotations; if anything, it exaggerated it. The orange-brown patina of the cast-bronze *Come*, for instance, draws out the sexual implications of the artist's choice of verb, while the declarative *Eat Meat* forms a repugnant image as a deliquescent pile of darkly patinated bronze (plate 24). Unlike the polyurethane pours, the surface modulations of the metal versions are more pronounced, painterly even, and sensuously charged. The result of a shift in materials rather than any overt manipulations on Benglis's part, these surface effects introduce a profusion of details that, somewhat perversely, inspire closer looking – perverse because the overall sculptural forms remain vaguely repugnant. The surface incidents do not elide so much as accentuate the works' bulk and materiality. In instances in which polish and patina are in evidence, however, Benglis's cast sculptures articulate a sensibility at odds with the standard position adopted by many artists of the period. As Richard Serra pronounced, for example, 'any exaggerated emphasis on surface for the sake of itself is decadent'.[39]

During this period, Benglis also cast one of her wall-mounted cantilevered pours in aluminium. Entitled *Wing* (1970/75), it now exists as a relic of sorts for a body of non-extant work. More pointedly, the artist wanted to see the formal virtuosity of the wall pieces translated into a more opulent material; as such, the choice of shiny aluminium was one way of imagining the cantilevered form 'in silver' in effect, if not in actuality (fig. 55).[40] In many respects, *Wing* encapsulates the distance between Benglis and many of the artists with whom she has shared the labels of process and postminimal art. Consider, for instance, Serra's *Prop* series (1968–87), which consist of lead plates and tubular struts propped against the wall and held in place by weight and gravity (fig. 56). Like *Wing*, the *Props* are animated by a play of opposing

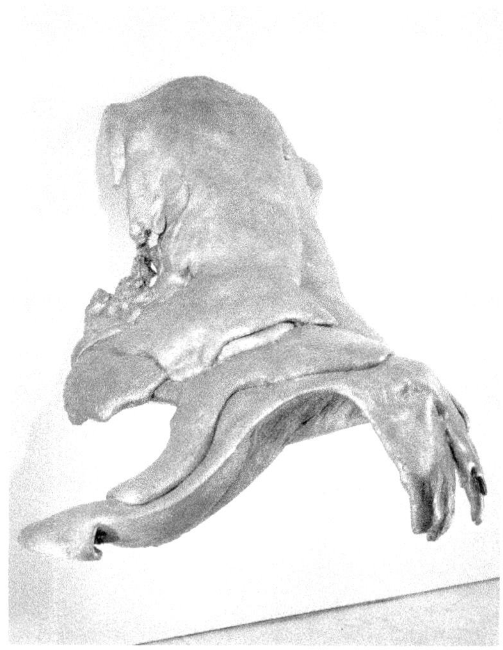

55. Lynda Benglis, *Wing*, 1970/75, cast aluminium, 67 x 59 ¼ x 60 in. (170.2 x 150.5 x 152.4 cm). Courtesy of the artist and Cheim & Read, New York. © Lynda Benglis/Licensed by VAGA, New York, NY.

forces, yet the literal mechanics of Serra's works, the precariousness of which induces a sense of unease, contrasts with the elegant and baroque illusionism of Benglis's aluminium relief, the latter held aloft as if by sheer willpower or sleight of hand. While both dramatise the viewer's encounter, *Wing* is much less aggressive and more openly theatrical in its address.

The casting of *Wing* foreshadowed a number of cantilevered bronze fountains Benglis has undertaken since the early 1980s. The first of these, *The Wave (The Wave of the World)*, was commissioned for the 1984 Louisiana World Exposition in New Orleans, the theme of which was 'The World of Rivers: Fresh Water as a Source of Life'.[41] Benglis's design, which essentially turned the biomorphic, cantilevered form on end, conveys water up and over a softly swelling arch, which she created by forming the casting mould over a weather balloon (plate 25). Like the artist's 1971 polyurethane installations, the fountain entailed considerable planning to ensure the stability and balance of the bronze form and its hydraulic component. Like the earlier work, too, the fountain engenders contradictory effects and connotations, as it seems by turns graceful and lumbering, lyrical and grotesque, sensual and vulgar.[42]

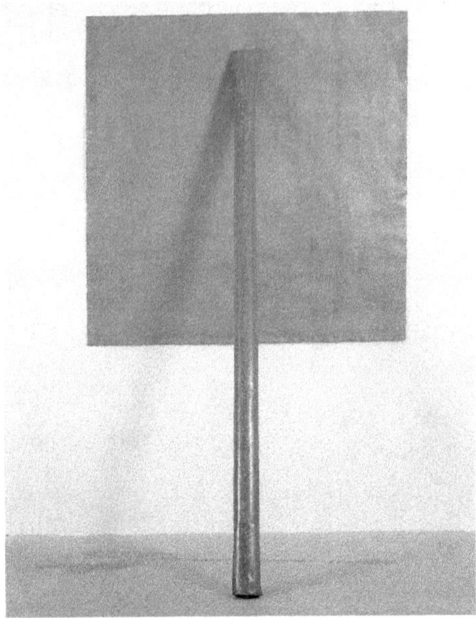

56. Richard Serra (b. 1939), *Prop*, 1968 (refabricated 2007), lead antimony and steel, overall: 89 ½ x 60 x 54 in., 1212.5lb. (227.3 x 152.4 x 137.2 cm, 550kg). Whitney Museum of American Art, New York; Purchase, with funds from the Howard and Jean Lipman Foundation, Inc. 69.20a-b. © 2011 Richard Serra/ Licensed by Artists Rights Society (ARS), New York. Photograph by Geoffrey Clements.

The added element of water underscores the impression of gestural and spontaneous process imparted by Benglis's biomorphic forms. More pointedly, the bronze component of *The Wave* appears to shift, even erode, under the effects of the water cascading up and over its variegated surface. This appearance of continual formation – and deformation – undermines the qualities of monumentality and permanence traditionally attending the history of public fountains. Significantly, it gives the impression that the process of making and unmaking is occurring in the viewer's time and space, not in some prior moment in the studio or foundry. The water element in *North South East West* conveys a similar sense of forming/unforming, as the single column of water rises between and then sprays down onto the huddled backs of the four bronze components (fig. 47).[43] Here, fluidity is literally and metaphorically conveyed through Benglis's 'frozen gestures'.

This notion of the sculptural surface as a site of continual activity in turn underscores the public, interactive nature of Benglis's fountains. When the artist envisages the water as the element that invites the viewer's participation, as she has noted to filmmaker Dermot Smyth, I believe she is speaking as much to its perceptual and affective charge as to the possibility that a viewer might literally reach in and touch the fountain.[44] The water, then, dramatises a dynamic that exists, however less overtly, in Benglis's later works as a whole, their detailed surfaces generating a compelling interplay between look and touch; it is an intensification now of surface, of skin, which nonetheless is internalised by and reverberates through the viewer's body.

an improper conclusion

The art critic Peter Schjeldahl once offered of Benglis's art that it 'invite[s] recognition, whether in the mind, at the fingertips or in the gut, of sensual feelings that might be mild or pleasant or wrenching or grotesque, but are in any case humanly true'.[45] It has been my goal throughout this book to illuminate some of the ways in which the artist's work solicits these contradictory and ambivalent sensations. More pointedly, however, I have also been concerned to with demonstrating that such feelings always have socio-historical contexts, such that to claim that anything is 'humanly true' is to say very little unless it is, to some degree, contextually and ideologically situated. Benglis's work generates highly elusive and subjective desires and associations that are nonetheless conditioned by specific socio-cultural practices of making and viewing art. Thus, throughout this book I have focused my attention on the specific word choices of other critics and art historians in order to identify some of the assumptions subtending them.

Another aim of this book has been to broaden understanding of Benglis's practice beyond accounts that tend to focus exclusively on the artist's 1974 *Artforum* ad, or conversely, on her procedural debt to Jackson Pollock. To some degree, the emphasis on these aspects of her career has functioned to keep the artist relevant to the photographic and performance-based practices and discourses that have dominated contemporary art since the 1980s; as I state in the introduction, they have secured Benglis's status as a 'bad mother' to younger generations of feminist and queer artists. Indeed, this is how I first learned of Benglis, and her legacy in this regard is not one I want to reject so much as resituate in relation to the artist's rich sculptural and video oeuvre. In turn, and in thinking about the subjective qualities of Benglis's work, I set out to articulate the potential significance of artistic process from the artist's as well as the viewer's perspective. Benglis's work, I argue throughout this book, offers up ambivalence as a means for enjoying and managing aesthetic experiences that the mainstream art world often denigrates or consigns to an inferior position.

Without a doubt, Benglis played a critical role in the re-evaluation of artistic processes and forms that occurred in the New York art world of the late 1960s. Her latex pours and polyurethane installations were indicative of the ways in which artists at the time reconceived the nature of making and viewing art. The problems that Benglis's latex pour raised for the curators of the 1969 *Anti-Illusion* exhibition at the Whitney Museum, however, were in many respects harbingers of the tendency over the years for the artist's practice to exceed art critical and curatorial frameworks. In addition to her artwork, the artist's negotiation of her identity as a 'woman artist' in the 1960s and 1970s likewise illuminates some of the ways in which Benglis both engaged with and worked against critical categories and labels. Her more recent move into the arena of craft production, and her ongoing commitment to decorative and sensuous aesthetic effects constitute yet another point of tension between the artist's multifaceted career and critical narratives of contemporary artistic production. In examining the specifics of Benglis's career, this book demonstrates how such narratives need to be opened up to further art historical assessment.

A final aim of mine has been to write as a feminist art historian on a subject who does not openly identify with feminism. My justification, if one is needed, is that questions of gender and sexuality have bearing on Benglis's practice and reception regardless of any open affiliations on my part or hers. In this regard, Benglis's ongoing flirtation with 'vulgarity' is instructive: though the term carries different inflections depending on its context, vulgarity broadly connotes an action of perceived impropriety, which is to say, it constitutes a gesture that is seen to bear an improper relationship to dominant tastes, social conventions, critical positions, and even time itself. I see the feminist problematic as integrally concerned with the 'improper', with identifying and interrogating its operations of inclusion and exclusion, and with its potential ability to trouble preconceptions. This in one of the lessons that I have taken away from Benglis's improper relation to both the mainstream art world and the contemporary feminist art movement – and one in turn that I hope to have instilled in my readers.

Notes

introduction

1. Robert Pincus-Witten, 'Lynda Benglis: The Frozen Gesture', *Artforum* 13, no. 3 (November 1974), p. 54.
2. Susan Krane, *Lynda Benglis: Dual Natures* (Atlanta, GA: High Museum of Art, 1991), p. 11.
3. The macharina snapshot was taken in 1973 when the artist was living in Los Angeles. It playfully parodies the California culture of cars and motorcycles with which a number of Benglis's male colleagues identified at the time. See Lucy R. Lippard, 'Making Up: Role-Playing and Transformation in Women's Art' (1975), reprinted in Lippard, *From the Center: Feminist Essays on Women's Art* (New York: E. P. Dutton, 1976), p. 104. The historian Sarah Schrank has also noted the similarities between Benglis's image and the artist Joe Goode's 1969 pinup calendar project, 'L.A. Artists in Their Cars', which includes snapshots of Goode, Ed Ruscha, Billy Al Bengston, Ken Price and eight other male artists posing with their vehicles. See Schrank, *Art and the City: Civic Imagination and Cultural Authority in Los Angeles* (Philadelphia: University of Pennsylvania Press, 2008), p. 133.
4. Benglis spent considerable time studying the history of female pinups before hiring Annie Leibovitz to photograph her. She, not the photographer, retains artistic control over the image.
5. In addition to the responses I discuss specifically, see John Corry, 'About New York: A Serious Dirty Picture?' *New York Times* (22 November 1974), p. 78; Annette Kuhn, 'Culture Shock', *Village Voice* (2 December 1974), p. 96; Cindy Nemser, 'Lynda Benglis – A Case of Sexual Nostalgia', *Feminist Art Journal* 3, no. 4 (Winter 1974/75), pp. 7, 23; and Dorothy Seiberling, 'The New Sexual Frankness: Goodbye to Hearts and Flowers', *New York Magazine* (17 February 1975), pp. 37–44.
6. For instance, see Brandon Taylor, *Contemporary Art: Art since 1970* (New York: Prentice Hall, 2004), p. 30; and Maria Elena Buszek, *Pin-Up Grrrls: Feminism, Sexuality, Popular Culture* (Durham, NC: Duke University Press, 2006), pp. 288–90.
7. Lawrence Alloway, Max Kozloff, Rosalind Krauss, Joseph Masheck, and Annette Michelson, 'Letter', *Artforum* 13, no. 4 (December 1974), p. 9. The sixth associate editor, Peter Plagens, wrote his own letter, also printed on p. 9.

8. By many accounts, the controversy over Benglis's ad contributed to the departure of Rosalind Krauss and Annette Michelson from *Artforum* and their subsequent establishment in 1976 of *October*. See the interviews collected in *Challenging Art: Artforum, 1962–1974*, ed. Amy Newman (New York: Soho Press, 2000), pp. 390–5, 413–23.
9. Amelia Jones, 'Postfeminism, Feminist Pleasures, and Embodied Theories of Art', in *New Feminist Criticism: Art, Identity, Action*, ed. Joanna Frueh, Cassandra Langer and Arlene Raven (New York: Icon Editions, 1994), p. 34. Jones reiterates her argument in her book *Body Art: Performing the Subject* (Minneapolis: University of Minnesota Press, 1998), p. 114.
10. Jones, 'Postfeminism', p. 34.
11. Ibid.
12. See Cindy Sherman's statement in *Lynda Benglis*, ed. Franck Gautherot, Caroline Hancock and Seungduk Kim (Dijon: Les presses du réel, 2009), p. 44; and Mike Kelley and Diedrich Diedrichsen's *Why I Got into Art: Vaseline Muses* (Cologne: Galerie Jablonka, 1991).
13. Joanna Frueh, 'The Body Through Women's Eyes,' in *The Power of Feminist Art: The American Movement of the 1970s, History and Impact*, ed. Norma Broude and Mary Garrard (New York: Abrams, 1994), p. 194. For an analysis of Benglis's ad as a popular icon of contemporary feminist art, see Susan Richmond, 'Sizing Up The Dildo: Lynda Benglis' *Artforum* Advertisement as a Feminist Icon', *n.paradoxa: international feminist art journal*, no. 15 (2005), pp. 24–34.
14. A handful of exhibitions showcased this art in Britain and the United States, including the 1993 *Bad Girls* at London's Institute of Contemporary Art and the 1994 *Bad Girls* and *Bad Girls West* at the New Museum in New York and the UCLA Wight Art Gallery, respectively.
15. Marcia Tanner, 'Mother Laughed: The Bad Girls' Avant-Garde', in *Bad Girls*, ed. Marcia Tucker (Cambridge, MA: MIT Press, 1994), p. 74.
16. Barbara Pollack, 'Letter on Good Girls, Bad Girls and Bad Boys' (1991), reprinted in *Meaning: An Anthology of Artists' Writings, Theory and Criticism*, ed. Susan Bee and Mira Schor (Durham, NC: Duke University Press, 2000), p. 50. For an extensive critique of the US *Bad Girls* exhibitions, see Laura Cottingham, *How Many 'Bad' Feminists Does It Take to Screw in a Lightbulb?* (New York: Sixty Percent Solution, 1994).
17. Jones, 'Postfeminism', p. 34; and Mira Schor, 'Representations of the Penis' (1988), reprinted in Schor, *Wet: On Painting, Feminism, and Art Culture* (Durham, NC: Duke University Press, 1997), p. 24. Fueling speculation about a possible romantic entanglement between the two artists, Morris and Benglis had previously exchanged videotapes of material shot in their studios; they also created a series of provocative Polaroid pictures together in which they are seen posing, along with the artist Ray Johnson, with the two-headed dildo. These photos were exhibited in 1975 at the Kitchen in New York, and again in the 2009–11 travelling retrospective, *Lynda Benglis*.

18. Barbara Rose in *Challenging Art*, p. 417. Also see comments by John Coplans and Rosalind Krauss, p. 415.
19. Benglis in *Challenging Art*, p. 415. Morris and Benglis agree that they discussed doing their respective projects with each other, but did not undertake them together, in 'Collage', *Art News* 73, no. 7 (September 1974), p. 44.
20. Irit Rogoff, 'Gossip as Testimony: A Postmodern Signature', in *Generations and Geographies in the Visual Arts: Feminist Readings*, ed. Griselda Pollock (London: Routledge, 1996), p. 82.
21. Ibid., p. 84.
22. Also see Buszek, *Pin-Up Grrrls*, p. 290. Interestingly, Jones notes in *Body Art* that Benglis objected to such a 'personal' reading and requested that the author not include a reproduction of the *Artforum* ad in that book (p. 287 n. 39).
23. Benglis in France Morin, 'Lynda Benglis in Conversation with France Morin', *Parachute* no. 6 (Spring 1977), p. 10.
24. Mary Kelly, 'Reviewing Modernist Criticism', *Screen* 22, no. 3 (1981), pp. 41–62.
25. Griselda Pollock, 'Feminism and Modernism', in *Framing Feminism: Art and the Women's Movement, 1970–1985*, ed. Rozsika Parker and Griselda Pollock (London: Pandora Press, 1987), p. 93.
26. For instance, see Griselda Pollock, 'Artists, Mythologies and Media – Genius, Madness and Art History', *Screen* 21, no. 3 (1980), pp. 57–96.
27. Amy Ingrid Schlegel, 'Codex Spero: Rethinking the Monograph as a Feminist', in *Singular Women: Writing the Artist*, ed. Kristen Frederickson and Sarah E. Webb (Berkeley: University of California Press, 2003), pp. 200–12. Schlegel notes that a thematic approach potentially avoids the pitfalls of hagiography as well as the impulse to construct a monograph 'like a submarine – streamlined, airtight, a microcosm unto itself' (p. 204).
28. Ibid., p. 203.

chapter 1

1. S. R. Dubrowin, 'Latex: One Artist's Raw Material', *Rubber Developments* 24, no. 1 (1971), p. 11.
2. Robert Pincus-Witten initially coined the term 'post-minimalism' in the late 1960s and subsequently expanded on it in *Postminimalism into Maximalism: American Art, 1966–1986* (Ann Arbor, MI: UMI Research Press, 1987); 'anti form' is associated with Robert Morris's 1968 essay bearing that title, which I discuss at length in this chapter.
3. Benglis in *Art in Process IV*, ed. Elayne Varian (New York: Finch College Museum of Art, 1969), n.p.
4. For instance, see Jeanne Siegel, 'Lynda Benglis, Jackson Pollock and Process', *ARTI* 34 (May–June 1997), pp. 75–82; Amelia Jones, *Body Art: Performing the*

Subject (Minneapolis: University of Minnesota Press, 1998), pp. 96–7; and Judith Tannenbaum, 'Lynda Benglis: Clandestine Performer', in *Lynda Benglis*, ed. Franck Gautherot, Caroline Hancock and Seungduk Kim (Dijon: Les presses du réel, 2009), pp. 104–24. The performative nature of her practice is also implied through the juxtaposition of photographs of Benglis creating a latex pour in 1969 and artist Janine Antoni performing *Loving Care* (1993), in Cornelia Butler, 'Art and feminism: an ideology of shifting criteria', in *WACK! Art and the Feminist Revolution*, ed. Butler (Los Angeles, CA: Museum of Contemporary Art, 2007), p. 18.

5. Susan Krane also argues for the need to address the 'object quality' of Benglis's art, in *Lynda Benglis: Dual Natures*, ed. Krane (Atlanta, GA: High Museum of Art, 1991), p. 13.
6. Benglis discusses Hesse's work in 'Interview: Linda [*sic*] Benglis', *Ocular* 4, no. 2 (Summer 1979), p. 36.
7. Benglis in *Art in Process IV*, n.p.
8. Benglis, quoted in Robert Pincus-Witten, 'Lynda Benglis: The Frozen Gesture', *Artforum* 13, no. 3 (November 1974), p. 57.
9. Benglis, quoted in Dubrowin, 'Latex', p. 12.
10. Peter Schjeldahl, 'Chronicles: New York Letter', *Art International* 13, no. 7 (September 1969), p. 72.
11. James Monte in *Anti-Illusion: Procedure/Materials*, ed. James Monte and Marcia Tucker (New York: Whitney Museum of American Art, 1969), p. 17.
12. Robert Morris, 'Anti Form', *Artforum* 6, no. 8 (April 1968), pp. 34–5.
13. Benglis, quoted in Vivien Raynor, 'The Art of Survival (and Vice Versa)', *New York Times Magazine* (17 February 1974), p. 50. For a similar account, see Carter Ratcliff, *Fate of a Gesture: Jackson Pollock and Postwar American Art* (New York: Farrar, Straus, and Giroux, 1996), p. 151.
14. Marcia Tucker, *A Short Life of Trouble: Forty Years in the New York Art World*, ed. Liza Lou (Berkeley: University of California Press, 2008), p. 84.
15. A Polaroid photograph in the *Anti-Illusion: Procedures/Materials* exhibition files at the Whitney Museum of American Art, New York, shows the installation of *Contraband* in progress.
16. Tucker in *Anti-Illusion*, p. 28. Since it was a last-minute decision, there does not appear to be any paperwork in the museum archives documenting Benglis's withdrawal.
17. Curator Caroline Hancock calls Benglis's latex pour a premonition of the health hazards of plastics. She refers to the film *Blue Vinyl* (directed by Judith Helfand and Daniel B. Gold, 2002), which documents the petrochemical pollution affecting the southern United States, including Benglis's childhood home of Lake Charles, Louisiana. See Hancock, 'Medusa in Ecstasy', in *Lynda Benglis*, ed. Gautherot, Hancock, and Kim, p. 139.
18. Benglis, quoted in Raynor, 'The Art of Survival', p. 50.
19. David Bourdon, 'Fling, Dribble and Dip', *Life* (27 February 1970), p. 62. Many authors incorrectly cite the essay's title as 'Fling, Dribble and Drip'.

20. Richard Serra in 'Richard Serra's Urban Sculpture: An Interview by Douglas Crimp' (1980), reprinted in Serra, *Writings/Interviews* (Chicago: University of Chicago Press, 1994), p. 129.
21. Benglis, quoted in Dubrowin, 'Latex', p. 11.
22. Benglis in an interview with Robert James Coad, in *Between Painting and Sculpture: A Study of the Work and Working Process of Lynda Benglis, Elizabeth Murray, Judy Pfaff and Gary Stephan* (Ann Arbor, MI: UMI Dissertation Information Service, 1988), p. 243.
23. Serra has noted that a 1969 set of photographs (taken by Gianfranco Gorgoni) documenting the creation of a lead splash in Leo Castelli's warehouse in New York gives the impression of expressive spontaneity, when in fact it took seven days to complete the project. See 'Interview by Peter Eisenmann' (1983), reprinted in Serra, *Writings/Interviews*, p. 148.
24. Robert Morris, 'Notes on Sculpture, Part IV: Beyond Objects', *Artforum* 7, no. 8 (April 1969), p. 54.
25. Schjeldahl, 'Chronicles: New York Letter', p. 72.
26. Emily Wasserman, 'Reviews: New York', *Artforum* 8, no. 1 (September 1969), p. 59; Klaus Kertess, 'Foam Structures', *Art and Artists* 7, no. 2 (May 1972), p. 33; Benglis has repeatedly cited Louisiana bayous as a reference point for her pours, and 'Contraband' is the name of one located near Lake Charles; for her comment about planets, see 'Interview with Lynda Benglis', in *The Context of Art, the Art of Context*, ed. Seth Sieglaub, Marion Fricke, and Roswitha Fricke (Trieste: Navado Press, 2004), p. 65.
27. Benglis in 'Interview with Lynda Benglis', *The Context of Art*, p. 65.
28. Peter Hutchinson, 'Mannerism in the Abstract' (1966), reprinted in *Minimal Art: A Critical Anthology*, ed. Gregory Battcock (New York: E. P. Dutton, 1968), pp. 187–94; quotes from pp. 187 and 194.
29. Wasserman, 'Reviews', pp. 59–60.
30. Benglis in 'Lynda Benglis: Interview by Ned Rifkin', in *Early Work: Lynda Benglis, Joan Brown, Luis Jimenez, Gary Stephan, Lawrence Weiner*, ed. Lynn Gumpert, Ned Rifkin, and Marcia Tucker (New York: New Museum, 1982), p. 11.
31. Benglis describes her technique in Jan Butterfield, 'Poured Art: Sculptor Reveals Technique, Approach to Style', *Fort Worth Star-Telegram* (14 June 1970), p. 6.
32. Benglis, quoted in Douglas Davis, 'The Invisible Woman is Visible', *Newsweek* (15 November 1971), pp. 130–1.
33. Roland Barthes, *Mythologies*, trans. Annette Lavers (New York: Hill and Wang, 1972), pp. 97–9.
34. Jeffrey Meikle provides a useful overview of the artistic use of plastics in the 1960s in *American Plastic: A Cultural History* (New Brunswick, NJ: Rutgers University Press, 1995), pp. 231–41.
35. Robert Pincus-Witten, 'Reviews: New York', *Artforum* 8, no. 5 (January 1970), p. 69.

36. For instance, these issues are touched on in Jean-Louis Bourgeois, 'Reviews: New York', *Artforum* 8, no. 8 (April 1970), p. 82.
37. Proprioception, which relies on bodily cues and is often called the 'sixth sense', is a sensory feedback mechanism tied to feelings of muscle tone, balance and equilibrium, and perceptions of physical effort.
38. Benglis in France Morin, 'Lynda Benglis in Conversation with France Morin', *Parachute*, no. 6 (Spring 1977), p. 9.
39. Jean Baudrillard, 'The Precession of Simulacra', in *Simulations*, trans. Paul Foss, Paul Patton, and Philip Beitchman (New York: Semiotexte, 1983), pp. 1–75.
40. Benglis cast this work in lead in 1975, entitling it *Quartered Meteor*. See my discussion in chapter 5.
41. Benglis in 'Lynda Benglis: Interview by Ned Rifkin', p. 11.
42. Benglis in 'Interview: Linda [*sic*] Benglis', p. 40.
43. Andre publicly refuted the idea that *Lever* could consist of more or fewer bricks in a letter to the editor, in *Artforum* 14, no. 9 (May 1976), p. 9.
44. Andre, quoted in David Bourdon, 'The Razed Sites of Carl Andre' (1966), reprinted in *Minimal Art*, p. 104.
45. For a comprehensive discussion of the *informe*, see Yve-Alain Bois and Rosalind Krauss, *Formless: A User's Guide* (New York: Zone Books, 1997). Despite its formless qualities, Benglis's work is not cited in this text.
46. Benglis, quoted in Raynor, 'The Art of Survival', p. 50.
47. *Phantom* was partially re-created for the 2009–11 travelling exhibition *Lynda Benglis*.
48. For instance, see Robert Pincus-Witten, 'Reviews: New York', *Artforum* 10, no. 4 (December 1971), p. 78; and Alfred Frankenstein, 'From Foam to Wax', *San Francisco Chronicle* (12 February 1972), p. 35.
49. Grace Glueck, 'New York: Trendless But Varied, The Season Starts', *Art in America* 59, no. 5 (September–October 1971), p. 122; and Hilton Kramer, 'Grace, Flexibility, Esthetic Tact', *New York Times* (30 May 1971), p. D19.
50. Kertess, 'Foam Structures', p. 35.
51. Benglis broached such connections in an interview with Susan Krane. See Krane, *Lynda Benglis*, p. 57 n. 40.
52. Martin Friedman has recently recounted that he was initially concerned that some of the artists invited to participate in the *New Works for New Spaces* exhibition would withdraw as a form of protest over the Vietnam War. See Friedman, 'Up Against the Wall with Lynda Benglis', *Art in America* 97, no. 11 (December 2009), p. 109.
53. Benglis also used phosphorescent salts in *Phantom*.
54. Skowhegan Lecture Archives (Benglis, 1978), Ernest G. Welch School of Art and Design, Georgia State University, Atlanta.
55. Krane, *Lynda Benglis*, p. 29.
56. In the late 1960s, Chrysler began to offer High Impact Paint in a range of bright rainbow colours.

57. Kertess, 'Foam Structures', p. 37. He provides thorough descriptions of all of Benglis's large-scale polyurethane projects.
58. Davis, 'The Invisible Woman is Visible', p. 130.
59. *Helen Frankenthaler*, Whitney Museum of American Art, New York, 20 February–6 April 1969; exhibition catalogue by E. C. Goossen.
60. Krane, *Lynda Benglis*, p. 25.
61. Anne Wagner posits Benglis as a likely inheritor of Frankenthaler's formal innovations in 'Pollock's Nature, Frankenthaler's Culture', in *Jackson Pollock: New Approaches*, ed. Kirk Varnedoe and Pepe Karmel (New York: Museum of Modern Art and Abrams, 1999), p. 196.
62. For example, Harold Rosenberg accused Frankenthaler of passivity and of failing to grasp 'the moral and metaphysical basis of action painting'. See Rosenberg, 'Art and Words', in *The De-definition of Art* (New York: Horizon Press, 1972), p. 64. A number of scholars, including Anne Wagner, have recently restored Frankenthaler's importance to postwar art. See, for instance, Lisa Saltzman, 'Reconsidering the Stain: On Gender and the Body in Helen Frankenthaler's Painting' in *Reclaiming Female Agency: Feminist Art History after Postmodernism*, ed. Norma Broude and Mary D. Garrard (Berkeley: University of California Press, 2005), pp. 372–83; and Alison Rowley, *Helen Frankenthaler: Painting History, Writing Painting* (London: I.B.Tauris, 2007).
63. Linda Nochlin, 'Why Have There Been No Great Women Artists?' *Art News* 69, no. 9 (January 1971), p. 22.
64. In addition to Benglis, the respondents were Eleanor Antin, Rosemarie Castoro, Rosalyn Drexler, Suzi Gablik, Elaine de Kooning, Louise Nevelson, and Marjorie Strider.
65. Louise Nevelson, 'Do Your Work', in 'Eight Artists Reply: Why Have There Been No Great Women Artists?' *Art News* 69, no. 9 (January 1971), p. 43.
66. Suzi Gablik, 'The Double Bind', in 'Eight Artists Reply', p. 45.
67. Benglis, 'Social Conditions Can Change', in 'Eight Artists Reply', p. 43.

chapter 2

1. Benglis in *Art in Process IV*, ed. Elayne Varian (New York: Finch College Museum of Art, 1969), n.p.
2. Gail Stavitsky, 'Waxing Poetic: Encaustic Art in America during the Twentieth Century', in *Waxing Poetic: Encaustic Art in America*, ed. Gail Stavitsky (Montclair, NJ: Montclair Art Museum, 1999), pp. 23–5.
3. Benglis in 'Lynda Benglis: Interview by Ned Rifkin', in *Early Work: Lynda Benglis, Joan Brown, Luis Jimenez, Gary Stephan, Lawrence Weiner*, ed. Lynn Gumpert, Ned Rifkin, and Marcia Tucker (New York: New Museum, 1982), p. 9.
4. 'Zip' is Newman's own term for the thin vertical elements in his work.

5. Newman, quoted in Gabrielle Schor, *The Prints of Barnett Newman, 1961–1969* (Ostfildern: Hatje Cantz, 1996), p. 23. *The Moment* forms part of an edition of prints entitled *Four on Plexiglas* to which Philip Guston, Claes Oldenburg, and Larry Rivers also contributed. Unfortunately, the qualities that Benglis admired in Newman's work do not translate well in reproduction.
6. Benglis knew the artist Dan Flavin and was familiar with his 1962 series of *Icons*, which consist of monochromatic paintings affixed with lightbulbs and fluorescent tubes.
7. Stavitsky, 'Waxing Poetic', p. 55.
8. Benglis developed her own encaustic recipe after consulting the formulas suggested in Ralph Mayer's well-known reference book, *The Artist's Handbook of Materials and Techniques*, originally published in 1940.
9. Benglis destroyed a number of these works, burning them in order to keep warm in her unheated studio. See 'Lynda Benglis: Interview by Ned Rifkin', p. 10.
10. Helen Molesworth, 'Lynda Benglis', in *Part Object Part Sculpture*, ed. Helen Molesworth (College Park: Pennsylvania State University Press, 2005), p. 173.
11. Susan Krane, *Lynda Benglis: Dual Natures* (Atlanta, GA: High Museum of Art, 1991), p. 32.
12. Philip Larson, *Painting: New Options* (Minneapolis, MN: Walker Art Center, 1972), p. 10; and Miles Beller, 'Albuquerque, Arnoldi, Benglis, Castoro, Steir', *Artweek* 7, no. 31 (18 September 1976), p. 3.
13. Klaus Kertess, 'Foam Structures', *Art and Artists* 7, no. 2 (May 1972), p. 33. Benglis and Kertess were professionally and romantically involved in the early 1970s.
14. For instance, bundi (or boondi) ladoo is a fried Indian dessert made from chickpeas.
15. Kertess, 'Foam Structures', p. 33.
16. Benglis in Karen Edwards, 'The Interview/99: Lynda Benglis', *Sunday Herald* (13 June 1971), p. 2:11.
17. Donald Judd, 'Specific Objects' (1965), reprinted in *Donald Judd: Complete Writings, 1959–1975* (Halifax and New York: Press of the Nova Scotia College of Art and Design and New York University Press, 1975), pp. 181–9.
18. For example, see Judd, 'Lee Bontecou' (1965), reprinted in ibid., pp. 178–80.
19. *Eccentric Abstraction* also included work by Alice Adams, Gary Kuehn, Don Potts, Keith Sonnier, and Frank Lincoln Viner.
20. Lucy R. Lippard, *Eccentric Abstraction* (New York: Fischbach Gallery, 1966), exhibition pamphlet, n.p.
21. Lucy R. Lippard, 'Eccentric abstraction', *Art International* 10, no. 9 (November 1966), pp. 28, 34.
22. Ibid., p. 39.
23. Mignon Nixon, *Fantastic Reality: Louise Bourgeois and a Story of Modern Art* (Cambridge, MA: MIT Press, 2005), p. 188.
24. Lippard, 'The Women Artists' Movement – What Next?' (1975), reprinted in Lippard, *From the Center: Feminist Essays on Women's Art* (New York: E. P. Dutton, 1976), p. 148.

25. Chicago and Schapiro co-authored an article in which they spelled out ideas they had been promoting for several years regarding the connection between body symbology and the visual expression of uniquely female experiences. See Judy Chicago and Miriam Schapiro, 'Female Imagery', *Womanspace Journal* 1, no. 3 (June 1973), pp. 11–14.
26. Ibid., p. 11.
27. Lippard, 'Prefaces to Catalogues of Women's Exhibition (Three Parts)' (1971–5), reprinted in Lippard, *From the Center*, p. 49.
28. Lippard never reviewed Benglis's encaustic paintings during this period; however, she included a reproduction of one, entitled *Grey* (1972), in *From the Center*, p. 72.
29. Benglis, quoted in Robert Pincus-Witten, 'Lynda Benglis: The Frozen Gesture', *Artforum* 13, no. 3 (November 1974), p. 55. Although this comment was made in specific reference to her encaustic paintings, both Benglis and others have subsequently extended the masturbatory trope to all her work.
30. Though Benglis did not have this in mind when she proffered her masturbatory comment, her words resonate with the French philosopher Luce Irigaray's assertion that 'woman "touches herself" all the time' since her genitals are 'formed of two lips in continuous contact'. See Irigaray, *This Sex Which Is Not One*, trans. Catherine Porter, ed. Carolyn Burke (Ithaca, NY: Cornell University Press, 1985), p. 24.
31. Griselda Pollock, 'Mary Kelly's *Ballad of Kastriot Rexhepi*: Virtual Trauma and Indexical Witness in the Age of Mediatic Spectacle', *Parallax* 10, no. 1 (2004), p. 110; Amelia Jones, *Body Art: Performing the Subject* (Minneapolis: University of Minnesota Press, 1998), p. 50.
32. Benglis, quoted in Pincus-Witten, 'Lynda Benglis', p. 55.
33. Benglis in France Morin, 'Lynda Benglis in Conversation with France Morin', *Parachute*, no. 6 (Spring 1977), p. 9.
34. Paula Webster, 'The Forbidden: Eroticism and Taboo', in *Pleasure and Danger: Exploring Female Sexuality*, ed. Carole S. Vance (London: Pandora Press, 1989), p. 385. In the 1970s, a number of feminist publications promoted the benefits of female sexual self-stimulation, including the Boston Women's Health Book Collective, *Our Bodies, Ourselves* (1973); Betty Dodson, *Liberating Masturbation* (1974); and Shere Hite, *The Hite Report* (1976).
35. Semmel, quoted in Dorothy Seiberling, 'The Female View of Erotica', *New York Magazine* (11 February 1974), p. 55.
36. Marsha Meskimmon, *The Art of Reflection: Women Artists' Self-Portraiture in the Twentieth Century* (New York: Columbia University Press, 1996), p. 7.
37. Judy Chicago in 'Judy Chicago, Talking to Lucy R. Lippard' (1974), reprinted in Lippard, *From the Center*, pp. 216–17.
38. Benglis, quoted in Pincus-Witten, 'Lynda Benglis', p. 58.
39. The scholarly literature on the gendering of artistic identity in postwar American art is extensive and ever growing; many authors have fruitfully reexamined the underlying anxieties that contributed to the masculinist discourse, the structures

through which it was maintained, and those instances in which it broke down or gave way to alternative narratives. In addition to the authors I discuss here, see Marcia Brennan, *Modernism's Masculine Subjects* (Cambridge, MA: MIT Press, 2005); Ann Gibson, *Abstract Expressionism: Other Politics* (New Haven, CT: Yale University Press, 1997); and Michael Leja, *Reframing Abstract Expressionism* (New Haven, CT: Yale University Press, 1993).

40. Roland Barthes, *Mythologies*, trans. Annette Lavers (New York: Hill and Wang, 1972), p. 127.
41. Julia Bryan-Wilson, *Art Workers: Radical Practice in the Vietnam War Era* (Berkeley: University of California Press, 2009), p. 89. Also see Anna Chave's astute analysis of gender politics in 'Minimalism and the Rhetoric of Power', *Arts Magazine* 64, no. 5 (January 1990), pp. 44–63.
42. Peter Plagens, cited in Bryan-Wilson, *Art Workers*, pp. 88–9. Plagens's review originally appeared in *Artforum* 8, no. 8 (April 1970), p. 86.
43. Jones, *Body Art*, p. 145. Though she does not discuss Benglis's encaustic paintings in this context, Jones characterises the artist's 1974 *Artforum* project and her latex pours of the late 1960s as instances in which the performing female body radically disrupts the coherence of modern masculinist selfhood.
44. See Acconci's description in Judith Kirshner, *Vito Acconci: A Retrospective, 1969–1980* (Chicago: Museum of Contemporary Art, 1980), p. 17. For equivocal reviews of *Seedbed*, see Denise Wolmer, 'In the Galleries', *Arts Magazine* 46, no. 7 (March 1972), p. 58; and Peter Schjeldahl, 'Vito Acconci at Sonnabend', *Art in America* 60, no. 2 (March–April 1972), p. 119.
45. Jones, *Body Art*, p. 105. Conversely, Acconci's performance may be said to reinforce the scholar Christine Battersby's contention that in the legacy handed down from the Romantic era, the great artist is always-already 'a *feminine male*'. See Battersby, *Gender and Genius: Towards a Feminist Aesthetic* (Bloomington: Indiana University Press, 1989), p. 4.
46. Patricia Waugh, *Feminine Fictions: Revisiting the Postmodern* (London: Taylor and Francis, 1989), pp. 12–13.
47. Jones, *Body Art*, p. 14.
48. 'The Two in the One' is a chapter heading in the Jungian analyst June Singer's widely read book *Androgyny: Toward a New Theory of Sexuality* (New York: Doubleday, 1976).
49. Tracy Hargreaves, *Androgyny in Modern Literature* (London: Palgrave, 2005), p. 3.
50. See *Collected Works of Plato*, trans. Benjamin Jowett (Oxford: Oxford University Press, 1953), pp. 520–5.
51. See Ovid, *Metamorphosis*, trans. Mary M. Innes (New York: Penguin, 1955), pp. 102–4.
52. Kari Weil usefully examines the rhetorical distinction between androgyny and hermaphroditism in *Androgyny and the Denial of Difference* (Charlottesville: University Press of Virginia, 1992).

53. Jung's concept of androgyny is loosely informed by a broad range of cultural traditions and belief systems, including Gnosticism, alchemy, Freudian psychoanalysis, and Taoism. Jung discusses the anima/animus of the collective unconscious in a number of contexts, including 'The Psychology of the Child Archetype', in *The Archetypes and the Collective Unconscious*, trans. R. F. C. Hull (Princeton, NJ: Princeton University Press, 1981), pp. 151–81.
54. Carolyn Heilbrun, *Toward a Recognition of Androgyny* (New York: Knopf, 1973), pp. x–xi.
55. Gayle Rubin, 'The Traffic in Women: Notes on the "Political Economy" of Sex', in *Toward an Anthropology of Women*, ed. Rayna R. Reiter (New York: Monthly Review Press, 1975), p. 204.
56. For example, see Robert Knott, 'The Myth of the Androgyne', *Artforum* 14, no. 3 (November 1975), pp. 38–45; Whitney Chadwick, 'Eros or Thanatos, the Surrealist Cult of Love Reexamined', *Artforum* 14, no. 3 (November 1975), pp. 46–56; Cindy Nemser, 'Four Artists of Sensuality', *Arts Magazine* 49, no. 7 (March 1975), pp. 73–5; and Michael Bonesteel, 'Art and the New Androgyny', *New Art Examiner* 6, no. 10 (Summer 1979), pp. 9, 11.
57. Bonesteel, 'Art and the New Androgyny', p. 9.
58. Wilke, quoted in Lynda Crawford, 'Women in the Erotic Arts', *Viva* 1, no. 4 (January 1974), p. 78.
59. Wilke in Chris Huestis and Marvin Jones, 'Hannah Wilke's Art, Politics, Religion, and Feminism', *The New Common Good* (May 1985), p. 1.
60. Saundra Goldman, *'Too Good Lookin' to Be Smart': Beauty, Performance and the Art of Hannah Wilke* (Ann Arbor, MI: UMI Dissertation Information Service, 2000), p. 27.
61. Eleanor Antin, 'An Autobiography of the Artist as an Autobiographer', *LAICA Journal*, no. 2 (October 1974), p. 20. Antin's reference to 'core images' should not be confused with Chicago and Schapiro's promotion of 'central-core imagery', an altogether different concept.
62. Barbara Charlesworth Gelpi, 'The Politics of Androgyny', *Women's Studies* 2, no. 2 (1974), pp. 151–60; Cynthia Secor, 'Androgyny: An Early Reappraisal', *Women's Studies* 2, no. 2 (1974), pp. 161–70.
63. Daniel Harris, 'Androgyny: The Sexist Myth in Disguise', *Women's Studies* 2, no. 2 (1974), pp. 171–84; Catharine Stimpson, 'The Androgyne and the Homosexual', *Women's Studies* 2, no. 2 (1974), pp. 237–48.
64. Mary Daly, *Gyn/Ecology: The Metaethics of Radical Feminism* (Boston: Beacon Press, 1990), p. 387.
65. Feminist and queer scholars continue to doubt androgyny's theoretical viability. For instance, in *Female Masculinity* (Durham, NC: Duke University Press, 1998), Judith Halberstam rejects the concept on the grounds that it 'always returns us to [a] humanist vision of the balanced binary in which maleness and femaleness are in complete accord' (p. 215).

66. Marjorie Garber, *Vice Versa: Bisexuality and the Eroticism of Everyday Life* (New York: Simon and Schuster, 1995), p. 233. Specifically, Garber aligns bad androgyny with bisexuality.
67. Hargreaves, *Androgyny in Modern Literature*, p. 67.
68. Francette Pacteau, 'The Impossible Referent: Representations of the Androgyne', in *Formations of Fantasy*, ed. Victor Burgin, James Donald and Cora Kaplan (New York: Methuen, 1986), pp. 77, 68. Pacteau considers androgyny to constitute a fantasy stemming from a repressed desire for a pre-oedipal state of undifferentiation.
69. Molesworth, 'Lynda Benglis', p. 173.
70. Anne M. Wagner, *Three Artists (Three Women): Modernism and the Art of Hesse, Krasner, and O'Keeffe* (Berkeley: University of California Press, 1996), pp. 272–3.
71. Ibid., p. 281.
72. Elisabeth Lebovici arrives at a similar conclusion, though argued differently, when noting that Benglis's work 'is not limited to the female identity of the artist nor to content or form but it operates to destabalise matter, or rather matters of aesthetics'. See Lebovici, 'Lynda Benglis: All that Matters ...', in *Lynda Benglis*, ed. Franck Gautherot, Caroline Hancock, and Seungduk Kim (Dijon: Les presses du réel, 2009), p. 100.
73. Though beyond the scope of this chapter, the dualism invoked in the two-brushstroke paintings bears affinity to Hélène Cixous's concept of an 'other bisexuality', which allows for the coexistence of the other in the self in a non-exclusive and non-deterministic manner. See Cixous, 'Sorties', in Hélène Cixous and Catherine Clément, *The Newly Born Woman*, trans. Betsy Wing (Manchester: Manchester University Press, 1986), esp. pp. 83–5.
74. Benglis in Morin, 'Lynda Benglis in Conversation with France Morin', p. 10.
75. Benglis, quoted in Sandy Ballatore, 'Lynda Benglis' Humanism', *Artweek* 7, no. 21 (22 May 1976), p. 6.

chapter 3

1. Benglis, quoted in *Video Art: An Anthology*, ed. Ira Schneider and Beryl Korot (New York: Harcourt Brace Jovanovich, 1976), p. 23.
2. Benglis's videos are distributed through Video Data Bank (www.vdb.org) and Electronic Arts Intermix (www.eai.org).
3. Benglis, quoted in Robert Pincus-Witten, 'Lynda Benglis: The Frozen Gesture', *Artforum* 13, no. 3 (November 1974), p. 58.
4. Ibid.
5. In addition to Tuttle, *Noise* features Gordon Hart, Robert Israel, Roberta Smith, and John Torreano.
6. Bruce Kurtz, 'Video is Being Invented', *Arts Magazine* 47, no. 3 (December–January 1973), p. 40.

7. I agree with Jayne Wark's contention that it is likely Kertess signifies a voice of authority in the art world, an authority that is asserted but also undermined by Benglis's video manipulations. See Wark, *Radical Gestures: Feminism and Performance Art in North America* (Montreal: McGill-Queen's University Press, 2006), p. 102.
8. Kurtz, 'Video is Being Invented', p. 40.
9. See Marshall McLuhan, *Understanding Media: The Extensions of Man* (Cambridge, MA: MIT Press, 1994), pp. 308–37.
10. See, for example, Laura U. Marks, *The Skin of Film: Intercultural Cinema, Embodiment, and the Senses* (Durham, NC: Duke University Press, 2000); and Amelia Jones, *Self/Image: Technology, Representation, and the Contemporary Subject* (London: Routledge, 2006), esp. chap. 4.
11. David Antin, 'Television: Video's Frightful Parent, Part 1', *Artforum* 14, no. 4 (December 1975), p. 38.
12. Samuel Weber, 'Television: Set and Screen,' in *Mass Mediauras: Forms, Technics, Media*, ed. Alan Cholodenko (Stanford, CA: Stanford University Press, 1996), p. 124.
13. Ibid., pp. 115, 117.
14. For instance, Bruce Boice characterises Benglis's work as 'boring, interesting and funny'. See Boice, 'Reviews: Lynda Benglis at Paula Cooper Gallery', *Artforum* 11, no. 9 (May 1973), p. 83.
15. Anne M. Wagner, 'Performance, Video, and the Rhetoric of Presence', *October* 91 (Winter 2000), pp. 69, 80.
16. Benglis's alterations to the photograph of her own face recall Marcel Duchamp's famous assisted ready-made, *LHOOQ* (1919), in which the French artist added a moustache and goatee to a postcard of the Mona Lisa. This reference to Duchamp's male and female alter egos likewise recalls Benglis's own investigation into androgyny at this time, discussed in chapter 2.
17. Rosalind Krauss, 'Video: The Aesthetics of Narcissism', *October* 1 (Spring 1976), p. 55.
18. Ibid., p. 59.
19. Lucy R. Lippard, 'The Pains and Pleasures of Rebirth: European and American Women's Body Art' (1976), reprinted in Lippard, *From the Center: Feminist Essays on Women's Art* (New York: E. P. Dutton, 1976), p. 126.
20. Stuart Marshall, 'Video Art, The Imaginary, and the Parole Vide', *Studio International* 191, no. 981 (May–June 1976), pp. 244–5.
21. Jeff Perrone, 'The Ins and Outs of Video', *Artforum* 14, no. 10 (June 1976), p. 55. In addition to Benglis's video work, Perrone refers to the sexuality in Bruce Nauman's *Manipulating a Fluorescent Tube* (1969), Douglas Davis's *The Austrian Tapes* (1974), and Nam June Paik's *TV Penis* (1972).
22. Ibid.
23. Lippard, 'The Pains and Pleasures of Rebirth', in *From the Center*, p. 125.
24. Semmel, quoted in Jamaica Kincaid, 'Erotica', *Ms.* (January 1975), p. 30.

25. For feminist-inflected critiques of Benglis's narcissism, see Micki McGee, 'Narcissism, Feminism and Video Art: Some Solutions to a Problem of Representation', *Heresies*, no. 12 (1981), pp. 88–91; and Cindy Nemser, 'Four Artists of Sensuality', *Arts Magazine* 49, no. 7 (March 1975), p. 74.
26. The video's colour has degraded over time to a bland, pinkish tonality.
27. Chris Straayer, 'Sexuality and Video Narrative', *Afterimage* 16, no. 10 (May 1989), p. 9.
28. Ibid., p. 8.
29. Amelia Jones, 'Interpreting Feminist Bodies: The Unframeability of Desire', in *The Rhetoric of the Frame: Beyond the Boundaries of the Framework*, ed. Paul Duro (Cambridge: Cambridge University Press, 1996), p. 223.
30. Wagner, 'Performance, Video, and the Rhetoric of Presence', p. 80.
31. See Judy Chicago and Miriam Schapiro, 'Female Imagery', *Womanspace Journal* 1, no. 3 (June 1973), pp. 11–14; and Patricia Mainardi and Janet Sawyer, 'A Feminine Sensibility? Two Views', *Feminist Art Journal* 1, no. 1 (April 1972), pp. 4, 25.
32. Linda Hutcheon, *A Theory of Parody: The Teachings of Twentieth-Century Art Forms* (New York: Methuen, 1985), p. 7.
33. Ibid., p. 63. Hutcheon uses the term 'bouncing' on p. 32.
34. Benglis uses the phrase 'visually sculpting' in an unpublished interview with Susan Krane (29 October 1989), transcript in *Lynda Benglis: Dual Natures* exhibition files, High Museum of Art, Atlanta, GA. Several minutes into *Female Sensibility*, there is a brief audio segment inserted between the radio programmes in which Benglis is heard taking on the phone about an upcoming sculpture show. This track reinforces her identity as a successful sculptor while simultaneously onscreen the artist stages an erotic 'sculptural' show with Lenkowksy.
35. 'Unskirting the Issue', *Art-Rite*, no. 2 (Summer 1974), pp. 6–7. *Art-Rite* was self-published by Edit DeAk and Walter Robinson between 1973 and 1978. The other respondents to 'Unskirting' were Laurie Anderson, Judy Chicago, Abigail Gerd, Nancy Graves, Joan Jonas, Agnes Martin, Lee Krasner, Sylvia Sleigh, Sylvia Stone, May Wilson, and Hannah Wilke. Chicago notes in her *Art-Rite* statement that a shared sensibility lies in making women's lives the subject matter of the art, though this subject matter is 'filtered through historic time, place and style' (p. 6). This deviates slightly from her promotion of central-core imagery as a universal and latent content of women's art.
36. Benglis in ibid., p. 6. Nonetheless, the feminist art critic Cindy Nemser repeated the quotation as evidence of Benglis's retrograde and anti-feminist agenda: 'What [Benglis] does not understand, and [feminists] do, is that women who are liberated do not primarily want to please'. See Nemser, 'Lynda Benglis – A Case of Sexual Nostalgia', *Feminist Art Journal* 3, no. 4 (Winter 1974–75), p. 23. Lucy Lippard likewise saw it as an example of how women were still conditioned by their psychological oppression to think of their sexuality in terms of pleasing others. See Lippard, 'Fragments', *From the Center*, p. 73.

37. Harmony Hammond, *Lesbian Art in America: A Contemporary History* (New York: Rizzoli, 2000), pp. 23–5.
38. Barbara Rose, 'Vaginal Iconology', *New York Magazine* (11 February 1974), p. 59. At this time, the adjective 'vaginal' was used more frequently to describe female body imagery than the more anatomically correct 'labial' or 'vulvic'.
39. Robert Pincus-Witten, 'Benglis's Videos: Medium to Media', in *Physical and Psychological Moments in Time: A First Retrospective of the Video Work of Lynda Benglis* (Oneonta, NY: Fine Arts Center Gallery, SUNY, 1975), n.p.
40. Katie King, 'The Situation of Lesbianism as Feminism's Magical Sign: Contests for Meaning and the US Women's Movement, 1968–1972', *Communications* 9 (1986), pp. 65–91.
41. For instance, see Sidney Abbott and Barbara Love, *Sappho Was a Right-On Woman: A Liberated View of Lesbianism* (New York: Stein and Day, 1972).
42. Radicalesbians, 'The Woman-Identified Woman', in *Notes from the Third Year: Women's Liberation*, ed. Shulamith Firestone and Anne Koedt (New York: Notes from the Second Year, 1971), p. 81.
43. Benglis, unpublished interview with Susan Krane (29 October 1989), transcript in *Lynda Benglis: Dual Natures* exhibition files.
44. Benglis has never revealed whether she engaged in a lesbian relationship during this time, however the point I am making is that her video should not be read as autobiographical.
45. Early filmmakers also utilised such scenes because they could elude censorship by producing explicit acts that did not feature penetration by an erect penis. See Linda Williams, *Hard Core: Power, Pleasure and the 'Frenzy of the Visible'* (Berkeley: University of California Press, 1989), p. 97.
46. Stephen Ziplow, *The Film Maker's Guide to Pornography* (New York: Drake, 1977), p. 31, cited in ibid., p. 127.
47. See Ralph Blumenthal, 'Porno Chic: "Hard Core" Grows Fashionable and Very Profitable', *New York Times Magazine* (21 January 1973), pp. 28–34.
48. Although Nora Ephron notes that not seeing *Deep Throat* seemed 'derelict', she was also highly critical of its treatment of women, as was Ellen Willis, who found the film 'exploitative'. See Ephron, 'Women', *Esquire* (February 1973), pp. 14, 22; and Willis, '*Deep Throat:* Hard to Swallow', *New York Review of Books* (25 January 1973), p. 22.
49. It is my argument here not that mainstream pornography forecloses the possibility of female viewing pleasure, but only that that genre is predominantly produced for and marketed to male heterosexual spectators.
50. Kaye is best known for his films *Georg* (1964) and *Brandy in the Wilderness* (1968).
51. Carrie Przybilla, 'Synopses of Videotapes', in *Lynda Benglis: Dual Natures*, ed. Susan Krane (Atlanta, GA: High Museum of Art, 1991), p. 111.
52. Other artists in residence at Artpark in the summer of 1976 appear in the video, including Pat Oleszko, Jim Roche, and Ree Morton (to whom the video is dedicated, following her untimely death in 1977 from an automobile accident).

53. Benglis in 'Interview: Linda [*sic*] Benglis', *Ocular* 4, no. 2 (Summer 1979), p. 35.
54. Benglis and Kaye in *Artpark: The Program in Visual Arts*, ed. Sharon Edelman (Lewiston, NY: Artpark, 1976), p. 138.
55. In 1993, Benglis used a photograph of Bow Wow to re-create the double-page layout of her 1974 dildo ad for an exhibition in book form entitled *Sex-Quake: Art After the Apocalypse* (New York: 1st Art-Genes Portable Museum, 1993). The recreation is also reproduced in *Lynda Benglis*, ed. Franck Gautherot, Caroline Hancock and Seungduk Kim (Dijon: Les presses du réel, 2009), pp. 102–3.
56. While these strategies have become a significant component of contemporary feminist and queer artistic practices, Benglis's videos uniquely anticipate them, laying the groundwork for younger artists ranging from Cheryl Donegan to Wynne Greenwood and Ryan Trecartin.

chapter 4

1. John Perreault, 'Celebrations Knotted and Dotted', *Village Voice* (16 May 1974), p. 44.
2. Benglis, quoted in Robert Pincus-Witten, 'Lynda Benglis: The Frozen Gesture', *Artforum* 13, no. 3 (November 1974), p. 55.
3. Benglis's collection of African art includes a Bamana Ntomo mask from Mali, Yoruba Ibeji twin figures, and a wooden dance mask from Western Cameroon. Of Gorchov, Benglis recently shared with an interviewer that she was drawn to his mark-making, and the manner in which he applied colour to his shaped canvases. See 'Lynda Benglis with Phong Bui', *Brooklyn Rail* (December 2009), http://www.brooklynrail.org/2009/12/art/lynda-benglis-with-phong-bui (accessed 15 March 2011).
4. With roots in European and African dance traditions, hoofing evolved on street corners and vaudeville stages before hitting its peak of popularity in the 1930s in Broadway and Hollywood musicals. See Richard Kislan, *Hoofing on Broadway: A History of Show Dancing* (New York: Prentice Hall, 1987).
5. Susan Krane, *Lynda Benglis: Dual Natures* (Atlanta, GA: High Museum of Art, 1991), p. 33.
6. Ann Daly, *Critical Gestures: Writings on Dance and Culture* (Middletown, CT: Wesleyan University Press, 2002), p. 312.
7. The film theorist Richard Dyer notes in *Only Entertainment* (New York: Routledge, 1992) that much of the subversive or utopian appeal of disdained forms of popular entertainment such as pantomime, musicals, burlesque, and cabaret occurs at the level of nonrepresentational signs, that is to say, through 'colour, texture, movement, rhythm, melody, camerawork' (p. 20).
8. Benglis, quoted in Krane, *Lynda Benglis*, p. 34.
9. The serial nature of the knots is now largely lost, as individual works have entered different collections. Originally, however, their group installation captured

Benglis's systematic exploration of the knotted motif in all its seemingly infinite mutations.

10. Cecile N. McCann, 'Linda [*sic*] Benglis: Dimensional Paintings', *Artweek* 4, no. 20 (19 May 1973), p. 3.
11. Benglis, quoted in Krane, *Lynda Benglis*, p. 33.
12. Benglis in France Morin, 'Lynda Benglis in Conversation with France Morin', *Parachute*, no. 6 (Spring 1977), p. 11.
13. Caroline Hancock suggests that the alphabetic names may have originated as a playful reference to the critic Barbara Rose's 1965 description of minimal and systemic works as 'ABC art' in an article of that title in *Art in America* 53, no. 5 (October–November 1965), pp. 57–69. See Hancock, 'Medusa in Ecstasy', in *Lynda Benglis*, ed. Franck Gautherot, Caroline Hancock and Seungduk Kim (Dijon: Les presses du réel, 2009), p. 140. This is a compelling suggestion, especially given Benglis's response to minimalism in her 1975 installation *Primary Structures (Paula's Props)*, discussed in the following pages.
14. For example, Benglis notes that a knot entitled *India* captures the lightness of the word when spoken. See Skowhegan Lecture Archives (Benglis, 1978), Ernest G. Welch School of Art and Design, Georgia State University, Atlanta. *India* is reproduced in *Lynda Benglis*, ed. Gautherot, Hancock and Kim, p. 292.
15. Perreault, 'Celebrations Knotted and Dotted', p. 44.
16. Peter Schjeldahl, 'Updated Data on the Adventure of being Human', *New York Times* (26 May 1974), p. D17.
17. Ann-Sargent Wooster, 'Reviews: Lynda Benglis at Paula Cooper', *Art in America* 62, no. 5 (September–October 1974), p. 106. Wooster's reference to schizophrenia may be an allusion to R. D. Laing's *Knots* (1970), a widely read pop psychology study of the mental impasses, or 'knots', that impede personal relationships.
18. Tom Wolfe's 'The Kandy-Kolored Tangerine-Flake Streamline Baby' was originally published in 1963 in *Esquire* and was reprinted in 1965 in an anthology of Wolfe's writings of the same title.
19. Pincus-Witten, 'Lynda Benglis', p. 59.
20. The art critic Peter Plagens usefully describes the LA Look as 'cool, semi-technological, industrially pretty art made in and around Los Angeles in the sixties by Larry Bell, Craig Kauffman, Ed Ruscha, Billy Al Bengston, Kenneth Price, John McCracken, Peter Alexander, DeWain Valentine, Robert Irwin, and Joe Goode, among others. The patented "look" was elegance and simplicity, and the material was plastic, including polyester resin, which has several attractions: permanence (indoors), an aura of difficulty and technical expertise, and a preciousness (when polished) rivalling bronze or marble'. See Plagens, *Sunshine Muse: Art on the West Coast, 1945–1970* (Berkeley: University of California Press, 1974), pp. 120–1.
21. Francis Colpitt, 'The Optimistic Object: LA art in the 1960s', in *Finish Fetish: L.A.'s Cool School*, ed. Frances Colpitt (Los Angeles: Fisher Gallery, University of Southern California, 1991), p. 7.

22. Barbara Rose, 'Los Angeles: The Second City', *Art in America* 54, no. 1 (January–February 1966), p. 114.
23. For instance, a 1964 Ferus Gallery exhibition poster publicising 'The Studs' features the names of Ed Moses, Ken Price, Robert Irwin, and Billy Al Bengston.
24. Laura Hoptman uses this phrase to describe the liquid metal surface of Benglis's knots, in 'For the Amusement of a Goddess', in *Lynda Benglis*, ed. Gautherot, Hancock and Kim, p. 230.
25. Artist's conversation with author, 29 May 2009, Santa Fe, NM.
26. Pincus-Witten, 'Lynda Benglis', p. 59.
27. Jane Livingston, 'East meets West... again... and again', in *Shift: LA/NY*, ed. Paul Schimmel (Newport Beach, CA: Newport Harbor Art Museum, 1982), p. 16.
28. Krane, *Lynda Benglis*, p. 48.
29. Thomas Albright, 'Three Major US Artists', *San Francisco Chronicle* (22 May 1973), p. 45.
30. Krane, *Lynda Benglis*, p. 35.
31. Judith L. Goldstein, 'The Female Aesthetic Community', *Poetics Today* 14, no. 1 (Spring 1993), p. 150.
32. Benglis's gallery announcement pointedly illustrates the gendered associations of cosmetics, regardless of whether the term is used to refer specifically to the use of makeup or more generally to any form of decorative alteration or addition. Such associations could operate independently of the gender of the artist. For example, John Chamberlain once characterised the applied colour in his sculptural work as 'flashy like lipstick or eyeshadow or something for a girl. Whatever people put on as colours, they put on so that somebody sees it'. Chamberlain was speaking specifically about his 1969 *Penthouse* series of resin-coated paper bag sculptures. See Phyllis Tuchman, 'An Interview with John Chamberlain', *Artforum* 10, no. 6 (February 1972), p. 40.
33. For an announcement card for the Clocktower show, Benglis used a 1952 childhood photograph of herself dressed in an evzone costume, the traditional uniform of the Greek soldier; the previous July she had used the same image to announce an exhibition at Jack Glenn Gallery in Corona Del Mar, Newport Beach, California. Benglis related the flounced cotton costume to the fabric-covered knots in both shows. The evzone photograph was also a precursor to the artist's 1974 sexual mockeries.
34. Krane, *Lynda Benglis*, p. 33.
35. Jeremy Gilbert-Rolfe, 'Reviews: Lynda Benglis, the Clocktower', *Artforum* 12, no. 6 (March 1974), pp. 69–70.
36. On a related note, Benglis has also compared her sparkle knots to the wilted floral wreaths adorning Greek houses at the end of May Day celebrations. See Krane, *Lynda Benglis*, p. 34.
37. The references to quipu and Chinese knotting appear in *American Artists '76: A Celebration* (San Antonio, TX: Marion Koogler McNay Art Institute, 1976), n.p. The reference to crocheting appears in *Modern Odysseys: Greek American Artists of*

the 20th Century, ed. Peter Selz and William Valerio (New York: Queens Museum of Art, 1999), p. 30.

38. As the scholar Peter Wollen has pointed out, the exotic, the ornamental, the decorative, the handmade, the historical, and the theatrical are lumped together as an 'other' inferior to modernist art and aesthetics. See Wollen, *Raiding the Icebox: Reflections of Twentieth-Century Culture* (Bloomington: Indiana University Press, 1993), pp. 1–34.
39. Hammond came out as a lesbian around the time she produced the *Floorpieces*. See Julia Bryan-Wilson, 'Queerly Made: Harmony Hammond's *Floorpieces*', *Journal of Modern Craft* 2, no. 1 (March 2009), p. 65.
40. Although Schapiro and Melissa Meyer write that 'femmage' refers to 'activities as they were practiced by women using traditional women's techniques to achieve their art – sewing, piecing, hooking, cutting, appliquéing, cooking and the like – activities also engaged in by men but assigned in history to women', they also outline fourteen criteria, at least half of which a work of art must meet to be considered femmage. See Schapiro and Meyer, 'Waste Not/Want Not: An Inquiry Into What Women Saved and Assembled', *Heresies*, no. 4 (Winter 1978), pp. 66–9.
41. For a 1977 exhibition at the New Orleans Museum of Art, Benglis collaborated with her former teacher Ida Kohlmeyer on a project entitled *Louisiana Prop Piece* (1977), which she subsequently called 'a super interior decoration job' (Skowhegan Lecture Archives). It involved an installation in the foyer of the museum of large papier-mâché heads from Mardi Gras floats. For a description and illustration of the project, see Krane, *Lynda Benglis*, p. 47.
42. At the time, many critics failed to identify Hammond's *Floorpieces* as art. For instance, Susan Heinemann claimed that they were 'too small and decorative to read as anything more than the rugs, which, in fact, they are.... Hammond's rugs don't even try to extend one's awareness of art; they seem to be involved with design and craftsmanship, problems of related decorative art and furniture'. See Heinemann, 'Review', *Artforum* 12, no. 6 (March 1974), p. 80.
43. Goldstein, 'The Female Aesthetic Community', p. 145.
44. Andreas Huyssen, *After the Great Divide: Modernism, Mass Culture, Postmodernism* (Bloomington: Indiana University Press, 1986), p. 47.
45. Tania Modleski, *Feminism without Women: Culture and Criticism in a 'Postfeminist' Age* (New York: Routledge, 1991), pp. 23–4.
46. Clement Greenberg, 'The Plight of Our Culture' (1953), reprinted in Greenberg, *The Collected Essays and Criticism, Volume 3: Affirmations and Refusals, 1950–1956*, ed. John O'Brian (Chicago: University of Chicago Press, 1993), p. 138. Also see Dwight Macdonald, 'Masscult and midcult' (1960), reprinted in Macdonald, *Against the American Grain*: *Essays on the Effects of Mass Culture* (New York: Random House, 1962), pp. 3–75.
47. For analyses of the feminine middlebrow in the US context, see Joan Shelley Rubin, *The Making of Middlebrow Culture* (Chapel Hill: University of North Carolina

Press, 1992); and Janice Radway, *A Feeling for Books: The Book-of-the-Month Club, Literary Taste, and Middle-Class Desire* (Chapel Hill: University of North Carolina Press, 1999).

48. Clement Greenberg, 'The Present Prospects in American Painting and Sculpture' (1947), reprinted in Greenberg, *The Collected Essays and Criticism, Volume 2: Arrogant Purpose, 1945–1949*, ed. John O'Brian (Chicago: University of Chicago Press, 1986), pp. 161–2. Greenberg's analysis is more nuanced than my choice of quotations suggests. The proliferation of middlebrow taste was double edged for the critic: on the one hand, the economic expansion of the middle class gave more Americans the means and inclination to pursue cultural pastimes and to become patrons of the arts, both essential to the survival of high culture; on the other hand, under capitalism, genuine culture investment and lasting aesthetic standards would always lose out to industrial standardization and market-driven novelty.
49. For a sustained analysis of the relation among decoration, craft, and femininity in Greenberg's writings, see Elissa Auther, 'The Decorative, Abstraction, and the Hierarchy of Art and Craft in the Art Criticism of Clement Greenberg', *Oxford Art Journal* 27, no. 3 (2004), pp. 341–64.
50. T. J. Clark, *Farewell to an Idea: Episodes from a History of Modernism* (New Haven, CT: Yale University Press, 2001), p. 397. Clark clarifies that his argument for the petty bourgeois vulgarity of the work does not extend to artistic intentionality: 'It was what Hofmann did, not what he discovered' (p. 400).
51. Radway notes in *A Feeling for Books* that while middlebrow culture 'defined itself, first, against academic ways of seeing', it also constituted a counter-practice to 'high cultural tastes and proclivities' (p. 9).
52. Shelley Nickles, 'More is Better: Mass Consumption, Gender, and Class Identity in Postwar America', *American Quarterly* 54, no. 4 (December 2002), pp. 581–622. Nickles suggests not that such tastes are inherent to working-class women but rather that they are fostered by a combination of material and social values that persist in spite of economic upward mobility.
53. In particular, Molesworth demonstrates how the work of Mary Heilmann, Joan Snyder, and Howardena Pindell invited critiques of vulgarity in 'Painting with Ambivalence', in *WACK! Art and the Feminist Revolution*, ed. Cornelia Butler (Los Angeles, CA: Museum of Contemporary Art, 2007), pp. 429–39.
54. Thomas Albright, 'Primarily Biological', *Art News* 78, no. 6 (Summer 1979), pp. 156–8.
55. Maureen Mullarkey, 'Dishing it Out: Judy Chicago's *Dinner Party*', *Commonweal* 108, no. 7 (April 1981), pp. 210–11; and Clara Weyergraf, 'The Holy Alliance: Populism and Feminism', *October* 16 (Spring 1981), pp. 23–4.
56. For an excellent overview of the circumstances surrounding both the production and reception of *The Dinner Party*, including feminist responses to Chicago's project, see the collection of essays in *Sexual Politics: Judy Chicago's "Dinner Party"*

in Feminist Art History, ed. Amelia Jones (Los Angeles, CA: Armand Hammer Museum of Art, UCLA, 1996).

57. Lucy R. Lippard, 'Making Something from Nothing (Toward a Definition of Women's "Hobby Art")', *Heresies*, no. 4 (Winter 1978), p. 63.
58. Glenn Adamson, *Thinking through Craft* (Oxford: Berg, 2007), p. 140.
59. Julia Bryan-Wilson, *Art Workers: Radical Practice in the Vietnam War Era* (Berkeley: University of California Press, 2009), p. 168.
60. Lippard, 'Making Something from Nothing', p. 65. Her description of the craft book *Feather Flowers and Arrangements* appears on p. 63.
61. Benglis in Seungduk Kim, 'Liquid Metal', in *Lynda Benglis*, ed. Gautherot, Hancock, and Kim, p. 175.
62. The critic Hilton Kramer accused Benglis of 'trafficking in [the] shopworn language of kitsch' with *Primary Structures (Paula's Props)*, in 'What Happens When Art is Confused with Publicity', *New York Times* (23 November 1975), p. D25.
63. Susan Sontag, 'Notes on Camp' (1964), reprinted in Sontag, *Against Interpretation and Other Essays* (New York: Noonday Press, 1965), p. 287.
64. The literature on camp is extensive, as are the critiques of Sontag's initial attempt to define it. For a useful starting place, see the collection of essays in *Camp: Queer Aesthetics and the Performing Subject: A Reader*, ed. Fabio Cleto (Edinburgh: Edinburgh University Press, 1999).
65. Sontag, "Notes on Camp', pp. 275, 280, 292.
66. See Andrew Ross, *No Respect: Intellectuals and Popular Culture* (New York: Routledge, 1989), pp. 135–70.
67. Ibid., p. 139. Ross also writes that camp's indulgence in bad taste entails a 'rediscovery of history's waste' (p. 151).
68. Donald Kuspit, 'Cosmetic Transcendentalism: Surface-Light in John Torreano, Rodney Ripps and Lynda Benglis', *Artforum* 18, no. 2 (October 1979), p. 38.
69. Julia Bryan-Wilson makes a related but distinct claim about Harmony Hammond's *Floorpieces*. In 'Queerly Made', she reads the burlesque or camp quality of Hammond's work as a 'queering' of the category of domestic craft and of the hybrid aesthetic position that craft occupies in modern artistic discourse.
70. Sontag, 'Notes on Camp', p. 291.
71. Andrew Ross states it more bluntly in *No Respect*: 'The fun and pleasure created by camp is often only enjoyed at the expense of others, and this is largely because camp's excess of pleasure, finally, has little to do with the (un)controlled hedonism of a consumer; it is the result of the (hard) *work* of a producer of taste, and "taste" is only possible through exclusion *and* depreciation' (p. 153).
72. My interest in connecting camp with a feminine middlebrow aesthetic has benefitted tremendously from the literary scholar Nicola Humble's work on women's interwar fiction in England. She posits, for example, that a camp sensibility is inherent in middlebrow fiction and the reading culture surrounding it. See Humble, 'The Queer Pleasures of Reading: Camp and the Middlebrow', *Working Papers on the Web*

11 (July 2008), http://extra.shu.ac.uk/wpw/middlebrow/Humble.html (accessed 10 January 2011).

73. Robertson points out that contemporary debates over camp have focused overwhelmingly on gay men's relationship to female culture, thus excluding women who 'are objects of camp and subject to it but are not camp subjects'. See Robertson, *Guilty Pleasures: Feminist Camp from Mae West to Madonna* (Durham, NC: Duke University Press, 1996), p. 5.
74. See Rita Felski, 'Nothing to Declare: Identity, Shame, and the Lower Middle Class', *PMLA* 115, no. 1 (January 2000), pp. 33–46.

chapter 5

1. *Lynda Benglis*, Van Abbemuseum, Eindhoven, 20 June–4 October 2009. It subsequently travelled to the Irish Museum of Modern Art, Dublin; Le Consortium, centre d'art contemporain, Dijon; Museum of Art, Rhode Island School of Art and Design, Providence; New Museum, New York; and the Museum of Contemporary Art, Los Angeles. See *Lynda Benglis*, ed. Franck Gautherot, Caroline Hancock, and Seungduk Kim (Dijon: Les presses du réel, 2009).
2. Ann Landi, 'Getting Paint off the Wall', *Art News* 109, no. 8 (September 2010), p. 85.
3. Benglis in conversation with Boston-based filmmaker Dermot Smyth, n.d. Smyth is currently completing a film on Benglis and the installation of *North South East West*. I am extremely grateful to him for sharing film footage and conversation with me.
4. As an eleven-year-old child and again as a young woman, Benglis travelled with her paternal grandmother to mainland Greece and to the family's ancestral home on the Greek island of Megisti (now Kastelorizo).
5. *Patang* is still in the collection of the Atlanta airport, but no longer on view. It has faded considerably and the Airport Art Program has no immediate plans to conserve or reinstall it. E-mail correspondence with Katherine Dirga, Airport Art Program manager, 20 May 2011.
6. On the importance of Matisse and textiles to P&D artists, see *Pattern and Decoration: An Ideal Vision in American Art, 1975–1985*, ed. Anne Swartz (Yonkers, NY: Hudson River Museum, 2007).
7. Matthew Kangas, 'Metamorphosis: Glass Sculptures by Lynda Benglis', *Glass: The UrbanGlass Quarterly*, no. 82 (Spring 2001), p. 22.
8. Paula Owen, 'Labels, Lingo, and Legacy: Crafts at a Crossroads', in *Objects and Meaning: New Perspectives on Art and Craft*, ed. M. Anna Fariello and Paula Owen (Lanham, MD: Scarecrow Press, 2004), p. 24; Glenn Adamson, *Thinking through Craft* (Oxford: Berg, 2007), p. 4.
9. M. Anna Fariello, 'Making and Naming: The Lexicon of Studio Craft', in *Extra/Ordinary: Craft and Contemporary Art*, ed. Maria Elena Buszek (Durham, NC: Duke University Press, 2011), p. 40.

10. Elissa Auther, *String, Felt, Thread: The Hierarchy of Art and Craft in American Art* (Minneapolis: University of Minnesota Press, 2010), esp. pp. 87–92.
11. As a reflection of this, perhaps, Benglis chose not to include any of her glassworks in the 1991 travelling retrospective *Lynda Benglis: Dual Natures*, at the time considering them secondary to her larger practice. See Amy Jinkner-Lloyd, 'Materials Girl: Lynda Benglis in Atlanta', *Arts Magazine* 65, no. 9 (May 1991), p. 55.
12. Paula Owen, 'Fabrication and Encounter: When Content Is a Verb', in *Extra/Ordinary*, p. 93.
13. Julian Kreimer, 'Shape Shifter: Lynda Benglis', *Art in America* 97, no. 11 (December 2009), p. 96; Andrew Bogle, 'From the Furnace', in *Lynda Benglis: From the Furnace*, ed. Priscilla Pitts (Auckland, NZ: Auckland City Art Gallery, 1993), p. 8.
14. Benglis in Marina Cashdan, 'Time and Tide', *Frieze*, no. 134 (October 2010), p. 218.
15. See *Glass: Material Matters*, ed. Howard Fox and Sarah Nichols (Los Angeles, CA: Los Angeles County Museum of Art, 2006).
16. Benglis, quoted in Kangas, 'Metamorphosis', p. 25.
17. Martha Drexler Lynn covers these points in *Sculpture, Glass and American Museums* (Philadelphia: University of Pennsylvania Press, 2005), p. 16.
18. 'Flocculent' is Roland Barthes' description of plastic in *Mythologies*, trans. Annette Lavers (New York: Hill and Wang, 1972). He writes: 'It is a "shaped" substance: whatever its final state, plastic keeps a flocculent appearance, something opaque, creamy and curdled, something powerless ever to achieve the triumphant smoothness of Nature' (p. 98).
19. While there is no consensus on the topic, some artists and scholars have proposed that functionality is a distinctive virtue of craft that needs to be maintained. See, for instance, John Perreault, 'Crafts Is Art: Tampering with Power', in *Objects and Meaning*, pp. 68–85; esp. p. 77; and Howard Risatti, *A Theory of Craft: Function and Aesthetic Expression* (Chapel Hill: University of North Carolina Press, 2007).
20. These objects can be viewed at www.eatitworld.com.
21. Benglis in Robert James Coad, *Between Painting and Sculpture: A Study of the Work and Working Process of Lynda Benglis, Elizabeth Murray, Judy Pfaff and Gary Stephan* (Ann Arbor, MI: UMI Dissertation Information Service, 1988), p. 247. Also see Susan Krane, *Lynda Benglis: Dual Natures* (Atlanta, GA: High Museum of Art, 1991), p. 50. Benglis saw the stele fragment in the 1979 exhibition of Aegean art, *Mer Egée, Grèce des Isles*, which originated at the Louvre before travelling to the Metropolitan Museum of Art under the title *Greek Art of the Aegean Islands*.
22. From 1977 to 1980, the world price of gold more than quadrupled, the sharp increase a result of a series of events unfolding since the early 1970s, including the oil crisis, the American defeat in Vietnam, and growing political unrest in the Mideast by the decade's end. Daily gold prices since 1970 are available at: http://www.usagold.com/reference/prices/history.html (accessed 3 March 2011).
23. Benglis discusses the issue of value in conversation with Seungduk Kim in 'Liquid Metal', in *Lynda Benglis*, ed. Gautherot, Hancock, and Kim, pp. 181–4.

24. Krane, *Lynda Benglis*, p. 54.
25. Ibid., pp. 52, 53.
26. Amy Jinkner-Lloyd, 'Materials Girl', p. 55. Marcia E. Vetrocq makes a similar point in 'Knots, Glitter and Funk', *Art in America* 9, no. 12 (December 1991), p. 94.
27. Peter Plagens, 'Objects of Affection', *Newsweek* (3 June 1991), p. 68.
28. The anti-aesthetic position is certainly more nuanced than my brief account allows. Nonetheless, it is often associated with the perspectives articulated in the anthology, *The Anti-Aesthetic: Essays on Postmodern Culture*, ed. Hal Foster (Port Townsend, WA: Bay Press, 1983). Though Foster does not discuss Benglis specifically, her work would probably constitute what he distinguishes as a 'reactive' rather than a 'resistant' mode of postmodernism (p. xii). Laura Mulvey's 'Visual Pleasure and Narrative Cinema', *Screen* 16, no. 3 (1975), pp. 6–18, was also an important catalyst for feminist theories of gendered spectatorship and critiques against visual pleasure in women's art in the 1980s and 1990s.
29. Fredric Jameson, 'Transformations of the Image in Postmodernity', in, *The Cultural Turn: Selected Writings on the Postmodern, 1983–1998* (London: Verso, 1998), p. 135. He also writes that 'The aesthetics of postmodernism generally can be characterized ... as the displacement of various modernist claims to "sublimity" by more modest and decorative practices in which sensory beauty is once again the heart of the matter' (p. 123).
30. The aforementioned quote by Jameson is targeted at the critical recuperation of beauty in the early 1990s. While the literature is wide ranging, frequently cited texts that advocate for beauty in contemporary art include: Dave Hickey, *The Invisible Dragon: Four Essays on Beauty* (Los Angeles, CA: Art Issues Press, 1993); Arthur C. Danto, *The Abuse of Beauty: Aesthetics and the Concept of Art* (Peru, IL: Open Court, 2003); and Wendy Steiner, *Venus in Exile: The Rejection of Beauty in Twentieth-Century Art* (Chicago: University of Chicago Press, 2001). Briefly, Hickey advocates the populist appeal of beauty and contrasts it with the elitism of the art establishment. Conversely, Danto proposes that beauty is a necessary condition for life, yet it has moral limitations and thus seems more suited to 'an era of taste' rather than 'an era of meaning' (pp. 6–7). Wendy Steiner reclaims the essential femininity of beauty from its status as secondary to the masculine sublime. Since none of these authors discusses Benglis's work in these contexts, they fall outside the scope of this chapter. However, Dave Hickey did write an essay on the artist's early work for the 2009 catalogue, *Lynda Benglis*, ed. Gautherot, Hancock, and Kim ('A House Built in a Body: Lynda Benglis's Early Work', pp. 10–21).
31. Jeremy Gilbert-Rolfe, 'Consistently Exciting', in *Lynda Benglis: Flow and Flesh* (Philadelphia: Locks Art Publications, 2010), pp. 13, 14.
32. Jeremy Gilbert-Rolfe, *Beauty and the Contemporary Sublime* (New York: Allworth Press, 1999), pp. 69, 73.
33. Gilbert-Rolfe, 'Consistently Exciting', p. 13.

34. Gilbert-Rolfe, *Beauty and the Contemporary Sublime*, p. 146.
35. Dave Beech, introduction to *Beauty*, ed. Dave Beech (Cambridge, MA: MIT Press, 2009), p. 17.
36. Kenneth Baker, 'Grimaces that have no faces', *San Francisco Chronicle* (10 March 2001), p. B1.
37. Non-Western art and architecture have also presented to the artist an alternative way of thinking about the function of decorative forms and surfaces; specifically, tantric symbolism and its rich heritage in Indian culture represent an important stimulus for a project Benglis completed in 2011 for the US Consulate in Mumbai, India. See Uttara Choudhury, 'It is my loving gift to Mumbai and the people of India', *dnaindia.com* (24 May 2009), http://www.dnaindia.com/world/report_it-is-my-loving-gift-to-mumbai-and-the-people-of-india_1258473-all (accessed 30 January 2011).
38. Benglis in 'Lynda Benglis: Interview by Ned Rifkin', in *Early Work: Lynda Benglis, Joan Brown, Luis Jimenez, Gary Stephan, Lawrence Weiner*, ed. Lynn Gumpert, Ned Rifkin, and Marcia Tucker (New York: New Museum, 1982), p. 12.
39. Richard Serra in 'Interview by Friedrich Teja Bach' (1978), reprinted in Serra, *Writings/Interviews* (Chicago: University of Chicago Press, 1994), p. 32.
40. Benglis in 'Lynda Benglis: Interview by Ned Rifkin', p. 12.
41. In addition to the public fountains I discuss here, Benglis has also installed *Chimera* (1988) at the Bass Museum of Art in Miami Beach, FL, and *Double Fountain* (2007) at Le Jardin Botanique de Dijon, France. See reproductions in *Lynda Benglis: Flow and Flesh*, pp. 47, 50–1.
42. In an unfortunate twist of fate, *The Wave* was one of many public works of art displaced when Hurricane Katrina devastated New Orleans in 2005. As of 2009, Benglis was still tracking down the different parts of the fountain, with the hope of restoring it to a new location.
43. Unfortunately, photographs of the fountain do not always capture this effect.
44. Benglis in interview with Smyth, n.d.
45. Peter Schjeldahl, 'Lynda Benglis: Body and Soul', in *Lynda Benglis: 1968–1978* (Tampa: University of South Florida, 1979), p. 4.

Bibliography

selected published sources

Abbott, Sidney and Barbara Love, *Sappho Was a Right-On Woman: A Liberated View of Lesbianism* (New York: Stein and Day, 1972).

Adamson, Glenn, *Thinking Through Craft* (Oxford: Berg, 2007).

Albright, Thomas, 'Three Major US Artists', *San Francisco Chronicle* (22 May 1973), p. 45.

—— 'Primarily Biological', *Art News* 78, no. 6 (Summer 1979), pp. 156–8.

Alloway, Lawrence, Max Kozloff, Rosalind Krauss, Joseph Masheck, and Annette Michelson, 'Letter', *Artforum* 13, no. 4 (December 1974), p. 9.

American Artists '76: A Celebration (San Antonio, TX: McNay Art Institute, 1976).

Andre, Carl, 'Letter', *Artforum* 14, no. 9 (May 1976), p. 9.

Antin, David, 'Television: Video's Frightful Parent, Part 1', *Artforum* 14, no. 4 (December 1975), pp. 36–45.

Antin, Eleanor, 'An Autobiography of the Artist as an Autobiographer', *LAICA Journal*, no. 2 (October 1974), pp. 18–20.

Auther, Elissa, 'The Decorative, Abstraction, and the Hierarchy of Art and Craft in the Art Criticism of Clement Greenberg', *Oxford Art Journal* 27, no. 3 (2004), pp. 339–64.

—— *String, Felt, Thread: The Hierarchy of Art and Craft in American Art* (Minneapolis: University of Minnesota Press, 2010).

Baker, Kenneth, 'Grimaces that have no faces', *San Francisco Chronicle* (10 March 2001), p. B1.

Ballatore, Sandy, 'Lynda Benglis' Humanism', *Artweek* 7, no. 21 (22 May 1976), pp. 5–6.

Barthes, Roland, *Mythologies*, trans. Annette Lavers (New York: Hill and Wang, 1972).

Battcock, Gregory, ed. *Minimal Art: A Critical Anthology* (New York: E. P. Dutton, 1968).

Beech, Dave ed. *Beauty* (Cambridge, MA: MIT Press, 2009).

Beller, Miles, 'Albuquerque, Arnoldi, Benglis, Castoro, Steir', *Artweek* 7, no. 31 (18 September 1976), p. 3.

Benglis, Lynda, 'Social Conditions Can Change', in 'Eight Artists Reply: Why Have There Been No Great Women Artists?' *Art News* 69, no. 9 (January 1971), p. 43.

—— 'Unskirting the Issue', *Art-Rite*, no. 2 (Summer 1974), pp. 6–7.

—— 'Interview: Linda [*sic*] Benglis', *Ocular* 4, no. 2 (Summer 1979), pp. 30–43.

Blumenthal, Ralph, 'Porno Chic: "Hard Core" Grows Fashionable and Very Profitable', *New York Times Magazine* (21 January 1973), pp. 28–34.

Boice, Bruce, 'Reviews: Lynda Benglis at Paula Cooper Gallery', *Artforum* 11, no. 9 (May 1973), p. 83.

Bonesteel, Michael, 'Art and the New Androgyny', *New Art Examiner* 6, no. 10 (Summer 1979), pp. 9, 11.

Bourdon, David, 'Fling, Dribble and Dip', *Life* (27 February 1970), pp. 62–6.

Bourgeois, Jean-Louis, 'Reviews: New York', *Artforum* 8, no. 8 (April 1970), p. 82.

Bryan-Wilson, Julia, *Art Workers: Radical Practice in the Vietnam War Era* (Berkeley: University of California Press, 2009).

—— 'Queerly Made: Harmony Hammond's *Floorpieces*', *Journal of Modern Craft* 2, no. 1 (March 2009), pp. 59–80.

Buszek, Maria Elena, ed. *Extra/Ordinary: Craft and Contemporary Art* (Durham, NC: Duke University Press, 2011).

Butler, Cornelia, ed. *WACK! Art and the Feminist Revolution* (Los Angeles, CA: Museum of Contemporary Art, 2007).

Butterfield, Jan, 'Poured Art: Sculptor Reveals Technique, Approach to Style', *Fort Worth Star-Telegram* (14 June 1970), p. 6.

Cashdan, Marina, 'Time and Tide', *Frieze*, no. 134 (October 2010), pp. 214–19.

Chave, Anna, 'Minimalism and the Rhetoric of Power', *Arts Magazine* 64, no. 5 (January 1990), pp. 44–63.

Chicago, Judy and Miriam Schapiro, 'Female Imagery', *Womanspace Journal* 1, no. 3 (June 1973), pp. 11–14.

Clark, T. J., *Farewell to an Idea: Episodes from a History of Modernism* (New Haven, CT: Yale University Press, 2001).

Cleto, Fabio, ed. *Camp: Queer Aesthetics and the Performing Subject: A Reader* (Edinburgh: Edinburgh University Press, 1999).

'Collage', *Art News* 73, no. 7 (September 1974), pp. 44–5.

Colpitt, Frances, ed. *Finish Fetish: L.A.'s Cool School* (Los Angeles: The Fisher Gallery, University of Southern California, 1991).

Corry, John, 'About New York: A Serious Dirty Picture?' *New York Times* (22 November 1974), p. 78.

Crawford, Lynda, 'Women in the Erotic Arts', *Viva* 1, no. 4 (January 1974), pp. 74–83.

Daly, Ann, *Critical Gestures: Writings on Dance and Culture* (Middletown, CT: Wesleyan University Press, 2002).

Daly, Mary, *Gyn/Ecology: The Metaethics of Radical Feminism* (Boston: Beacon Press, 1990).

Davis, Douglas, 'The Invisible Woman is Visible', *Newsweek* (15 November 1971), pp. 130–1.

Dubrowin, S. R., 'Latex: One Artist's Raw Material', *Rubber Developments* 24, no. 1 (1971), pp. 10–12.

Edelman, Sharon ed. *Artpark: The Program in Visual Arts* (Lewiston, NY: Artpark, 1976).

Edwards, Karen, 'The Interview/99: Lynda Benglis', *The Sunday Herald* (13 June 1971), p. 2:11.

Fariello M. Anna, and Paula Owen, eds. *Objects and Meaning: New Perspectives on Art and Craft*, (Lanham, MD: Scarecrow Press, 2004).

Felski, Rita, 'Nothing to Declare: Identity, Shame and the Lower Middle Class', *PMLA* 115, no. 1 (January 2000), pp. 33–46.

Firestone, Shulamith, *A Dialectic of Sex: The Case for Feminist Revolution* (New York: Bantam Books, 1971).

Frankenstein, Alfred, 'From Foam to Wax', *San Francisco Chronicle* (12 February 1972), p. 35.

Friedman, Martin, 'Up Against the Wall with Lynda Benglis', *Art in America* 97, no. 11 (December 2009), pp. 102–9.

Frueh, Joanna, 'The Body through Women's Eyes', in *The Power of Feminist Art: The American Movement of the 1970s, History and Impact*, ed. Norma Broude and Mary Garrard (New York: Abrams, 1994), pp. 190–207.

Gablik, Suzi, 'The Double Bind', in 'Eight Artists Reply: Why Have There Been No Great Women Artists?' *Art News* 69, no. 9 (January 1971), pp. 43–5.

Garber, Marjorie, *Vice Versa: Bisexuality and the Eroticism of Everyday Life* (New York: Simon and Schuster, 1995).

Gautherot, Franck, Caroline Hancock, and Seungduk Kim, ed. *Lynda Benglis* (Dijon: Les presses du réel, 2009).

Gelpi, Barbara Charlesworth, 'The Politics of Androgyny', *Women's Studies* 2, no. 2 (1974), pp. 151–60

Gilbert-Rolfe, Jeremy, 'Reviews: Lynda Benglis, The Clocktower', *Artforum* 12, no. 6 (March 1974), pp. 69–70.

—— *Beauty and the Contemporary Sublime* (New York Allworth Press, 1999).

Glueck, Grace, 'New York: Trendless But Varied, The Season Starts', *Art in America* 59, no. 5 (September–October 1971), pp. 121–3.

Goldin, Amy, 'Patterns, Grids and Painting', *Artforum* 14, no. 1 (September 1974), pp. 50–4.

Goldstein, Judith L., 'The Female Aesthetic Community', *Poetics Today* 14, no. 1 (Spring 1993), pp. 143–63.

Greenberg, Clement, *The Collected Essays and Criticism, Volume 2: Arrogant Purpose, 1945–1949*, ed. John O'Brian (Chicago: University of Chicago Press, 1986).

—— *The Collected Essays and Criticism, Volume 3: Affirmations and Refusals, 1950–1956*, ed. John O'Brian (Chicago: University of Chicago Press, 1993).

Gumpert, Lynn, Ned Rifkin, and Marcia Tucker, ed. *Early Work: Lynda Benglis, Joan Brown, Luis Jimenez, Gary Stephan, Lawrence Weiner*, (New York: New Museum, 1982).

Hammond, Harmony, *Lesbian Art in America: A Contemporary History* (New York: Rizzoli, 2000).

Hargreaves, Tracy, *Androgyny in Modern Literature* (London: Palgrave, 2005).

Harris, Daniel, 'Androgyny: The Sexist Myth in Disguise', *Women's Studies* 2, no. 2 (1974), pp. 171–84.

Heilbrun, Carolyn, *Toward a Recognition of Androgyny* (New York: Knopf, 1973).

Huestis, Chris and Marvin Jones, 'Hannah Wilke's Art, Politics, Religion and Feminism', *The New Common Good* (May 1985), pp. 1, 9–11.

Hutcheon, Linda, *A Theory of Parody: The Teachings of Twentieth-Century Art Forms* (New York: Methuen, 1985).

Huyssen, Andreas, *After the Great Divide: Modernism, Mass Culture Postmodernism* (Bloomington: Indiana University Press, 1986).

Jameson, Fredric, 'Transformations of the Image in Postmodernity', in *The Cultural Turn: Selected Writings on the Postmodern 1983–1998* (London: Verso, 1998), pp. 93–135.

Jinkner-Lloyd, Amy, 'Materials Girl: Lynda Benglis in Atlanta', *Arts Magazine* 65, no. 9 (May 1991), pp. 53–5.

Jones, Amelia, ed. *Sexual Politics: Judy Chicago's Dinner Party in Feminist Art History*, (Los Angeles: Armand Hammer Museum of Art, UCLA, 1996).

Jones, Amelia, 'Postfeminism, Feminist Pleasures, and Embodied Theories of Art', in *New Feminist Criticism: Art, Identity, Action*, ed. Joanna Frueh, Cassandra Langer and Arlene Raven (New York: Icon Editions, 1994), pp. 16–41.

—— 'Interpreting Female Bodies: The Unframeability of Desire', in *The Rhetoric of the Frame: Essays on the Boundaries of the Artwork*, ed. Paul Duro (Cambridge: Cambridge University Press, 1996), pp. 223–41.

—— *Body Art: Performing the Subject* (Minneapolis: Minnesota University Press, 1998).

—— *Self/Image: Technology, Representation, and the Contemporary Subject* (New York: Routledge, 2006).

Judd, Donald, *Donald Judd: Complete Writings 1959–1975: Gallery Reviews, Book Reviews, Articles, Letters to the Editor, Reports, Statements, Complaints* (Halifax and New York: Press of the Nova Scotia College of Art and Design and New York University Press, 1975).

Jung, Carl Gustav, *The Archetypes and the Collective Unconscious (Collected Works of C. G. Jung, Volume 9, Part 1)* (Princeton: Princeton University Press, 1981).

Kangas, Matthew, 'Metamorphosis: Glass Sculptures by Lynda Benglis', *GLASS: The UrbanGlass Quarterly*, no. 82 (Spring 2001), pp. 22–7.

Kelly, Mary, 'Reviewing Modernist Criticism', *Screen* 22, no. 3 (1981), pp. 41–62.

Kertess, Klaus, 'Foam Structures', *Art and Artists* 7, no. 2 (May 1972), pp. 33–7.

Kincaid, Jamaica, 'Erotica', *Ms.* (January 1975), pp. 30–3.

King, Katie, 'The Situation of Lesbianism as Feminism's Magical Sign: Contests for Meaning and the US Women's Movement, 1968–1972', *Communications* 9 (1986), pp. 65–91.

Kirshner, Judith, *Vito Acconci: A Retrospective, 1969–1980* (Chicago: Museum of Contemporary Art, 1980).

Knott, Robert, 'The Myth of the Androgyne', *Artforum* 14, no. 3 (November 1975), pp. 38–45.

Kramer, Hilton, 'Grace, Flexibility, Esthetic Tact', *New York Times* (30 May 1971), p. D19.

—— 'What Happens When Art is Confused with Publicity?' *New York Times* (23 November 1975), p. D25.

Krane, Susan, *Lynda Benglis: Dual Natures* (Atlanta, GA: High Museum of Art, 1991).

Krauss, Rosalind, 'Video: The Aesthetics of Narcissism', *October* 1 (Spring 1976), pp. 51–64.

Kreimer, Julian, 'Shape Shifter: Lynda Benglis', *Art in America* 97, no. 11 (December 2009), pp. 94–105.

Kuhn, Annette, 'Culture Shock', *Village Voice* (2 December 1974), p. 96.
Kurtz, Bruce, 'Video is being Invented', *Arts Magazine* 47, no. 3 (December–January 1973), pp. 37–44.
Kuspit, Donald, 'Cosmetic Transcendentalism: Surface-Light in John Torreano, Rodney Ripps and Lynda Benglis', *Artforum* 18, no. 2 (October 1979), pp. 38–40.
Landi, Ann, 'Getting Paint Off the Wall', *Art News* 109, no. 8 (September 2010), pp. 84–9.
Larson, Philip, *Painting: New Options* (Minneapolis: Walker Art Center, 1972).
Lippard, Lucy R., *Eccentric Abstraction* (New York: Fischbach Gallery, 1966), exhibition pamphlet, n.p.
—— 'Eccentric Abstraction', *Art International* 10, no. 9 (November 1966), pp. 28, 34–40.
—— *From the Center: Feminist Essays on Women's Art* (New York: E. P. Dutton, 1976).
—— 'Making Something From Nothing (Toward a Definition of Women's "Hobby Art")', *Heresies*, no. 4 (Winter 1978), pp. 62–5.
Lynda Benglis: 1968–1978 (Tampa: University of South Florida, 1980).
Lynda Benglis: Flow and Flesh (Philadelphia: Locks Art Publications, 2010).
Lynn, Martha Drexler, *Sculpture, Glass and American Museums* (Philadelphia: University of Pennsylvania Press, 2005).
Mainardi, Patricia and Janet Sawyer, 'A Feminine Sensibility? Two Views', *Feminist Art Journal* 1, no. 1 (April 1972), pp. 4, 25.
Marks, Laura U., *The Skin of Film: Intercultural Cinema, Embodiment, and the Senses* (Durham, NC: Duke University Press, 2000).
Marcia, Tucker, ed. *Bad Girls*, (Cambridge, MA: MIT Press, 1994).
Marshall, Stuart, 'Video Art, the Imaginary, and the Parole Vide', *Studio International* 191, no. 981 (May–June 1976), pp. 243–7.
McCann, Cecile N., 'Linda [*sic*] Benglis: Dimensional Paintings', *Artweek* 4, no. 20 (19 May 1973), p. 3.
McGee, Micki, 'Narcissism, Feminism and Video Art: Some Solutions to a Problem of Representation', *Heresies*, no. 12 (1981), pp. 88–91.
McLuhan, Marshall, *Understanding Media: The Extensions of Man* (Cambridge, MA: MIT Press, 1994).
Meikle, Jeffrey, *American Plastic: A Cultural History* (New Brunswick, NJ: Rutgers University Press, 1995).
Meskimmon, Marsha, *The Art of Reflection: Women Artists' Self-Portraiture in the Twentieth Century* (New York: Columbia University Press, 1996).
Modleski, Tania, *Feminism without Women: Culture and Criticism in a 'Postfeminist' Age* (New York: Routledge, 1991).
Molesworth, Helen, ed. *Part Object Part Sculpture* (College Park: Pennsylvania State University Press, 2005).
Monte, James and Marcia Tucker, ed. *Anti-Illusion: Procedures/Materials* (New York: Whitney Museum of American Art, 1969).
Morin, France, 'Lynda Benglis in Conversation with France Morin', *Parachute*, no. 6 (Spring 1977), pp. 9–11.
Morris, Robert, 'Anti Form', *Artforum* 6, no. 8 (April 1968), pp. 33–5.

—— 'Notes on Sculpture, Part IV: Beyond Objects', *Artforum* 7, no. 8 (April 1969), pp. 50–4.

Mullarkey, Maureen, 'Dishing It Out: Judy Chicago's *Dinner Party*', *Commonweal* 108, no. 7 (April 1981), pp. 210–11.

Nemser, Cindy, 'Lynda Benglis – A Case of Sexual Nostalgia', *Feminist Art Journal* 3, no. 4 (Winter 1974/75), pp. 7, 23.

Nevelson, Louise, 'Do Your Work', in 'Eight Artists Reply: Why Have There Been No Great Women Artists?' *Art News* 69, no. 9 (January 1971), pp. 41–2.

Newman, Amy, ed. *Challenging Art: Artforum, 1962–1974* (New York: Soho Press, 2000).

Nickles, Shelley, 'More is Better: Mass Consumption, Gender, and Class Identity in Postwar America', *American Quarterly* 54, no. 4 (December 2002), pp. 581–622.

Nixon, Mignon, *Fantastic Reality: Louise Bourgeois and a Story of Modern Art* (Cambridge, MA: MIT Press, 2005).

Nochlin, Linda, 'Why Have There Been No Great Women Artists?' *Art News* 69, no. 9 (January 1971), pp. 22–39, 67–71.

Pacteau, Francette, 'The Impossible Referent: Representations of the Androgyne', in *Formations of Fantasy*, ed. Victor Burgin, James Donald and Cora Kaplan (New York: Methuen, 1986), pp. 62–84.

Parker, Rozsika and Griselda Pollock, ed. *Framing Feminism: Art and the Women's Movement, 1970–1985* (London: Pandora Press, 1987).

Perreault, John, 'Celebrations Knotted and Dotted', *Village Voice* (16 May 1974), p. 44.

Perrone, Jeff, 'The Ins and Outs of Video', *Artforum* 14, no. 10 (June 1976), pp. 53–7.

Pincus-Witten, Robert, 'Reviews: New York', *Artforum* 8, no. 5 (January 1970), p. 69.

—— 'Reviews: New York', *Artforum* 10, no. 4 (December 1971), pp. 78–9.

—— 'Lynda Benglis: The Frozen Gesture', *Artforum* 13, no. 3 (November 1974), pp. 54–9.

—— 'Benglis' Video: Medium to Media', in *Physical and Psychological Moments in Time: A First Retrospective of the Video Work of Lynda Benglis* (Oneonta, NY: Fine Arts Center Gallery, SUNY, 1975).

Pitts, Priscilla, ed. *Lynda Benglis: From the Furnace* (Auckland, New Zealand: Auckland City Art Gallery, 1993).

Plagens, Peter, 'Letter', *Artforum* 13, no. 4 (December 1974), p. 9.

—— 'Objects of Affection', *Newsweek* (3 June 1991), p. 68.

Pollack, Barbara, 'Letter on Good Girls, Bad Girls and Bad Boys' (1991), reprinted in *Meaning: An Anthology of Artists' Writings, Theory and Criticism*, ed. Susan Bee and Mira Schor (Durham, NC: Duke University Press, 2000), pp. 46–50.

Pollock, Griselda, 'Artists, Mythologies and Media – Genius, Madness and Art History', *Screen* 21, no. 3 (1980), pp. 57–96.

—— 'Mary Kelly's *Ballad of Kastriot Rexhepi*: Virtual Trauma and Indexical Witness in the Age of Mediatic Spectacle', *Parallax* 10, no. 1 (2004), pp. 100–12.

Radicalesbians, 'The Woman-Identified Woman', in *Notes from the Third Year: Women's Liberation*, ed. Shulamith Firestone and Anne Koedt (New York: Notes from the Second Year, 1971), p. 81.

Radway, Janice, *A Feeling for Books: The Book-of-the-Month Club, Literary Taste, and Middle-Class Desire* (Chapel Hill: University of North Carolina Press, 1999).

Ratcliff, Carter, *Fate of a Gesture: Jackson Pollock and Postwar American Art* (New York: Farrar, Straus, and Giroux, 1996).

Raynor, Vivien, 'The Art of Survival (and Vice Versa)', *New York Times Magazine* (17 February 1974), pp. 8–9, 50, 52–5.

Richmond, Susan, 'Sizing Up the Dildo: Lynda Benglis' *Artforum* Advertisement as a Feminist Icon', *n.paradoxa: international feminist art journal*, no. 15 (2005), pp. 24–34.

Robertson, Pamela, *Guilty Pleasures: Feminist Camp from Mae West to Madonna* (Durham, NC: Duke University Press, 1996).

Rogoff, Irit, 'Gossip as Testimony: A Postmodern Signature', in *Generations and Geographies in the Visual Arts: Feminist Readings*, ed. Griselda Pollock (London: Routledge, 1996), pp. 75–85.

Rose, Barbara, 'Los Angeles: The Second City', *Art in America* 54, no. 1 (January–February 1966), p. 110–15.

—— 'Vaginal Iconology', *New York Magazine* (11 February 1974), p. 59.

Ross, Andrew, *No Respect: Intellectuals and Popular Culture* (New York: Routledge, 1989).

Rubin, Gayle, 'The Traffic in Women: Notes on the "Political Economy" of Sex', in *Toward an Anthropology of Women*, ed. Rayna R. Reiter (New York: Monthly Review Press, 1975), pp. 157–211.

Rubin, Joan Shelley, *The Making of Middlebrow Culture* (Chapel Hill: University of North Carolina Press, 1992).

Schapiro, Miriam and Melissa Meyer, 'Waste Not/Want Not: An Inquiry into What Women Saved and Assembled', *Heresies*, no. 4 (Winter 1978), pp. 66–9.

Schimmel, Paul, ed. *Shift: LA/NY* (Newport Beach, CA: Newport Harbor Art Museum, 1982).

Schjeldahl, Peter, 'Chronicles: New York Letter', *Art International* 13, no. 7 (September 1969), pp. 70–3.

—— 'Updated Data on the Adventure of being Human', *New York Times* (26 May 1974), p. D17.

Schlegel, Amy Ingrid, 'Codex Spero: Rethinking the Monograph as a Feminist', in *Singular Women: Writing the Artist*, ed. Kristen Frederickson and Sarah E. Webb (Berkeley: University of California Press, 2003), pp. 200–12.

Schneider Ira and Beryl Korot, ed. *Video Art: An Anthology* (New York and London: Harcourt Brace Jovanovich, 1976).

Schor, Gabrielle, *The Prints of Barnett Newman, 1961–1969* (Ostfildern: Hatje Cantz, 1996).

Schor, Mira, 'Representations of the Penis' (1988), reprinted in Schor, *Wet: On Painting, Feminism, and Art Culture* (Durham, NC: Duke University Press, 1997), pp. 13–25.

Schwartz, Bruce, 'Adhesive Product', *The Tech* (16 November 1971), p. 11.

Secor, Cynthia, 'Androgyny: An Early Reappraisal', *Women's Studies* 2, no. 2 (1974), pp. 161–70.

Seiberling, Dorothy, 'The Female View of Erotica', *New York Magazine* (11 February 1974), pp. 54–8.

—— 'The New Sexual Frankness: Good-bye to Hearts and Flowers', *New York Magazine* (17 February 1975), pp. 37–44.

Selz, Peter and William Valerio, ed. *Modern Odysseys: Greek American Artists of the 20th Century* (New York: Queens Museum of Art, 1999).

Serra, Richard, *Writings/Interviews* (Chicago: University of Chicago Press, 1994).

Sieglaub, Seth, Marion Fricke and Roswitha Fricke, ed. *The Context of Art, The Art of Context* (Trieste: Navado Press, 2004).

Siegel, Jeanne, 'Lynda Benglis, Jackson Pollock and Process', *ARTI* 34 (May–June 1997), pp. 75–82.

Singer, June, *Androgyny: Toward a New Theory of Sexuality* (New York: Doubleday, 1976).

Smith, Michael H., *Jack Brogan: Projects* (Pasadena: Baxter Art Gallery, California Institute of Technology, 1980).

Sontag, Susan, 'Notes on Camp' (1964), reprinted in Sontag, *Against Interpretation and Other Essays* (New York: Noonday Press, 1965).

Stimpson, Catharine, 'The Androgyne and the Homosexual', *Women's Studies* 2, no. 2 (1974), pp. 237–48.

Straayer, Chris, 'Sexuality and Video Narrative', *Afterimage* 16, no. 10 (May 1989), pp. 8–11.

Suares, Jean-Claude, 'The Designer's Guide to Schlock, Camp and Kitsch – and the Taste of Things to Come', *Print* 29 (January 1975), pp. 25–35.

Stavitsky, Gail, ed. *Waxing Poetic: Encaustic Art in America* (Montclair, NJ: Montclair Art Museum, 1999).

Tucker, Marcia, *A Short Life of Trouble: Forty Years in the New York Art World*, ed. Liza Lou (Berkeley: University of California Press, 2008).

Varian, Elayne, ed. *Art in Process IV* (New York: Finch College Museum of Art, 1969).

Wagner, Anne M., *Three Artists (Three Women): Modernism and the Art of Hesse, Krasner, and O'Keeffe* (Berkeley: University of California Press, 1996).

—— 'Pollock's Nature, Frankenthaler's Culture', in *Jackson Pollock: New Approaches*, ed. Kirk Varnedoe and Pepe Karmel (New York: Museum of Modern Art and Abrams, 1999), pp. 181–200.

—— 'Performance, Video, and the Rhetoric of Presence', *October* 91 (Winter 2000), pp. 59–80.

Wark, Jayne, *Radical Gestures: Feminism and Performance Art in North America* (Montreal and Kingston: McGill-Queen's University Press, 2006).

Wasserman, Emily, 'Reviews: New York', *Artforum* 8, no. 1 (September 1969), pp. 56–62.

Waugh, Patricia, *Feminine Fictions: Revisiting the Postmodern* (London: Taylor and Francis, 1989).

Weber, Samuel, 'Television: Set and Screen', in *Mass Mediauras: Forms, Technics, Media*, ed. Alan Cholodenko (Stanford: Stanford University Press, 1996), pp. 108–28.

Webster, Paula, 'The Forbidden: Eroticism and Taboo', in *Pleasure and Danger: Exploring Female Sexuality*, ed. Carole S. Vance (London: Pandora Press, 1989), pp. 385–98.

Weil, Kari, *Androgyny and the Denial of Difference* (Charlottesville: University of Virginia Press, 1992).

Weyergraf, Clara, 'The Holy Alliance: Populism and Feminism', *October*, no. 16 (Spring 1981), pp. 23–34.

Williams, Linda, *Hard Core: Power, Pleasure and the 'Frenzy of the Visible'* (Berkeley: University of California Press, 1989).

Wooster, Ann-Sargent, 'Reviews: Lynda Benglis at Paula Cooper', *Art in America* 62, no. 5 (September–October 1974), p. 106.

archives, dissertations and films

Anti-Illusion: Procedures/Materials exhibition files, Whitney Museum of American Art Archives, New York, NY.

Coad, Robert James, *Between Painting and Sculpture: A Study of the Work and Working Process of Lynda Benglis, Elizabeth Murray, Judy Pfaff and Gary Stephan* (Ann Arbor, MI: UMI Dissertation Information Service, 1988).

Goldman, Saundra, *'Too Good Lookin' to be Smart': Beauty, Performance and the Art of Hannah Wilke* (Ann Arbor, MI: UMI Dissertation Information Service, 2000).

Lynda Benglis: Dual Natures exhibition files, High Museum of Art Archives, Atlanta History Center, Atlanta, GA.

Skowhegan Lecture Archives (Benglis, 1978), Ernest G. Welch School of Art and Design, Georgia State University, Atlanta, GA.

Smyth, Dermot, dir. *Lynda Benglis* (working title), film in production, 2011.

Index

www.ingramcontent.com/pod-product-compliance
Lightning Source LLC
LaVergne TN
LVHW010603110826
845149LV00003B/748

9781350290068